NIKKI DE CARTERET

SOUL POWER

THE TRANSFORMATION THAT HAPPENS WHEN YOU **KNOW**

Copyright © 2003 O Books
46A West Street, Alresford, Hants SO24 9AU, U.K.
Tel: +44 (0) 1962 736880 Fax: +44 (0) 1962 736881
E-mail: office@johnhunt-publishing.com
www.o-books.net

Text: © 2003 Nikki de Carteret

Designed by Krave Limited, London
Soul Power logo by MedDesign, Jordan
Author's Photograph by Eclipse Photography, Vancouver

ISBN 1 903816 36 X

A CIP catalogue record for this book is available from the British Library.

Printed in the UK by Ashford Colour Press

CONTENTS

Acknowledgements I

Introduction V

Stage One: Awakening
The light 2
The path opens 6
Newness 11

Stage Two: Spiritual knowledge
Connecting to soul 20
The peace within 25
Knowing God 31
Yoga -- mystic union 37
Golden thread 42
Sometimes push, sometimes pull 48

Stage Three: Spiritual practice
Silence 54
Meditation - the loving way 59
Master of mind, master of self 64
Higher consciousness 69
Practice makes perfect 74
The game of remembering and forgetting 80

Stage Four: Dark night of the soul
Walking the path 90
The fall 96
The alchemy tale 102
The dark night 107
Spiritual warrior 113
The handless maiden 120

Stage Five: Illumination

Silent witness 132

Achilles heel 138

Ego crunch 145

True heart 153

Faith 159

Soul power 166

Stage Six: Surrender

Healing into wholeness 178

Letting go 183

The Beloved 191

God's vision 198

A work of Grandeur 205

Stage Seven: Walking the talk

The power of virtue 216

The authentic self 221

One family 228

Stage Eight: Bliss

The drama of life 240

Living in the presence of God 248

Truth 256

Stage Nine: Perfection of spirit

The humble server 264

Peak of perfection 270

A light for the world 274

Epilogue: Your right to soul power 281

About the Author 283

Sources 284

To my Beloved,
eternally yours,

ACKNOWLEDGEMENTS

When you begin a book you are alone. There is just you, the pen, and the page. The task would prove quite daunting if it were not for the unseen hands stretching out to hold and support. I am indebted to Baba who has been my Inspiration, Guide, Friend and constant Companion. I also thank *Soul Power* for being a generous and patient teacher.

I am particularly grateful to three amazing modern mystics who have influenced and guided my spiritual growth, Dadi Prakashmani, Dadi Gulzar, and especially Dadi Janki who always kept faith in me. Sister Jayanti has been a wise and noble teacher.

To the many students, colleagues, and friends who have informed my learning, and shared with me their personal stories, I would like to extend my heartfelt appreciation. The power of story has enriched us all. I would like to honor my spiritual family worldwide for their unfailing commitment to spiritual growth and global transformation. You continue to inspire me. Special thanks to family members in Vancouver, London, Calgary, and Amman for giving me space to do what I needed to do. You know who you are and what this has meant to me.

Many people contributed directly to the evolvement of this book. I would like to thank Fi Lakin, Judi Rich, Loretta Rymer, Rita Cleary, and Nizar Juma for reading parts of the earlier manuscript; Meisa Batayneh for her love of creativity and third-dimensional input into the seminar materials; Sameer Patro for his stunning design work and Jaymini Patel for her constant support of the project. Barbara Shipka, who extended her hand of friendship and wise editorial comments, your support at the beginning of this project was invaluable. Many others not mentioned here also retain a place in my heart.

Joy Parker, my dear spiritual and electronic friend has been a constant source of insight, story-telling, and sharp editorial guidance. Thank you for giving me the courage to keep on writing during the "dark night of the book." I am especially grateful to Shobna Obhrai for keeping the vision and holding the fort when it mattered. Cheryl Van Blerk, my agent, your knowledge and enthusiasm brought a breath of fresh air during the publishing process. A big thank you to my publisher John Hunt and editor Michael Mann for their kind spirits and noble vision.

Finally, words are insufficient to express my sincere gratitude to Carole Hart, my mother and spiritual sister, who was a clear and sensitive critic and guiding companion during the re-shaping and editorial process. Your patience, tolerance, wisdom, and love are astounding.

ENDORSEMENTS

"I HAVE, QUITE SIMPLY, never before read a book that made me feel so keenly the love of God or sense so many possibilities for a relationship with the Divine. De Carteret's special gift is taking spiritual concepts that other writers make difficult, and putting them into language that flows directly to our understanding. Many of these chapters resonate deeply within my heart, and I have become so much more vibrantly alive from reading them. Some say we live in a secular age, but the power of this book is that it shows how contemporary men and women, caught up in all the complexities and paradoxes of our times, can still experience a deepening commitment to spiritual growth, service, and joy."

Joy Parker, co-author of *Woman Who Glows in the Dark* and *Maya Cosmos*

"SOUL POWER is straight from the heart from a true spiritual teacher. De Carteret writes powerfully and credibly about spirituality because she lives spirituality not just day by day, but minute by minute."

Alan Hobson, Mount Everest climber and summiteer, author of *From Everest to Enlightenment - An Adventure of Soul*

"IN THIS BEAUTIFUL and touching expression of the spiritual journey, Ms. de Carteret shares her own experiences and observations of the path of the mystic at the same time that she integrates her knowledge and wisdom. I found myself receiving nourishment for my own spiritual journey as I read different sections of de Carteret's book. Given where I was at the particular time, some stages offered me reflection of where I've been, others gave me encouragement for where I am, and yet others presented me with a glimpse into where I will go as I quest for a deeper, more personal relationship with God and a greater fullness of authenticity within myself."

Barbara Shipka, author of *Leadership in a Challenging World*

"Nikki de Carteret has taken a life-time's experience of spiritual exploration and poured it into one book. It's a unique combination of scholarly research and hands-on experience. By no means a 'starter manual', Soul Power is a fascinating and useful manual for those already on the path to spiritual realization."

Michael Rymer, *Hollywood film director*

INTRODUCTION

ABOUT FIVE YEARS AGO I went with some friends on a four-wheel trek in the southern deserts of Jordan looking for a Bedouin called Mohammed. Now Mohammed had no fixed address, he moved his tent, wife, children, camels and goats according to the feeding needs of his animals. Since there are no pathways the desert, we took along another Bedouin called Omar as our guide. We began our journey in Wadi Rum, the beautiful red desert made famous in the film *Laurence of Arabia*. Then we drove east for three hours through the crushing sands of a desolate landscape that eventually leads to the border of Saudi Arabia.

Any one who has been to the desert can tell you that it is a dangerous place. The floor of the desert is just sand. There is no road, you make the road as you travel. You have to be well equipped with water, blankets, and tools in case of vehicle breakdown. It's not as if you can expect a mobile gas station to appear just over the hill. For the first part of the journey, I couldn't tell where we were going. The terrain all looked the same, barring a few extra trees and rocks. Even though we had a guide, after three hours of driving I began to feel nervous. It was a ridiculous notion to think we could find a man and a tent in the middle of nowhere, like trying to find a needle in a haystack.

To make myself feel better I began to closely observe Omar when he called out, "Turn left. Now turn right. Go this way. Now go over there." I tried to look at the terrain through his eyes, to see what he was seeing. To my untrained eye it appeared as if we were going through the same endless sea of shimmering sand. But after a while I started to spot the coded messages that the Bedouins left for each other. I noticed stones turned in a certain way, or a small pile of rocks on a hill, or black markings on an acacia tree. Soon I too could pick out the landmarks of the journey through the desert.

With renewed faith I realized that we were sailing right on course to our destination. What a discovery! About fifteen minutes after we passed a tiny oasis boasting a single palm tree, we saw Mohammed's tent. He waved as we approached. It was as if he had been expecting us. His wife had lit the fire and a kettle was boiling. We were invited to sit on the ground and have a well-deserved cup of tea!

Just as the Bedouin landmarks are necessary for navigating a desert, it is useful for people on the spiritual path to have a road map detailing the landmarks of that journey. What this book attempts to do is to chart the passages or stages of growth that most of us go through when traveling on the spiritual path. I do not see these stages as a blueprint for spiritual development, but rather as signposts to illuminate the spiritual process. Spiritual process means the journey to the core of the self, namely the soul.

Process intrigues me. In a world that has become too prescriptive, the tendency is to promote "the cure" for a malady before finding the "cause." The pressure is to find a quick fix for the ailments of the heart and soul without allowing sufficient time for healing and a return to wholeness. In spite of cultural brainwashing, more and more people are discovering that spirituality is a process. There is no such thing as a quick route to enlightenment. Transformation doesn't happen overnight, but over months and years of learning and discovering.

Like most seekers of truth, I have sought to find myself. My questioning of the meaning and purpose of life began in my teens. I read books, went to courses in positive thinking, and took up meditation, all in an attempt to find the answers.

A friend once told me I should have called this book, "How I survived a car crash and found God." At the age of twenty-two while studying at the Sorbonne in Paris, I had a strange encounter with the Light after I had been severely injured in an automobile accident. I wasn't looking for God but it seemed that during that life-shattering crisis God came looking for me. The full implications of this experience weren't clear at the time. Later I understood that the accident was a significant landmark that took me from the periphery of my quest right into the heart of my spiritual adventure.

The spiritual quest is a search for insight. It is a mystical journey and, like all journeys, is strangely cyclical. We think we are setting out to go somewhere and discover something new only to find that we have arrived at the place we have known all along. That place is the self. Most of us hunger to know ourselves. When we chose to become awakened to an awareness of each moment, we re-discover aspects of the soul that previously were hidden or shut down. My belief is that, as souls, we are all spiritually powerful. It's just that we have forgotten this. It is as if we have been asleep for a long time and our internal clock is now signaling us to awaken to our Soul Power.

Soul Power is the ultimate spiritual intelligence. It comes from the knowledge of the true self and a clear understanding of the nature and function of the soul. Soul Power is the spiritual energy that is found within, rooted in the essential self and nurtured through our unfolding relationship with the Divine.

During our journey back to Soul Power, we come to understand the dynamics of spiritual growth, what factors drain spiritual energy and what practices and transformational forces restore it. The re-discovery of Soul Power unleashes the power of love, self-acceptance, and spiritual healing. When you tap into your Soul Power you will receive insights about yourself, your energy will increase, and you will feel more alive and alert to the joy of living.

Soul Power, which is fundamental to each one of us, is not about having control over others. Soul Power cannot be taught but is strengthened through spiritual practices such as silence, reflection, inquiry, prayer or meditation. Only through the understanding and application of spiritual principles and truths is our consciousness raised sufficiently to release the experience of that inner power. Recapturing and restoring Soul Power is a powerful illustration of the redemptive power of renewal.

I *am* a soul, I do not *have* a soul. Though it is grammatically correct in the English language to say "my soul," spiritually it is not considered correct. Other languages do not require the use of the possessive term and this is also true of spiritual language. In this book I have used the phrase "I, the soul," to release the soul from its linguistic entrapment. At other times I have used the term "the soul" when referring to the dynamics and functions of the soul that apply to us all spiritually.

A recent survey in North America indicates that most people believe in God or a Higher Power. I do not offer any excuse for my assumption that God exists and leave it to other writers to prove that God does not. Most of us are tired of theory. We just want a God that is accessible. For me God is Light, a Being with whom I can have a direct and personal relationship. I use the words God, the Divine and Higher Power interchangeably. You may want to substitute your own term for and understanding of this energy. Though I see God as beyond gender, I have mostly relied on convention though at times, I have used both genders, describing God as both Mother and Father.

One of the reasons I wanted to write this book was to help demystify the "mystical" dimensions of the spiritual journey. Sometimes when we go through personal or spiritual crises we cannot easily accept why such things happen or that they can happen to us at any time, even when we believe we have become spiritually advanced. After many years on my own spiritual journey I went through a dramatic and unexpected spiritual crisis. Not even my closest spiritual teachers and friends were able to help me. Since I was normally positive and enthusiastic about life, this crisis was disturbing. What on earth was going on?

This question prompted the beginnings of this book. I began to look back over my spiritual journey, searching for answers. Were there signposts along the way that I hadn't noticed? Had I taken the wrong turn? Were there earlier signals that could have helped me? Was I alone in all of this or had others experienced something similar? When you are physically ill you go to a doctor for a diagnosis. When you are spiritually ill what do you do?

Searching for clues I began to re-read the lives of the ancient mystics whose writings I had studied at university. These mystics were men and women from all faith traditions who had real and direct experiences of the Divine. The road they traveled was not a straight one, it was full of bumps, and twists and turns. Reading their accounts was like delving into a personal diary where all the details of their thoughts and feelings, their despair and joy, their personal revelations and insights were explicitly exposed. In the company of these mystics I no longer felt alone.

Around this time I began keeping a journal on the nature of spiritual process. This book has unfolded as my life unfolded. In part, it is a record of the maze of experience through which I journeyed to find my route to Soul Power. For nine years this book has traveled with me to New York, Nairobi, Toronto, Paris, Delhi, Los Angeles, Athens, Tehran, Guatemala City, and many other places. If I mention these places it is because they have informed me and informed the feelings of this book. I give thanks to the places where I have been and the people who have entered my life and contributed to my learning. Spirituality is universal and global and can be lived and practiced in any place and at any time.

The many students and participants who attended my workshops also contributed to this book through their own specific questions about their own process. I have also drawn on many people's personal stories. In some cases, with permission, original names and details are revealed. In other instances, names, places, and circumstances have been altered to maintain confidentiality.

Since childhood I have had a love affair with the power of story. I loved Greek and Roman myths, Celtic and Viking legends, Indian and old European tales. I was captivated by the magic and mystery of an unfolding story, of hidden elements that produced continuity and discontinuity in people's lives. My fascination extended to journeys to the Otherworld, to places unseen, and battles between good and evil as part of the hero or heroine's noble quest for personal empowerment.

I consider numerous symbols used in mythology, literature, and spiritual autobiography relevant to the third dimension of the spiritual journey. In these stories there are dangerous descents to dark underworlds, journeys across the ocean to enchanted lands, ascents up spiral staircases, even forays through rooms of an interior castle. I have used all of these symbols at various times to clarify my own process. And in my workshops I have frequently used modern images such as escalators, gardens, and inner mansions to help participants explore their inner world. Seeing the look on people's faces when they light up with some re-discovery about themselves is a constant delight.

Stories teach us that there are consequences to our thoughts and actions and that some things in life are just meant to be. Are we ruled by fate or do we consciously choose our destiny? And how is it that we attract synchronistic events into our lives that can totally change our course of direction? These paradoxes lie at the heart of our personal stories. They are reconciled through the understanding and experience of Soul Power. With Soul Power you develop the ability to live with contradiction, to recognize the shadow while living in the light and seeing the possibilities in everything.

This book is a tapestry of nine stages of spiritual growth, interwoven with the experiences of the ancient and modern mystics and the colorful threads of my own story. In inviting you to journey with me through these nine stages to Soul Power, I point out the ups and downs, the setbacks and victories that you can expect to encounter. I have designed this tapestry to draw you, the reader, into ever deepening levels of awareness, self-discovery, and insight.

Throughout the nine stages important themes are explored, such as, love, compassion, acceptance, the beauty of silence, contentment, the dark night of the soul, etc. Spiritual process is not logical or linear, but associative and re-iterative. This is why themes in one stage of the book are revisited and discussed at a later stage, thus mirroring at a deeper level of consciousness an earlier theme. For example, I found I could not write a single chapter on dissolving the ego because spiritually we do not close the chapter on the ego and then never have to come back to it again. On our journey we discover deeper levels at which the ego must be dissolved. This is how we learn spiritually, by going more subtly into what we already know.

We shall not cease from exploration
and the end of our exploring
will be to arrive where we started
and know the place for the first time.
– TS Eliot

Someone in a workshop once asked me, "Do we all go through the nine stages?" These stages are not definitive and are not experienced by everyone in the same way or at the same point in their lives. Yet all serious spiritual seekers will go through some form of an awakening or dramatic self-realization, an inevitable encounter with their dark side, followed by a redemptive return to spiritual power.

Some people will stay longer in some stages than others. Others will move through some stages quickly only to find themselves revisiting an earlier stage before moving on. Some people don't like the idea of going through a process that has a set course. They believe that we advance spiritually in a spontaneous way. Other people fight with all their might against what is happening to them, resisting the way their journey unfolds. The secret is to trust in your own process.

I do not believe that the spiritual journey is something esoteric, only for the chosen few or that sacred knowledge is secret and exclusive, but a person definitely has to be ready for it. Sometimes we have to become strengthened before receiving spiritual insights. Insights don't always come automatically. Yet when they do, they come as gifts from God.

Though I began my spiritual search twenty-four years ago, it wasn't until five years into my journey that I discovered a path especially designed for me. Raja Yoga is an ancient meditation taught by the Brahma Kumaris World Spiritual Organization that encourages each person to become a self-master. I am deeply grateful for the wisdom and teachings that I have received and consider myself fortunate for having some wonderful spiritual mentors. The details of my personal story are a reflection of my own experiences and not an official representation of these teachings.

It is my hope that Soul Power will encourage those who are at the start of their spiritual journey. It is also written for those have journeyed for some time and are seeking deeper meaning and levels to their spiritual understanding. For this purpose, I have included at the end of each chapter some reflective questions, spiritual exercises, and meditations to help strengthen your Soul Power.

In discussing the various stages leading to Soul Power I have left some elements unspoken. These silent places are designed to create a space -- a space in which you can awaken to your own discovery. Like the undercurrents of the sea, barely seen but certainly felt, much of spiritual growth goes on subtly underneath the surface and for this reason is difficult to pinpoint or describe. My intention is that the things I do not talk about will speak to you as much as what I have said. What I have outlined in this book is merely a lay of the land, with various signposts and familiar landmarks of the journey that you may eventually recognize and claim as your own.

STAGE ONE

AWAKENING

Holy Spirit,
giving life to all life,
moving all creatures,
root of all things,
washing them clean,
wiping out their mistakes,
healing their wounds,
you are our true life,
luminous, wonderful,
awakening the heart
from its ancient sleep.

– St Hildegard of Bingen –

THE LIGHT

The greatest authority is that of experience.

SOMETHING WAS WRONG. I knew it the moment Vince said, "We're running out of gas." It was as if a film was being replayed, and we were acting out the same scene all over again.

Vince, the relative of a Laotian Prince, was driving me home through one of the northern suburbs of Paris. We had been at his cousin's wedding. It was early in the evening, but already dark and rainy. At first I didn't recognize the streets. But then I did. Some future memory stabbing at the pit of my stomach told me that I had been here before.

"Turn left," I said, pointing a finger, "there's a gas station." Vince shook his head and carried on. I started to break out in a warm sweat. My eyes searched out another station. "There's one," I shouted. "Turn left."

Vince hesitated. "Go on, turn left." I was begging him now. "Vince, please!" He turned his ashen face toward me apologetically, as if in that split second he were powerless to turn the wheel, powerless to save me from my destiny...

I looked up to see an approaching car crashing into the passenger side, my face open to the shards of glass that rained in on us. Glancing down at my yellow party dress, I saw that it was bathed in red. "Oh God," I whimpered. Blood was pouring out of me. My head started to spin. Soon, people were pulling at the car door, grabbing my arm, making me lie down on the wet pavement.

"Someone cover her head," I heard them say. A woman came close and screamed.

"Vince, Vince," I said in a strangled voice, "What's happening? I can't see. My eye... I can't see."

"For God sake," someone protested, "find a blanket to cover her."

I remember the French anesthetist. His voice was kind and soft, "Don't worry, this isn't going to hurt." It didn't. Yet I was hurting inside. I was alone in a big city, a foreigner without any rights. And I was not in control.

"What about my eye?" I asked, struggling to catch his response beneath the fog of numbing drugs. He wheeled me swiftly into the operating theater. The surgeon came and stood over my head. I tried to communicate with him, but my tongue was frozen.

"Oh, God," my mind pleaded, "help me!" With my head in the surgeon's hands, I was powerless. Somehow I had to trust. I felt myself relaxing and letting go as I drifted in and out of a haze of unformulated thought.

From behind shut lids, I could vaguely perceive the shadowy form of the surgeon's hands working effortlessly on my face. Slowly, my mind found its focus. Rather than resisting the surgeon I began to work with him, sending him positive thoughts. "He'll do a good job," I assured myself. As if in response the surgeon warmed with satisfaction. Only when I caught his thought, "It's done. It's good," did I finally drift off to sleep.

I don't know which was worse, standing before the mirror the next morning staring for an eternity at my turbaned head, or plucking up the courage to lift the bandages. I shrieked at the sight of the purple monster reflected in my own image: right eye sealed with zigzag stitches, nose squashed into black pulp and volcanic mounds of flesh rising up from all sides of my face.

My feet were rooted. I couldn't move. But I couldn't keep looking either. Somehow, I crawled back into the hospital bed, covered my head with coarse gray blankets, and sobbed my terrified heart to sleep.

It was midday. Light streamed in through the loosely curtained windows. A nurse poked her head around the door. "My eye," I called out in French, "I want to know if I still have my eye." She shrugged her shoulders and disappeared. I got up, wandered into a corridor, found a telephone, and called my mother in London.

"I'll come right now," she said.

"Don't bother, it's not serious. I'll see you soon."

I didn't go to London right away. Once out of hospital, I watched spring descend on Paris from the wooden frame of my bed. I could look out through the shuttered window that opened onto the gardens of the students' residence. The chestnut trees were magnificent this time of year. The rain had stopped and a sparrow was pecking at the glass, looking for the yogurt cartons I normally left to chill on the window ledge.

Vince didn't come to see me. The Polish student next door didn't tap on my door as he used to. He was organizing *solidarnosc* marches outside La Bastille. The French Canadians on the top floor were also out every night, or so I imagined, because they didn't come to my room either. People have a way of avoiding sights they do not wish to see.

For a long while, I stopped looking at myself in the mirror. It was particularly hard in the morning when I stood over the washbasin to brush my teeth and wash the left side of my face. The right eye was still intact, but it remained closed for weeks, walled in by a mound of protruding flesh and ugly scars. Soon I was facing the reality that, at twenty-two years old, I would be scarred for life.

My studies were on hold. I didn't go out. I didn't have either the energy or the will to do so. And anyway, I couldn't bear the thought of people looking at me. An Egyptian doctor called Hazem brought me groceries and news from outside. Hours went by in silence. The days lengthened, the light became sharper, but in my room nothing seemed to change.

I lay in bed and tried to heal my face. I wasn't clear on how to go about it, but a book I had once read said that blue is the color of healing. So I started with blue, the color of sky.

I began by visualizing a blue and white light around my face. In my mind's eye I saw purple scars receding into healthy pink cheeks. I was looking at my face through an inner mirror; there were no more marks on the skin, but underneath the skin were dark, ugly patches. In silence I began to understand how, by thinking negatively, people pull negative events toward themselves. For months, I'd had recurring thoughts about being involved in an accident. And then, as if by design, the accident had occurred.

I thought of Vincent Van Gogh, the brilliant artist. He had cut off his ear and sent it in a letter to his lover. I had seen his mocking self-portraits at an exhibition in Amsterdam. Self-inflicted wounds are always the hardest to bear. They hide under the guise of external circumstances, and we have to look at ourselves with honesty before admitting they are our own creation, and not something that life has cruelly forced on us.

With that realization came a flood of tears, bitter tears for the passing of spring and a face men would no longer look at or admire. I thought of my boyfriend in Canada. Would he still want me? Would I ever go out in public again?

One evening, around eight, I was lying in bed, visualizing the usual blue and white light around my face. My body was warm and still. It seemed to hang like a coat off its skeletal hanger. Such warmth and loose-ness had a calming effect. I wasn't afraid to play with the light as it danced over my skin and formed a protective aura around my body.

All of a sudden, this healing energy concentrated in a spot at the cen-ter of my forehead. A beautiful beam of white light emerged from a place between my brows. Moving away from me, it pushed out from the confines of my matchbox room and shot into space. The farther the beam traveled, the more intense the light became. I was no longer 'present' in the room, but seemed to be floating away from my body, detached from the restric-tions that normally keep the self in limitation.

From a distance, I could see myself. I was both the observer and the observed. My battered face was bathed with light, and my consciousness was riding this light beam as it stretched out into limitless space, racing beyond the sun, moon, and stars. And further still, into a world of immeas-urable light.

Then, without warning, the beam stopped. Something was in the way; rather, *Someone* was in the way. I was in another dimension, in the presence of an extraordinary Being. The Being was silent and strong, like the sun in a clear, patient sky. It seemed to know me and wanted to pull me close. At first I was afraid, but the Being sent out rays of love that melted my fear and weakened my resistance. Some kind of magnetic force was drawing me into an ocean of light. Not only was I contained by the light, I realized that I too was made of light. All thoughts about what was happening disap-peared. Only this moment was real. I was lifted out of rational thinking and gently wrapped in a soft cradle of love and joy.

A healing love penetrated my thoughts, feelings, and every nerve of my being. I was soothed by love, revitalized by love. And it was not my own energy at work. Certainly, I had ignited the light, but what was filling me now in wave after wave was not of my own making.

Love! Power! Light! All of these beautifully intense waves of energy were coming to me from infinite space and time. But who was filling me? Who was healing me? Surely, it wasn't my own imagination?

When the waves finally stopped and I found myself cushioned in the body again, a scary thought flashed into my awareness: "God!" The thought was painful at first because I didn't want to acknowledge Him/Her. This meeting was unexpected, uninvited, not of my own intention.

Only the thought kept repeating: "It must be God. It must be God."

THE PATH OPENS

God is recognized through the heart.

AFTER THE ACCIDENT LIFE WASN'T THE SAME. Paris, one of the most beautiful cities in the world, had lost its enchantment. No longer did I want to saunter down by the Seine, drink coffee in the crowded cafes, or view exhibitions in the Grand Palais on a rainy Sunday afternoon.

With a scar-ridden face I had lost all confidence in going out and being seen in public. Each time that I caught my reflection in the mirror above the sink, I felt a pang of dread and fear. The initial panic when I had first lifted my bandages in hospital and seen the vision of my battered unrecognizable face hadn't gone away. It kept coming back like a haunted dream.

I knew I had to get out of Paris, away from these memories of loneliness and pain. The cheerful open spaces of Alberta were calling me and I longed for the security of the Rocky Mountains against my back. I raced to finish my thesis on medieval visionary and mystical literature, said goodbye to my professors, and caught the earliest plane home to Canada.

Back in Calgary life was flat. I felt alienated from the world. All the things that I had previously loved, such as going to the theatre, lively conversation with friends, or adventures in the great outdoors, no longer captured my interest. It was as if I had arrived on the planet from Mars, not Venus, with a heart full of contradictory emotions and no means of communicating them.

One day, the man in my life said, "Honey, you're heading down a path I don't understand and I can't follow you." I was speechless. What path had I embarked on? Where was I heading? Obviously, he had seen something that I hadn't recognized myself. I hadn't yet begun to connect my growing dissatisfaction with the world to my strange 'meeting' with God. But he had.

Soon afterward, he let me go. He opened the door of our nest, pushed me out, and said with tears in his eyes, "Fly!" It was the beginning of spring, just after all the snow had melted, when I boarded a plane for London to start a new life. I was hurt, confused, and worried about the future. Where was all this upheaval leading me?

Clearly, not where I wanted to go, but ultimately where I needed to be.

Without realizing it, I had stumbled into an ancient initiation that happens to many at the start of their spiritual journey. This awakening to spirituality is often marked by a separation from familiar situations and ways of being. For me, it involved a gradual disenchantment with life as I knew it, the break-up of an intimate relationship, and the opening up to realms of consciousness I had only read about, yet was still to experience.

I had no intention of pursuing a spiritual life. All signs were in my favor to follow a career in television journalism. At twenty-four I started working for the BBC in London. My first job was as a researcher for the Russell Harty Show. It was a prime-time evening chat show, a British 'male' equivalent of Oprah Winfrey, presenting the serious and zany along with celebrity interviews and human-interest stories.

My greatest achievement was a satellite feed (the latest technology back in the early 80s) of a life-saving operation on a turtle in Florida. This poor turtle had lost his flipper in a skirmish with a shark. Thanks to a generous donation by Dunlop, the turtle was having a new flipper made of rubber sewn on by an American surgeon.

My editor was over the moon. We had a scoop. We snatched the story from under our competitors' feet, and even had our own news channels begging us for footage. I was elated!

This victory gave me the confidence to turn my hand to another equally bizarre event from across the Atlantic: the launch of Shirley MacLaine's book on reincarnation, titled *Out on a Limb*. Our charismatic young editor was itching to ridicule the book's contents. Somehow, reincarnation didn't agree with his brain cells. I volunteered to do the necessary research. But behind his back I vowed, that while I didn't fully agree with all Ms. MacLaine's views on reincarnation, I would do my best to produce a quality show and prove to Tom that reincarnation was no laughing matter.

I traveled the length and breadth of England looking for articulate people who could authenticate their own past births. I found experts to refute them and experts to back them up. We ended up producing two evening shows, including live phone-ins for the public to voice their opinions. Shirley MacLaine was accused of devil-worship and also proclaimed a saint. Sacks of letters flooded into the office after the show, which for many months consumed the attention of both my producer and myself.

By then my attention was being consumed by another matter, which was also related. During my research I had stumbled across a small suburban house in North London where women yogis taught the famous Raja Yoga of India. This was the yoga that had been part of the original training of the ancient rulers of India.

I wanted to talk to the sisters about reincarnation. They talked about soul, meditation, and God. At the time, I didn't realize there was a connection.

I was invited into a small upstairs room that seemed vaguely familiar, but also a little strange. I sat in an old brown armchair across from one of the sisters who must have been no more than thirty. She had curled her feet up underneath her white sari, and looked more like a little girl settling into a good novel than a highly experienced yogi. The carpet was a speckled white-brown that somehow matched the chairs. And on the wall hung a picture of a yogi meditating.

"Yogi in Bliss," Sister Jayanti said.

I couldn't help staring at the picture. There was nothing unusual about it, or even stunningly beautiful. Just a beam of light that was joined from the yogi's forehead to a small bright star in an expansive golden-red sky. "We meditate by linking the soul to the Supreme Soul. In this way, we open ourselves to experiencing God's love and power."

No one had ever spoken to me so simply or sweetly about the soul and God. I was ready to give it a go. Without even trying, as if by magic, I was transported back to Paris, to the dark matchbox room, to the beam of light that had propelled my consciousness beyond space and time and into a meeting with God. And there, in London, on the comfy brown chair, it all came tumbling back. Actually, it was happening again in a fresh, unexpected way.

As the room filled up with light, I was being showered with love. An immense, otherworldly energy had scooped me up and was filling me with light and joy. I wanted to cry but couldn't. The recognition was too deep.

Then I remembered a winter's night in Calgary when I was nineteen years old. I had taken a bus from the university campus and gotten out on 16th Avenue. Feeling depressed, I looked up at the stars for courage and hope. In that moment I asked myself an important philosophical question: "Nikki, if ever you hear the truth, will you have the courage to follow it?"

The question stuck in my throat. I was choked up, yet alive, and suddenly no longer depressed. Under a cold, starry Canadian sky I made a difficult promise to myself. I vowed that if ever I heard the truth, somehow - - I didn't know how -- I would muster the courage to follow it.

Five years later, a yogi in Bliss was laughing at me...

God had pulled me to Himself again and, before such magnitude, I was powerless to withstand. My legs, heart, and head, all of me caved in before the solidity of His soft presence.

If I had known then what I know now, maybe I wouldn't have surrendered so quickly. I had no idea about the various stages of spiritual growth, of the 'dark night of the soul,' or of the transformation and lessons that awaited me. At the time, there was nothing else I could have done with my life. Instinctively, I embraced what came toward me, completely and utterly, without looking back, without thinking ahead.

From some immeasurably secure place, I sensed that God was offering Himself to me, but equally, I was being returned to the Divine. I was the prodigal daughter coming home.

Within three days of beginning instruction in Raja Yoga, I intuitively stopped eating meat and drinking alcohol. For a journalist it was an incredible decision. After a short internal review, I just said, "Yes! This is what I need and want to do."

Friends and family thought I was crazy getting up early in the morning to meditate, then racing off over Hammersmith Bridge in my little gold Volkswagen Beetle to attend spiritual class at six before putting in a twelve-hour day at work. To them, this was manic behavior. At the time, I guess it was.

But God was calling. The prayer bells were silent and sweet; only my ears seemed to hear them. Suddenly, I was filled with a desperate longing to know God as God really is, without theology or words. I wanted to know the Being, not the concept or theory. "Love, I want Thee, the whole of Thee," the great mystic Catherine of Genoa had exclaimed five hundred years ago, aptly describing the intensity of this longing.

On the second day of my meditation lessons, I had what amounted to a small 'visionary' experience. It was like going through a doorway and stepping out into the future. In a flash, I saw all six billion souls on the planet waking up, as if from some hallucinatory sleep, and realizing that they were 'souls.' It was as if they could see themselves as souls who had come to earth and taken bodies, rather than as bodies that had souls. Their realization of 'soul' was so profound, it transformed them into wondrous beings of light, alert, serene, and elegantly poised before the light of God as He pulled them into blissful union.

I was ecstatic beyond words. The world I had just stepped into was awash with light. There was no fear, no uncertainty, only a calm surrendering to the inevitability of God's light. Through light there was a complete transformation. God, the Alchemist, was doing His silent business, turning base metal into gold. The planet, all living creatures, all human souls, were being cleansed and transformed by Divine Love.

Nothing in my wildest imagination could have prepared me for the truth that I saw. Intellectually, it didn't make sense. But in my heart, I knew that my spiritual path was opening for me and would open for all souls. They would find their own way home.

Bear in mind, this was happening in the early 80s, at the height of the Cold War. The young people of my generation were living under threat of nuclear attack. We knew the world was in a crisis, yet felt paralyzed to do anything about it. Every day, the headlines carried stories about protesters chaining themselves up at Greenham Common, a nuclear cruise missile site in southern England. While some of my colleagues at the BBC joked about their seemingly futile efforts, I silently wondered what joke I would be the butt of if they only knew of the future that I was entertaining.

After that visionary experience, I felt as if a load as heavy as the centuries had lifted from my head. For once, I didn't feel different or separate from the rest of humanity. My life was connected to the whole. I was part of a Divine plan and each soul was included in that Divine plan.

The enormity of this understanding washed through me, opening my heart. For too long my heart had been separated from God. Now the strength of His love moved me. It was this love that set me on my spiritual journey. Immediately I experienced a shift in attitude toward others. I saw the uniqueness and sacredness of each human heart.

And I was humbled.

NEWNESS

Bring newness into your mind, speech, actions, and relationships.
Newness in yourself will automatically bring newness into effect.

THERE ARE NO RULES to spiritual awakening.

The need for happiness and fulfillment sets many people on a quest for purpose and meaning in their lives. They read books, go to workshops and retreats, and begin to attract into their company other spiritually minded people. Their search opens them to new ways of thinking, changes in lifestyle, and helps them begin the process of finding their true spiritual home and practice.

Each person's awakening is programmed from within, characterized by his or her own special circumstances. Some people come to spirituality early in life, others when they are mature. Some seekers spend years experimenting with different spiritual methods and teachings. They begin to question old beliefs about the Divine and find themselves drawn to God in a completely different way. Others are guided automatically to their path. I've heard that some people discover spirituality leafing through the yellow pages, others from a program on TV. Some awaken through practices such as meditation, prayer, or chanting; others like Alex go through a life-altering crisis and come out of it with a renewed sense of purpose and mission. Each person is led by destiny and choice.

A few months ago Alex experienced a serious heart attack. At that time, she wanted to die because her life had seemed so meaningless to her. She decided to attend an African Spirit Medicine workshop that was being held outside of San Francisco, California. During the workshop, she underwent a spiritual ritual in which she took back her life and prayed that it would become sacred again. Within two months her relationship with her husband had transformed, her health had improved, and she had found a new job that fulfilled and excited her.

Sometimes the quest involves a spiritual adventure. People travel to exotic locations wanting to explore indigenous cultures or the spirituality of an ancient past. At other times, truths are discovered by staying at home. Zeynep, a woman in her 50s, said she had everything, yet still she wasn't satisfied. "On the surface, all was fine when you looked at me. I was educated, loved, healthy, had a family, plenty of friends, and no financial difficulties. But one day I packed my bags. I was leaving my home, family, everything. I thought that by running away, I could fill the emptiness within myself. I was the victim and I had to do something about it.

"Having prepared my bags I was ready for a dramatic exit. One minute before the exit, something made me stop and visualize myself in the various new locations I was considering. All of a sudden, I could see that I would still be the same person but only in a different environment. I realized that wherever I went, I would only be taking myself there. It was not the place that was wrong, but myself. A voice said, 'Cancel all arrangements and stay.' And I did. In poured the books, and I read for three years. Other people had been through the same thing. I was not alone. God was there for me. When I was ready, God took me by the hand and showered me with truths in the form of other people, experiences and realizations. The emptiness I had felt was no longer there. I had found God, my soul, and the miracle of my life."

As you read this, take time to appreciate and validate your own spiritual awakening. It is important not to compare your experiences with those of others but to trust implicitly in your own unfolding process. Other people's experiences are their own and unique, just as yours are your own and unique. I've had some people say to me, when they hear of my Paris experience, "Why couldn't I have had a wake-up call from God like you had?" They were impressed by the theatrics of it, amazed by the way God pulled me to Himself without any apparent effort on my part. I tell them: "You weren't meant to wake up like that. You had to come to spirituality in your own way." And so it is for everyone.

Spiritual life is a journey, a process that evolves through various stages of growth. While trying to piece together my own story and discover the underlying principles and truths that help to shape spiritual growth, I started to reread the lives of the ancient mystics. These were men and women from all spiritual traditions who sought enlightenment. I was amazed to discover patterns in their stories to which I could relate, patterns that gave meaning to my own journey. Their experiences were not outdated, nor were their writings like dusty old parchments covered in cobwebs. Many of these ancient mystics had led very real and colorful lives. Although they came from different cultures and faith traditions, they shared similar struggles and insights.

I am thinking particularly of the unknown author of *The Way of the Pilgrim*, whose earnest account of his spiritual journey across Russia and Siberia in the nineteenth century is filled with self-awareness, honesty, and compassion. After attempting the first spiritual exercise set for him by his teacher, he wrote, "At first things seemed to go very well. But then it tired me very much. I felt lazy and bored and overwhelmingly sleepy, and a cloud of all sorts of other thoughts closed round me."

During my research the more I read of the mystics, the more I warmed to the humor with which they viewed themselves and the spiritual process. They literally jumped out of the pages of their lives and became my spiritual friends. In their company I didn't feel alone.

At the same time I also searched out and interviewed people whom I consider to be modern mystics, people such as my teachers Dadi Prakashmani and Dadi Janki, whom I met in India and London respectively. As living portraits of spirituality, these wise women yogis taught me not so much by what they said but through the extraordinary presence of their being. Having been called to their spiritual path in the 1930s, they have been teaching and modeling spiritual practices for more than sixty-five years.

Only a lucky few enter spiritual life fully aware. They hear the call and consciously seek out the mystic way. Their awakening happens quickly and cleanly because they are ready for it. The fourteenth-century mystic Julian of Norwich, for example, was spiritually inclined from an early age. Her initiation into contemplative life was like the flowing of an on-course river into an expectant ocean, instinctive and sure.

Other people are not so prepared to embrace change. For this reason they tend to awaken in stages. Often it takes a few of life's hard knocks to draw them out spiritually. This is what happened to Angela of Foligna, an Italian mystic who lived in the thirteenth century. Angela went through a harrowing awakening that was exacerbated by the conflict she felt between her love of the world and her love of prayer. This is a conflict experienced by many people who are pulled to be spiritual but who also wish to remain in the world. Angela came from a well-off family and was comfortably married with children. She had to overcome a complex personality that was easily attached to luxuries and social standing. She suffered other forms of hardship such as ill health before she could embrace spiritual life with conviction and enthusiasm.

It took Angela twenty years and eighteen spiritual steps to resolve all her inner conflicts. In *Conversion and Penitence*, she candidly revealed the depth of her unwillingness to change, and how each event that unmasked her non-spiritual self was a painful but necessary part of the process of spiritual growth.

Why do some of us resist change? Why do we kick and scream every time something happens to us that we do not like or which does not fit our preconceived notion of how life should unfold? I believe that resistance to change comes from a lack of acceptance of anything new. We tend to be frightened of the new and prefer the comfort of the old, no matter how restrictive it may be.

Instead of 'change,' I prefer to use the word 'renewal.' Renewal is a principle of life. It underpins how both the physical and spiritual worlds work. The energy that is found in any system eventually runs out and must be renewed. The body's cells, for instance, regenerate every seven years. The need for renewal, therefore, is the inherent force that propels change.

Just as in our physical lives, we pass from childhood to adolescence to maturity, similarly, we go through various stages of spiritual growth that involve leaving behind the old and embracing the new. Just as a snake sheds its old skin so that the new one can emerge, so too leaving behind old thoughts, patterns, and activities is a way of stepping forward spiritually, releasing what is no longer useful to our growth. For only then can the spirit move.

This was the case of Rebecca, a woman who for many years has opened her home to troubled teenagers. Rebecca said, "I had reached a point in my life back in 1985 when I had about one drop of self-confidence and self-worth left. I had finally left my abusive husband and taken refuge for about six weeks in a shelter for battered women. My four-year-old son, who was terribly angry and frightened, had backed me into a closet and begun to scream at me using terrible profanity. That was the moment of truth when I realized that I had sunk so low I could be backed into a corner by my own small son. That's when I realized that I needed to get my life together and heal. From then on, it was as if I was filled with a spiritual hunger, and I just kept reading, and seeking, and trying to fill it. The things I needed were given to me, and my teachers appeared along the way. And now I feel that I am very blessed, and that I live in true joy."

In being pushed to the limit Rebecca had to look at herself and change. Spiritual awakening is usually accompanied by some kind of energy renewal, involving a separation from the old and an awakening to the new. This awakening can be internalized, implying a change of attitude or belief, or it can be externalized, implying a separation from familiar surroundings, activities and people. Often it is preceded by some kind of crisis or challenging event. People can go through the loss of a valued job, the break-up of a relationship, even serious illness. They think they are in hell, when in fact they are coming out of it.

Alan Hobson, a Canadian mountaineer, reached the top of Mt Everest in 1997 on his third attempt. But he paid a heavy price. Because of the intensity of his focus to succeed, his fiancee broke off their engagement while accompanying him to base camp. After they returned from the mountain, his climbing partner also decided it was time for them to part ways. "It was the most difficult, emotional climb of my life," Alan told me. "You come down from the highest summit on earth, and everyone thinks you should be on top of the world, but I wasn't. I had lost my future wife, my best friend, and my dream. Once you achieve your dream you also lose it." All of these losses pushed Alan into an emotional crisis. He was forced, like many of us during spiritual awakening, to re-examine his life, look inward for answers, and become more spiritually aware.

Releasing the old is essential to the transformational work we do on our path. The spiritual journey is a powerful process of creation, decay, and renewal. New experiences ultimately lose their power. This is why we need to learn to move on from these experiences, utilizing the wisdom gained from them as compost for new growth. Renewal is the benchmark that distinguishes between different phases of growth as well different levels of consciousness. By understanding the importance of letting go of the old we can awaken gracefully to the knowledge that we are moving forward.

At the age of thirty-four, Jeannie, a former stockbroker in Vancouver, lost her job, her apartment, and her partner all in the same week. It was a big wake-up call. She phoned her mother who said, "Come home. Come back to the mountains." Jeannie spent the next six months in Fairmont, British Columbia reading every spiritual book she could lay her hands on. She now believes that what happened to her was for the best. "You have to trust that the universe is supporting you," she told me.

So do not despair if you are quietly going broke or if a relationship turns sour. You are not alone, you are not going mad. You may be encountering what author and medical intuitive Caroline Myss calls 'spiritual madness.' This is something that can happen especially in times of uncertainty and chaos. Whether we are making a transition into sacred awareness, or from one phase of spiritual growth to another, we will inevitably encounter destabilizing forces. The vacuum created by our consciousness as it separates from the old to adopt the new, is disorientating. And the chaos that ensues cannot be prevented or ignored, it simply has to be lived through.

Yet, somehow it is important to trust -- really trust -- that any upheavals we encounter happen for a good reason and come to make us stronger. Crises are opportunities in disguise. They alert us to the fact that our energies have dissipated and it's time once again for them to be renewed.

Some people's readiness to embrace change allows them to adopt alternative ways of leading their lives. Their spiritual calling can also involve the strong urge to help humanity. Take the case of Tom, a successful dentist in New Orleans who drove racing cars and was a stunt flyer. His story reveals the power that comes from embracing change and redirecting energy positively. During a mid-life crisis, Tom gave up his practice to go back to school and earn a Ph.D. Something propelled him to renew his energy by creating newness in his life. Today, Tom runs one of the most successful prison after-care services in the U.S. His spiritual awakening cost him his marriage, a good many friends, a big salary and success in worldly terms. But in return, he gained peace of mind and an opportunity to serve society in a new and meaningful way.

New beginnings are only a thought away. Alfred, Lord Tennyson once wrote, "The shell must break before the bird can fly." At any moment we can wake up with a new attitude or approach to life, and leave behind the dark hours of yesterday.

> *Look to this day...*
> *for yesterday is but a dream,*
> *and tomorrow is only a vision*
> *but today, well-lived, makes*
> *every yesterday a dream of happiness,*
> *and every tomorrow a vision of hope.*
> *Look well therefore to this day.*
> *Such is the salutation of the dawn.*
> *– Sanskrit poem*

NOTE TO THE READER

If you would like to explore your own awakening process in more depth, use the following questions, exercises, and short meditation. Write down your answers and observations, or start your own *Soul Power* journal. By reflecting and journaling you will gain many spiritual insights. Each stage is accompanied by a set of questions, exercises, and meditations to facilitate your spiritual development.

REFLECTIONS ON AWAKENING

Reflective Questions

1. What dramatic changes have occurred recently, or are occurring at this moment in your life?
2. Is there a pattern in the changes that you can see?
3. What do you think these changing circumstances are trying to tell you?
4. What new attitudes, values, and beliefs are emerging in your life at this time? Or what newness would you like to emerge?

Exercises for Spiritual Practice

1. Spend five to ten minutes a day in quiet reflection. Observe your awakening process -- your thoughts, feelings, hopes, and dreams.
2. When unexpected changes come into your life, do not worry or be afraid. Change is a part of life. Welcome it. Say to yourself, "I open myself to each changing moment. I see the importance and benefit of each event in my life."
3. Feelings of alienation or separation are part of the awakening process. Consider how they are a preparation for spiritual life.
4. Trust the process. Whatever happens is for the best. Whatever you need to know will be revealed to you.
5. Think deeply about the ways in which "spiritual madness" marks the transition from the profane world to the sacred.

Meditation on Light

Sit quietly on a chair. Focus your eyes on a specific spot in the room and allow them to rest there. Lay your hands gently in your lap. Become aware of your breath. Take a slow, deep breath into your abdomen. As you breathe in, imagine light filling your abdomen, moving into your lungs, spreading to every cell of your body. As you breathe out, feel as if all tension is leaving you. Again, breathe in deeply. Feel yourself filling with newness, enthusiasm, and light. As you exhale, allow each breath to massage your whole being. Push out feelings of worry, doubt, and confusion. Inhale light. Exhale all that holds you back spiritually.

STAGE TWO

SPIRITUAL KNOWLEDGE

Desire for God leads us to want to know God.
Knowledge of God causes us to love Him.
It is impossible to love God if you have
a false conception of Him. But those who possess true
knowledge of God cannot help loving Him.

– Rumi –

CONNECTING TO SOUL

No one can see the soul. The soul is realized.

IN SEPTEMBER 1992 I went to Romania to participate in a United Nations conference on human development. It was my first visit to a communist country. After the conference I stayed on for another week to meet with people who were interested in learning to meditate. Katerina, a charming professional woman in her early thirties, was the first to invite me to her home.

"We Romanians carry a lot of guilt," Katerina told me as we sipped coffee at her kitchen table in Bucharest. "Some of us did things we are not proud of, and we can't speak about them even to our close friends and family."

Three years had passed since the dramatic revolution when the Romanian people rose up against their hated dictator Ilieu Ceausescu, and shot him and his wife dead. Yet the fear instilled by the old regime still haunted the country. "Whenever I had extra food, I gave some of it away. But if I was down to my last piece of bread, I don't know if I would have given it." Katerina looked at me earnestly, "Would you?"

I was struck by the depth of her honesty, by the weight of her moral investigation. I shook my head. Coming from a privileged life in the West, these were not problems I'd ever had to face.

Katerina's friends who had been with us earlier that evening were part of a new generation of thinkers and activists. The day before I saw their political slogans plastered on the walls of the *Piata Universitatii*, the University Square. With three weeks to go before the country's first election, they were determined to overcome the old communist order and lay the ghosts to rest. Katerina was different from them, but she didn't know why.

"Life isn't getting any better, it's getting worse," she said. "Something has to change. I have to change. I can't live with the shadow of the past any more. Will you teach me to meditate?"

The next morning Katerina's husband took the children for a walk so we could be alone. Katerina took up a position on the white couch. I settled into the solid, dark armchair opposite her.

I started by explaining some basic concepts, that meditation is more than just relaxation or mind control. It is a way of life, a means of deeply knowing ourselves. By understanding how consciousness works we regain spiritual power. "The soul is our spiritual identity. It is who we are," I said, slowly. "You may think that you are Katerina, but that is just the name of your body. As a soul, you are more than the sum total of your physical being. The soul is so tiny it cannot be seen with these physical eyes. It can only be realized."

Katerina looked at me intently. She understood and spoke English well. But since she came from a respected communist family, I could not be sure whether 'soul' fitted into her vocabulary. I continued, "The soul is the conscious being, the life-force that makes the body work. It is a minute point of energy, just like a sparkling star, but smaller than the tiniest pinpoint. The form of the soul is a point. As a soul you sit inside this body and look out at the world from behind these eyes. The eyes are the window of the soul." I pointed to my forehead, to a place between my brows. "This is the seat of the soul..."

But my explanation was cut short. Katerina had put her head in her hands, and was slowly rocking back and forth on the couch. Tears streamed down her face.

"The soul really exists?" she exclaimed. "You mean it really exists?" A little girl's expression crept over her face. She put her husband's large handkerchief to her eyes. "I can't believe it..." she sobbed. There was a long pregnant pause. Then she said, "I knew all along, I knew it. I just needed someone to confirm it."

Silence again. Then, with the tears all gone, she whispered, "It is such a relief to know."

I remember when I first heard about the soul and began to meditate. All I had to do was pull my attention away from externals and focus on the light within, the soul. Instantly, I connected to the source of my spiritual energy and power.

It was a simple change of consciousness. Instead of identifying myself as a physical body that operates according to a complex system of chemical impulses, I became aware of myself as a soul, totally distinct from my body. I was a wondrous point of light -- a conscious, thinking, feeling being. The body was my vehicle and I, the soul, was like the driver of a car, sitting at the wheel -- in this case inside the brain -- and directing my activities through the body.

It was a beautiful feeling to connect to my real self. I was aware that all of my energy emanated from this one tiny, powerful point -- the soul. And instead of feeling scattered, now I was centered. I could actually feel the subtlety of my own spiritual energy pulsating gently from this still point behind my forehead. With attention, I could also begin to direct the flow of this energy, simply by maintaining an inner focus.

This shift from physical to spiritual awareness changed the way I thought about myself. I realized that I was light, not dense; I was eternal, not mortal. I was not weak or a victim of circumstance. I was a powerful soul in my own right, a master of my own destiny.

As soon as I heard this knowledge of soul, I couldn't stop thinking about it. I skipped, flew down the streets of south London where I lived at the time, laughing at passers-by like some crazy woman who had just won the lottery. Every now and then, as I stopped to look at my reflection in the shop windows, I half expected that I would look different, the child in me totally enraptured by the thought, "I am a soul, a beautiful shining star."

I had rediscovered my eternal identity and that discovery released in me a surge of energy, softer, warmer, more subtle than I had previously known. I felt invincible, energized, and suddenly acutely aware and present with myself.

"The first lesson of Raja Yoga is to understand who you are," my teacher Sister Jayanti told me during our session together earlier that morning. "For this you need knowledge of the soul." Then she tapped her forehead lightly and smiled. "It's what the ancient seers called the third eye of knowledge."

Whatever 'eye' it was, I knew wanted it. I wanted the peace, happiness, and exhilaration that came each time I connected. "Meditation means to focus inward on the soul," Sister Jayanti said. "When your third eye opens, you will realize many things about yourself. This is called self-realization."

So that was it. I had arrived at the place most mystics talk about. This was the origin of mysticism: the age-old desire to know the self. Throughout history, philosophers and the spiritually inclined sought divine knowledge as a means of unraveling the great mysteries of life. When the Greek philosopher Socrates went to the Oracle at Delphi and asked, "What is the highest knowledge?" he was told, "Know thyself."

At some point in our lives each of us needs to turn within. For it is here beyond the superficial layers of physical, social, and psychological constructs, that we discover the essence of our being and the meaning of life. "Do not go abroad," advised St Augustine, one of the early Christian mystics, "but turn within, for in the inner man dwells truth."

This inner way is the mystic way, the way to soul power. It is attained through knowledge of self and knowledge of God. Knowledge of one is incomplete without knowledge of the other. In discovering the self, there is the natural pull to want to know God, the Source and Seed of life. By knowing God, the soul gains in strength, and moves toward deeper levels of understanding. In his *Confessions* St Augustine asked, "But what is my God?" A paragraph later, he wrote, "And I turned to myself and said, 'And who are you?'" These seminal questions are ones that you will ask at the beginning of your journey, return to in the middle, and maybe answer at the end. One yogi I know spent five years meditating on just this one question: Who am I?

So, who am I? I am a soul. What is soul? The conscious being. The eternal being. The being who radiates light.

After my first week of experiencing the happiness of soul-connection, my critical mind began to question. How could I know if this knowledge of soul was true? What was the proof? So the women yogis claimed that the soul was a tiny point-source of metaphysical energy, totally distinct from the energy of matter, and that it housed all of the functions of consciousness, including rational and intuitive thinking, as well as a record of feelings and emotions, memories, and personality traits. By accepting this knowledge how did I know I wasn't deluding myself?

After a second week of internal wrestling, I came to an important realization. No matter how persuasive this knowledge was, I still had to figure it out for myself. No one could make me realize the soul, or help to verify my eternal existence. As it suggests, self-realization has to do with the self. It is an internalized process, arrived at on one's own through self-exploration. If I wanted realization I would have to resort to my own inner laboratory. "Experiment with this knowledge of soul and see if it works," I told my mind. "You've got nothing to lose if it doesn't." As my mind listened, my heart opened. I tested the knowledge in meditation, then observed the results.

What I found is this: by connecting to soul, the memory of soul returns. Knowledge of it already lies within. Katerina knew that she was a soul, even though in this lifetime she had had no religious or spiritual instruction. The knowledge I shared with Katerina gave her the tools to remember. Basically, I had gone to Bucharest to jog her memory.

Each soul has a memory of soul. In the deepest recesses of our being, we know that we are luminous. We know, but at the same time we forget. A forgetful fog shields us from the truth.

With spiritual knowledge we can cut through this lack of clarity. The moment we wake up and realize that we are souls, we are empowered. In Katerina's case, knowledge gave her a new identity, a spiritual center no person or regime could ever touch or harm. From those brief moments of quiet in her tiny living room, her mind began to expand in ways she didn't think were possible. She started to tackle her dependency on cigarettes, became more patient with her children, worried less about the future. Connecting to soul was her path to freedom.

While shifting into spiritual awareness can happen in seconds, maintaining a spiritual focus requires concentrated effort. It's not as simple as saying, "Gee, I'm a soul," and thinking that you have found a quick route to spirituality. Connecting to soul is a profoundly sacred act, not a superficial switch of vocabulary.

Where to begin? Stop for a few minutes every day. As you turn your attention inward, become aware of who you are. Say to yourself, "I am soul, a tiny beautiful star, radiating light." Hold this awareness for a while.

Allow yourself time to remember...

THE PEACE WITHIN

Peace is the original religion of the soul.

NAVIGATING MY BAG through the jostling crowd Anna and I made our way toward the check-in counter. We were late. The attendant from Olympic Airways was stressed-out and unhelpful. "Your flight out of Athens is overbooked," she said. "The in-coming flight hasn't yet arrived. You will have to wait."

"Do I have any guarantee of getting on the flight?" I asked.

The attendant smirked, "It's the day before New Year. What do you expect, a miracle?"

My friend Anna, who has wavy blond hair, lifted her hands and shoulders apologetically, "This is Athens, what can I say?"

I nodded. There was nothing we could do. As meditators, we knew that these kinds of aggravations weren't won by fighting. Besides, we had just come from the meditation center where I had spoken to students about the benefits of maintaining calm in stressful situations. Now, my own words were being put to the test. So to pass the time, I asked Anna to teach me Greek.

"Ime mia galina psihi."

"What?"

"Ime mia galina psihi," she repeated. "I am a peaceful soul."

I laughed. The words seemed to drop casually out of her mouth. I tried to repeat them, "Im galin psi..."

At first I couldn't stretch my cheek muscles wide enough, and the words bottled up inside of me, hard and unsatisfying. But the more I practiced "Ime mia galina psihi," the softer the words fell from my lips, and the more peaceful I became.

The airport atmosphere was hot and tense. Passengers were bumping into bags, almost kicking each other. I must have stood at the check-in counter for forty-five minutes, smiling at the attendant, repeating intermittently under my breath so she didn't hear me, "I am a peaceful soul."

Anna and I gave each other knowing looks. We were conspirators, spreading vibrations of peace. My Greek was appalling, but it didn't matter. These were no longer words, but wings my mind could fly on. The attendant could have told me anything and I would have been happy.

After a while, she went away to consult a supervisor. When she returned to the counter, the woman handed me my ticket and boarding pass, "You're on the flight," she said, and waved me aside.

I am a peaceful soul. This was the first transformative thought I consciously created. My teacher, Sister Jayanti, had taught me how to use it as the basis for my meditation. It was simple. I just focused my attention inward, and said to myself, "I am a peaceful soul. Peace is who I am." Not only did I create a peaceful thought, but in the silence that followed feelings of peace and tranquility also emerged. It was the most calming thing I had ever done with my mind.

Peace lies within. At the deepest level of the soul there is a huge reservoir of peace waiting to be tapped. Try it. By experiencing yourself as soul in meditation, this quality of peace is naturally released. Simply maintain the awareness "I am a peaceful soul." This consciousness opens the channel allowing peace to flow.

Peace is not the absence of war or violence. It is an inner state of quietness and calm, a freedom from internal agitation and worry. Things outside of yourself cannot give you peace, not even nature. The mountains cannot give you peace, nor can the pine trees. Their stillness can only remind you that *you* are peace.

Once you have tasted the peace within, you won't want to step back into a non-peaceful state. Somehow, being without peace will seem as if you are going against the grain, like chalk scraping across the surface of a blackboard. Whereas being peaceful is like coming home.

We all long for peace. I haven't heard anyone say that he or she seeks anger or wants to experience pain. We search for peace because it is our original state. We know it as soon as we experience it. Peace is contagious. All it takes is for one person to be peaceful and to emanate that quality of peace, and soon many others are inspired to experience the peace within. When I told my friend Carmen about the soul, she loved the idea of being naturally peaceful. Before going to sleep at night, she created the thought "I am a peaceful soul." She slept peacefully, and when she woke up, she felt peaceful.

Carmen had a friend who was under a lot of stress at home. She told her friend, "Look, just create the thought, 'I am a peaceful soul,' and you will start to realize that this is who you are." Carmen's friend rang her the next day, "It's amazing, I feel so peaceful, so relaxed. This peaceful soul thing really works." Carmen's friend then told another friend about being a peaceful soul. After that I lost track, but I am sure the 'peace-thing' didn't end there.

Try it and see. Say to yourself, "I am a peaceful soul." Repeat this thought again, quietly, confidently, "I am a peaceful soul." Do not say it mindlessly, say it from the depth of your being. As well as thinking and saying this thought, feel the reality behind it. Feel that you are a peaceful soul, and because you are peaceful, everything around you is also touched by your peace.

Thoughts create reality. As you think, so you become. I'll give you an example. Before I discovered that I was a peaceful soul, I used to become irritated in traffic jams. Particularly when driving to work I used to jump up and down in my seat and thump the steering wheel anytime I got stuck behind a line of cars for longer than five minutes. In my early days of learning to meditate, I took up thinking, "I am a peaceful soul." I would practice this as I went bumper to bumper over Hammersmith Bridge in London on my way back from work in Shepherd's Bush. After three months, I noticed a huge change. Instead of my normal impatience, I sat quietly behind the wheel and observed the other drivers from a place of peace. I saw the fists, the fingers, the glint of sunlight on metallic fenders, yet I remained undisturbed. Even when the traffic was backed up for miles, I didn't lose my cool or calm. I was a peaceful soul. Peace was my true nature.

What also helped me to undergo this dramatic change was a radical shift of consciousness. This came about not from having adopted a different attitude or affirming a positive thought, rather it was related to the way I now saw myself. Having meditated deeply for three months on the fact that I was a peaceful soul, I was now learning to act peacefully in thought, word, and deed. This awareness of soul in action was strengthened as I held the steering wheel of my car, and looked out through the windows as a peaceful observer at the chaos of traffic going on around me. I was no longer a physical being getting caught up in the irritations of the world. I was a spiritual being interacting with the physical world, fully in control.

In this way, I began to shift out of what is called in Raja Yoga 'body consciousness' into the realm of 'soul consciousness.' These two terms refer to the lens through which a person views him or herself, others, and the world. A person's worldview and vision of self is either outer-directed and shaped according to what he or she perceives through the senses, or it is inner-directed and shaped from the perspective of soul.

In body consciousness, we define ourselves and others as either male or female, black or brown, red or white, rich or poor, young or old, skilled or unskilled. In soul consciousness, each person is seen as a soul. Each one is recognized for the light and peace within, and for all the innate qualities that make the soul shine such as contentment, patience, joy, wisdom, truth, etc. Whereas body consciousness is concerned with physical identity, soul consciousness is the experience of one's spiritual identity.

Take time now to go within. Check the vision you have of yourself. If you are basing your identity -- and as a consequence your reality -- on externals, such as the way you look, the position you hold in society, or the opinions others have of you, then you are operating in body consciousness. If, on the other hand, your identity is based on a vision of soul, then you are operating in soul consciousness.

As a soul, you are light, bright, and eternal. You have no age, no color, no gender or ethnicity. You are free from limitations. As a soul, you take on a body, be it male or female and, and you play a part as an actor on the stage of life. You can play the part of a mother, father, son, daughter, plumber, or clerk. The role doesn't matter. Just as long as you operate consciously as a soul, you will be at peace. But if you do not know your spiritual identity, you will experience the pain of living in a material world that defines you according to various physical attributes, such as your looks, job description, and the size of your pay check.

In this media-driven age of glitz and glamour, the pressure to identify with one's body is intense. The young are especially vulnerable. Nine years ago, I had a conversation about this with a government minister in Zimbabwe. She related to me the following story: "One morning a friend of mine went into the bathroom. She found her five-year-old daughter sitting on the floor scraping her skin with a razor. 'Mummy,' said the little girl, 'I don't want to be black any more.' The little girl's elder sister had fairer skin. She thought her sister was more beautiful and wanted to be like her."

What makes this story all the more shocking is that it happened in Africa, and not in a Western culture where people of African descent are more in the minority. I told the minister that if the little girl had had some knowledge of soul, she might have been spared this grief. The minister replied, "Had the mother known, both would have been spared."

This strong urge to identify with our bodies and physical attributes is one of the primary causes of human suffering. Body consciousness places us in a transitory world, open to the fluctuating forces of nature. At any moment, our bodies can fail us. We can go bankrupt, our children can leave home, we can lose our jobs, looks, credibility, even our country. Nothing is safe or predictable, except the eternal soul. Peace comes from knowing who we are; the lack of peace comes from believing we are just mortal beings.

Many years ago I visited a film studio in Los Angeles. A friend and I were sitting in the little tour train, waiting to take off. Suddenly a burst of yelling and screaming came from the back of the train. Turning around I saw a huge gorilla shaking the bars and gnashing his teeth. The children screamed in terror, while their parents laughed. The other passengers began to smile. Unlike the children, the adults knew there was a man inside that gorilla's outfit. We had nothing to fear. We could afford to laugh and smile because we knew about costumes and movie sets. The children did not.

At the time, I felt for those children and wished their parents had been quicker to explain and comfort them. Watching their fearful faces reminded me how devastating it is to be uninformed. I often use this story as an analogy in lectures to illustrate the importance of spiritual knowledge for this is what helps to distinguish between illusion and reality. The adults on that train knew the difference between what was real and what was not. The children, on the other hand, due to their ignorance and inexperience, couldn't make the distinction. By taking the gorilla at face value, they 'bought' the illusion, and as a consequence experienced fear.

Think about it: What makes you afraid? What takes away your peace? What causes you to be unhappy? Most, if not all, of your answers will be linked to a false perception of yourself and others. Seeing ourselves as bodies that have souls rather than as souls with bodies is the ultimate illusion.

To move away from body consciousness, consider this knowledge of soul to be like a laser beam of light. Imagine you can use this beam of light to penetrate the layers of false identity that keep the real you hidden from yourself. With this light, you can illuminate your core, touch the peace within, and know with absolute certainty this is who you are.

The more you practice soul consciousness, the more you will awaken to the subtlety of energy, beauty, light; the soft interplay of your thoughts, feelings, qualities and vibrations. As you maintain the awareness of being a soul while walking, talking, and moving around, you will notice a change in the use of your energy, and a greater ability to stay focused and calm.

Then instead of being worried or agitated, you will be at peace, able to generate an atmosphere of peace and well-being around you. As a peaceful soul you will be naturally drawn to God, more easily able to attain the peace that comes from the Divine.

Try this: When you get out of bed in the morning, stop for a moment, turn your attention inward, and create the awareness, "I am a peaceful soul." As you jump into the car, or onto a bus or bike, say to yourself, "I am a soul, a peaceful soul." As you make a cup of coffee, turn on the computer, sort through your mail, stop for a second and remember, "I am a peaceful soul."

Whether you are in ordinary, everyday situations, or difficult, distressing situations, do not worry. Stay cool, stay calm. Before doing anything, say to yourself, "I am a peaceful soul."

Remember, a peaceful soul is at peace even when there is chaos all around.

KNOWING GOD

Very few know Me as I really am.

WHO IS GOD? Can God be known?

Over the centuries people of all backgrounds, cultures and faiths have turned to God. Many were looking for strength and support from a Divine Source, even though at times that Source may have seemed distant and surreal. Others climbed mountains, went on pilgrimages, performed rituals and fasts, penance, and prayers -- did the most extraordinary things in their quests to find God and know God.

Of all the mysteries in the universe, perhaps God is the most mysterious. While each faith tradition has its own teachings about God, even strong adherents to those traditions have professed to not knowing God as well as they would have liked. Apparently when St Francis of Assisi was once praying, he was heard to say over and over again, "My God! My God! What are You? And what am I?" Striving to know God was a recurrent theme among the ancient mystics. Many of them spent a lifetime trying to fathom the depth of the Supreme.

And today -- in churches, mosques, meditation centers, and other places of worship, in homes, and on the streets -- the same questions that the mystics posed down through the ages are still being asked, "What is God? Where is God? How can I come close to God?"

The journey to God is both universal and personal. God belongs to all souls, but each person has to find his or her own way to the Source. And yet any seeker's attempt to know God is complicated by the fact that in today's world there is a plethora of beliefs about the Divine. The information age has produced an abundance of books and websites on all matters related to the spiritual. Even within the same faith tradition there are many different views, making it difficult for the spiritual seeker to come to any clear comprehension. Hence my own trepidation in writing these words and venturing into an arena that for centuries has been at the center of debate and conflict.

Can anyone really know God, except God Himself?

Last week my friend Annabel went to a lecture given by a Catholic priest on mysticism and multiculturalism. The priest said that he had read most of the mystical literature from Hinduism, Buddhism, Judaism, Christianity, and Islam and had come to the conclusion that it was impossible to know God.

My friend was speechless. After all, weren't the mystics those contemplative types who had gone into silence to commune with God? If they couldn't know God, what hope was there for the rest of us? Finally, unwilling to accept the premise that God could not be known, Annabel decided not to take the priest's word for it. "The mystics may not have had all the answers. It still doesn't mean God is unknowable," Annabel said. "That's like saying God is dead."

I agreed. But I also understood where the priest was coming from. There is a substantial body of mystical literature expounding the idea that God transcends all thoughts and human conceptions. In the Jewish mystical tradition of the Kabbalah, for instance, God, the absolute essence, lies beyond human comprehension. The term *Ein-Sof* meaning Infinite was used to convey this unknowable and transcendental aspect of the Divine "which has no end" and is above or beyond thought. For some of the Christian mystics God was equally unknowable. For example, Richard Rolle, the fourteenth-century English mystic, said that the question "What is God?" could not be answered. "How can you seek to know what is essentially beyond knowledge and cannot be conveyed to anyone?" Rolle wrote in his book, *The Fire of Love.* "Even God himself, who can do all things, cannot teach you what He is... Only God knows Himself or has the ability to know Himself."

A slightly different viewpoint was offered by the unknown author of the *Cloud of Unknowing,* a fourteenth century book of contemplation. The author admitted to having no idea as to the identity of God. Yet he said that God could be approached provided a person rid him or herself of any preconceived ideas and entered into the "darkness of the absence of knowing." In this way, the author sought to distinguish between an intellectual knowing of God based on limited human thinking, and an emotive knowing of a personal God based on the language of the heart.

"Every single rational creature has two faculties: the power of knowledge and the power of love," he wrote. "God is always quite unable to be comprehended by the first faculty, that of intelligence, but he is totally and perfectly comprehensible by the second, the power of love." In other words, in his view, God could not be intellectualized, only understood through the vehicle of love.

This distinction is important for anyone on the mystic path today. To be drawn to the mystical side of the spiritual journey means to be concerned with the direct experience of God, rather than any dry conceptions of the Divine. Indeed, mystics of the past paid less attention to theories about Divine Love, and more attention to attracting the infusion of God's Love into their lives. Through prayer and contemplation, poetry and song, mystics of India such as Meera and Kabir, Sufis such as Rabi'a and Rumi, Christian saints such as Hildegard of Bingen and John of the Cross expressed their love and longing for God. All of their devotion was dedicated to achieving a total union with the One they loved.

Love has appeared from Eternity and will continue till Eternity and none has been found in eighty thousand worlds who could drink one drop of it until at last he is united with God.
– Rabi'a

Much of what the mystics discovered about God came to them through revelations and visionary experiences. Many admitted that they just caught glimpses, and then were left to interpret what they saw, felt or heard. In *Revelations of Divine Love*, Julian of Norwich wrote, "From the time that it [the revelation] was showed I desired oftentimes to learn what was our Lord's meaning." Fifteen years later Julian said she came to understand that "Love was our Lord's meaning."

Even the great sixteenth-century Spanish mystic St Teresa of Avila who achieved profound levels of union with God, in accordance with her own tradition's definition of this state, wrote about her inadequacies in realizing all there was to know about the Divine. For many of the ancient mystics, penetrating the mysteries of God did not always lie within their control. Many of the insights they gleaned came, as St Teresa said, as a 'favor' or 'mercy' from God.

So maybe when the priest said it was impossible to know God, what he really meant is that there are different levels at which God can be known. God is knowable and attainable in the ultimate sense, but the extent of that attainment varies from person to person. There is also another factor that needs to be taken into consideration: the probability that God has not revealed everything to us about the Divine, but could do so at any moment.

From all of the mystical literature I have studied, two important details about God stand out in my mind. I select these two aspects because they resonate most with my own experiences and with the experiences of others that I know.

The first is the recurring description of God as light. St Hildegard of Bingen, the twelfth-century German mystic, had visions of God as "The Living Light." In *Scivias*, she described having an experience of "a bright light which without any flaw of illusion, deficiency, or deception designates the Father." This imagery of light can be found in most religious and spiritual traditions. It is also the dominant image used by people who claim to have 'encountered' God during near death experiences.

The second is the experience of God through His qualities. For Catherine of Genoa, God was Light, Love, and Peace. Evelyn Underhill in *Mystics of the Church* quotes her as saying, "Wouldst thou that I should show thee what God is? Peace; that peace which no man finds, who departs from Him." St Teresa of Avila named her God according to His attributes, "Truth," "My Good," "My Mercy." And St John of the Cross, a contemporary of St Teresa, described his experience of God as an in-taking of God's qualities into the soul. In *Flame of Love*, he wrote, "Contemplation is nothing other than the peaceful and loving infusion of God, which, if accepted, inflames the soul with the spirit of love." God's qualities are also seen to be endless. Many mystics write that there are no limits to the depth of God.

When I was doing research for *Soul Power*, I came across a large leather-bound book in a friend's library in Jerusalem. In it were lines from a liturgical hymn, the *Akdamut Millin*, praising God's greatness and grandeur. The hymn was originally written in Aramaic by the eleventh-century Jewish preacher Meir ben Isaac Nehora'i. It goes like this:

> *Could we with ink the ocean fill*
> *Were every blade of grass a quill*
> *Were the world of parchment made*
> *And every man a scribe by trade.*
> *To write with love*
> *Of God above*
> *Would drain the ocean dry;*
> *Nor would the scroll*
> *Contain the whole*
> *Though stretched from sky to sky.*

These descriptions of God match my own experiences. Before my 'out of body experience' in Paris, I had no real comprehension of God -- I believed in God and had an indistinct faith, but I was basically naive in matters of the Divine. Then, when I least expected it, God pulled me to Himself. I experienced God as a Being of pure energy, not an indistinct energy, but a Being of Higher Consciousness. Through the rays of Love and Light, I felt the magnitude of a Divine presence. Looking back, I knew it was God because of the strength of that energy that flooded my being. No energy can be compared to God's. God is not in this world, nor of this world, not even in nature. The pure vibrations that emanate from God's Being are the highest and of an essence that is beyond this world.

After my meeting with God, even though I had been filled with His light, I was left dangling in the dark. For some years afterward I was confused. I didn't have the necessary tools to assimilate my experience. Nor did I have any idea how to connect with God again.

When the women yogis introduced me to their teachings, they provided me with the necessary spiritual knowledge to understand God and also a key to experience the Divine. "Just as we souls are beings of pure energy, so too the Supreme Soul is a tiny point of conscious energy, radiating light," Sister Jayanti explained to me during one of my lessons. Her words hit my heart. "Yes," I thought, "I have seen God as light."

Sister Jayanti continued, "As the Supreme Source, God is smaller than a dot on a page, tinier than a pinhead." She pressed her thumb and index finger together and held it up to her eye. "So tiny," she smiled, "but more powerful in terms of energy than an atom bomb. Condensed energy is always the most powerful." I nodded. In my mind's eye, I saw God as the silent, tiny point around which all things revolved. Instinctively, I knew that the Light I'd encountered radiated out from a single point. It was a conscious Being who had drawn me close, not some uncontained amorphous light.

"God is the Seed, the eternal Source. As Supreme Soul, God is full of all knowledge and wisdom, all virtues and powers. God is like the sun spreading rays of peace and love, happiness and joy, purity, and power." Just talking about God made Sister Jayanti's eyes sparkle.

"How do you know?" I asked. It was a silly question. And for a moment I thought that I had disturbed her flow because she didn't answer. A few seconds passed, maybe more. Sister Jayanti had gone silent, totally still. The focus of her attention seemed to have turned inward and upward, and yet she was looking at me with such clarity that her face beamed with light.

"These are God's qualities," she said simply. "People of all religions remember God as Love, Happiness, Peace, Mercy, Compassion." I nodded. I had been set alight by God's love, overcome by an indescribable joy, so I knew what she said was true. "We come to know God through His qualities," Sister Jayanti continued. "God is a conscious Being with a distinct personality, someone with whom we can experience a close relationship. Both masculine and feminine qualities are found in God. As our Mother, God is loving and nurturing; as our Father, protecting and giving; as our Friend, constant and loyal. Moreover, God knows us more intimately than we know ourselves."

By the end of the lesson, I was dancing in happiness. Something amazing had just happened. A woman had spoken to me for an hour about God. It was a God she knew. And what she told me had corroborated my own experience. Later, as I began to meditate using the knowledge she had given me, I was able to connect with God again. "It's simple," I thought to myself. "All I needed was a method to help me find my way back to God."

Many years have passed since those early lessons. Over time what I have come to realize is this: to know God means to develop a personal and intimate relationship. This requires a complete approach, an engagement of both head and heart. It is possible to know God on the basis of spiritual knowledge but only through spiritual experience do we claim God as our own. A little child learns to walk using both legs, placing one foot in front of the other. Similarly, as souls we totter our way back to God, using the foot of knowledge as the foundation for our experience, and the foot of experience as the confirmation of our knowledge.

And the One who inspires us to walk guides our tentative steps.

YOGA-MYSTIC UNION

Understand yourself to be a soul and remember Me. To have yoga means for a soul to have a meeting with the Father.

IMAGINE A WORLD OF SILENCE far beyond this physical plane. Imagine a vast dimension of light without any limits, where there is no noise, no speech, no movement, only silence. This is God's domain -- the eternal realm -- and also the Home of all souls. There are various names for this place: soul world, supreme region, nirvana, heaven above, the eternal land, the world beyond sound. It is not accessible through physical means. Only the soul can go there.

To reach this world of silence, let go of the restrictions that normally bind you to your body and to this earth, and allow your consciousness to extend beyond time and physical space. As a soul you are like a tiny rocket. With your thoughts you can move beyond the sun, moon, stars and universe, and enter a timeless dimension.

To 'travel' in this way does not mean that you actually leave your body -- if you did, your body would cease to function. Instead, you project your consciousness beyond the physical realm to the place where you, as a soul, originate. And there, in the silence of eternity, you reconnect with God.

At first, it might seem difficult to conceive of this dimension where God resides. Ordinary consciousness restricts spiritual vision. When it comes to the comprehension of things, we are accustomed to relying on physical evidence to construct our reality. We know that the physical world exists because we can see it, smell it, and feel it (even though no two people ever experience the world in exactly the same way). However, to experience God in His domain requires a different kind of perception. It suggests a willingness to accept there is another Reality beyond this everyday world. To enter a dimension that is invisible to the human eye, and connect with a Being who is not of this world, requires the full concentration of inner sight. It is understood that soul consciousness leads to the Source. Yogis refer to this concentrated awareness as the "opening of the third eye."

Yoga means link, connection, union. There are many different kinds of yoga, both physical and spiritual. The one I practice is a form of meditation that links soul to God. If God is the target, and thoughts the arrows of concentration, connection is achieved by focusing our thoughts on the target. Where our thoughts go so too go our energy and attention. Since connection ultimately leads to union -- the meeting of two souls -- then God, the Supreme Soul, who is aware of our intent also draws us near. Just as when the eyes of two friends meet, and there is a discernible exchange, similarly, when we connect to God there is an automatic transmission of energy.

When this first happened to me I thought, "Wow! I've just touched God, and God has touched me." Of course, I didn't touch God physically. I simply reached out with my thoughts and connected to the Being of light. Then when a current of pure energy came back to me from God, I found that I was energized. After learning that God does not live in the physical world, I understood that He is not bound by the physical laws of change. As the only constantly stable Source of energy, God's role is to energize all those who seek to connect. Yoga, therefore, is the means for the soul to plug into God and receive whatever it is lacking, whether it is knowledge or peace, happiness or spiritual power.

Some people complain that they love God but aren't able to connect. This is because connection requires an ability to focus. A little bit of concentration won't do. If you sit to meditate and cannot still your mind, or if you are overly affected by the sights, sounds, smells, and whirl of daily activities, then you will only be able to think of God but you wont be able to connect and be filled by God. Hence, the importance of learning to meditate with discipline but also with passion. Each of us is filled to the extent we maintain the link.

Whether from East or West, mystics of the past viewed total union with God as their ultimate aim. A variety of opinions existed within the different mystical traditions about the nature of that state and how it could be achieved. One popular concept was to view union as a state of self-forgetfulness or self-loss. In the *Upanishads*, one of India's earliest religious texts, it is said, "Be lost altogether in Brahma [God] like an arrow that has completely penetrated its target." The idea was that by emptying oneself into God, it was possible to become One with God and thus achieve lasting liberation.

This desire for Oneness also lay at the heart of Jewish, Islamic, and Christian mysticism. Some of the Jewish mystics considered union with the Infinite as an ultimate experience that first required a total abandoning of oneself into a "state of nothing." While the Sufis, Islamic mystics, believed that to attain perfection and ultimate union with the Beloved, a person's sense of individuality had to be sacrificed in the fire of love.

Knock,
And He'll open the door.
Vanish,
And He'll make you shine like the Sun.
Fall,
And He'll raise you to the heavens.
Become nothing,
And He'll turn you into everything.

– Rumi

The concept of union involving a merging into God was taken up by the fourteenth-century Christian mystic Suso in his *Book of Truth*. Suso wrote, "Like a being which loses itself in an indescribable intoxication, the spirit ceases to be itself, divests itself of itself, passes into God, and becomes wholly one with Him, as a drop of water mingled with a cask of wine."

However, Ruysbroeck, another fourteenth-century Christian mystic, had a different view. He said that although the soul could attain union with God through love, it was nevertheless impossible for the soul to divest itself of its essence and merge with God and disappear. In the *Book of Supreme Truth*, Ruysbroeck wrote, "...no created essence can become one with God's Essence and pass away from its own substance. For so the creature would become God, which is impossible; for the Divine Essence can neither wax nor wane, nor can anything be added to It or taken from It." In other words, soul and God have separate identities; they are totally distinct. This view is the closest to my own understanding and experience based on the spiritual teachings I have received.

Although human souls are similar in size to the Supreme Soul and to each other -- each being an infinitesimal point of conscious energy -- no two souls are identical. Nor are we chips off the old block. God is unique, Supreme in terms of qualities, knowledge, energy, and power. God is not bound by time or space. Since God is One, He cannot be divided into parts, and therefore does not exist in all things. God is not in us, nor are we in God, nor can we become God or merge into Him through a state of union. However, in relationship with God we can acquire similar qualities and attributes through the simple act of Him filling us with Divine wisdom and strength.

The feeling of Oneness described by the mystics, therefore, is not the merged state of one plus One equals One as is often suggested. Rather, it is the overwhelming feeling of God's love that makes the soul feel as though two were One. Union means being united by love, not joined at the hip. It is the ultimate state of soul power.

What's surprising for those who have experienced it is that God desires this meeting of hearts as much as we do. In the Talmud, it is written, "God wants the heart." Indeed, God wants to fill us to the brim. As the eternal Seed, God is indivisible and intact, constantly full. God is the Benevolent Source who is constantly giving, nurturing, and renewing. God's pure intent is to make us souls as strong and beautiful as we can be, complete in all the beauty and divine qualities that come to us from Him. In *Revelations of Divine Love*, the English mystic Julian of Norwich expressed the intensity of love that God had shown her. She wrote, "It is I that thou lovest, that thou enjoyest, that thou servest. It is I that thou longest for, it is I that is all."

This desire to be united is reciprocal. Our human longing is to expand and feel God's presence. Through this link of yoga, a mighty flame envelops us, a sweet flame of love leaps from God's heart into ours, wiping away all other thoughts save of the Divine. When our link of love is secure -- unbroken for moments of timeless joy -- our connection is complete. As souls we do not lose ourselves in these outpourings of God's Love, instead we are made whole.

It is a process. First, we learn to link to God, then we form a relationship with God. The extent to which we contemplate God's qualities, and open ourselves to being filled by them, the more we feel in tune and stay connected. Being in relationship gives us the gift of Divine company. It is an intimacy that can last throughout the day, from the time we get up until we go to bed. God can even fill our dreams. Only when we are filled and transformed by Divine love, can God make use of us in the world. For the modern mystic, union with God does not isolate us from the world, but allows us to become co-partners with God in its stewardship.

For such a transformation to take place, we need to connect with God in the world beyond sound. For it is here, beyond the pull of ordinary consciousness, that we can concentrate on receiving light and strength from the

Supreme. Once empowered in this way, God's light shines in our lives and serves as a beacon for others. Connecting to God in the world of light is not the only way to experience connection, but it is by far the most powerful.

When I first learned of this mystic union, I would connect, then disconnect. I was afraid, perhaps unsure, of what would happen if I stayed with God for a long time. Over the years, I have learned to "ascend to the Light" and drink from God's never-ending fountain.

Now I cannot live a day without doing this.

"Come close, child!" You say.
"But You seem far, my God."
"I am far only from your mind."
"I must concentrate to reach You," I protest.
"Do other matters pull you so much?" God asks.
"Sometimes my mind won't stay still."
"Is your heart open?"
"I am willing, my Lord."

When I abandon mundane thoughts of the everyday world, and turn my attention inward and upward, I experience God's help. He puts a fatherly hand under my feet, and lifts me up high above the walls of this physical domain. In God's world, my world, we are alone, soul to Soul, point to Point, light to Light.

"All I need is contained right here, with You," I whisper. "You are the Seed of my life, my never-ending Source of strength."

As my Father, God fills me up, as my Mother, She cools me down. She nurtures me with the waves of Her deep peace. I dive into this cool, calm Ocean, submerse myself in the silent underwaters of Her presence.

And when I resurface, my Mother dries my face. She colors me pink with Her fragrant love and dresses me up for the start of another day.

GOLDEN THREAD

You make God belong to you in all relationships by tying Him with the thread of your love.

I MUST HAVE BEEN around eleven or twelve years of age, when my mother first told me the story of my birth. But I have added details to it, which I gleaned from her later on when I was much older and wanting to understand...

"The room was dark. Your father was away and I was alone. The pain of the contractions was intensifying. All of a sudden, my stomach heaved forward, the water burst, and I knew my time had come. I pulled myself off the bed, opened the door, and started down the long dark corridor shouting for help. And as I screamed I felt something coming through -- the top of your head -- and I knew it was useless to go further. No one could hear me in such a big house.

"My breath was short, my mouth dry. I stumbled from one wall to the next trying to get back to the room. I didn't know what to do, except to make my way back to the bed. I had an uncontrollable urge to push, but I had never done this before. You were my first child. As the contractions continued, fear mounted my body in clumps of sweat, my shouts mingling with tears of helplessness and pain. Still no one came. 'Oh, God,' I pleaded, 'Who will help my child?'

"In the midst of all my fear, I felt an extraordinary presence, as if two enormous arms had stretched out from underneath either side of the bed and enveloped me. These were strong arms, beautiful arms, and they wrapped themselves around me as you were squeezed through my dark tunnel into the world. The presence grew stronger and brighter, so much so that I knew we were not alone. Slowly my fears subsided, washed away by the light. As I was held, so too you were held. Together God cradled us.

"All at once you were there, fuzzy head, with your face squashed into the bed sheets, inert, lifeless. And I didn't have the strength to turn you over and help you to breathe. 'God, please make the child breathe,' I prayed. 'Don't let it die.'

"Suddenly she was there, at the end of the bed, coming from I don't know where. The old woman entered the room, picked you up and turned you on your back. You breathed."

When I first heard this story, I blocked my ears. I didn't want to hear how one night in September 1959, my paternal grandmother had left my mother alone at the far end of her house, and how the housekeeper had come in at the last moment and turned me over. I was repulsed by the thought of my mother struggling alone in an isolated room, and guilty about the pain she went through to give me birth.

The worst part was the God bit. I was sure my mother had made it up. Whoever heard of God playing midwife? It was some kind of sick joke.

Many years later, I realized that my reluctance to hear about God's role at my birth did stem from a sickness of sorts -- an inability to accept and receive divine love. Most of us believe in the power of love, but at the subconscious level we reject it. This is strange. We want love, crave love, but the beliefs we hold about ourselves and God prevent our hearts from opening. What is also lacking is the ability to relate to God in a deeply personal way. Many of us have learnt to keep God at a distance, to view the Divine in theological terms, or to call out only in times of need or despair. To commune with God as a living Being -- someone with whom we can form a close relationship -- is appealing but also frightening. In a way, it is far less threatening to wave at God from a distance than having a meeting face-to-face.

Like many people I've met, Tanya, a performer from Toronto, was resistant to organized spirituality and religion. "God was just a story to me," Tanya told me last winter. "There were so many barriers between us, I couldn't relate. Finally, after many years, I realized that in order to form a relationship with God, I had to let go of the old images and concepts I had of Him." The gentleness of meditation appealed to Tanya. Gradually, as she learned to reflect on God's pure qualities, her beliefs about Him changed.

Other people are less open to change. One meditation student told me, "To think of God in a personal way as my Father or Friend is disrespectful."

This student believed that God could only be understood as the

Creator. And as Creator, God is so powerful and mighty, the creation must be in awe of Him. I tried to explain, "But if you don't accept that you can have a relationship with God, then God will remain far from you. You will think of God with fear, not with love."

"I know," the man replied, "but I can't change the way I think."

Often the beliefs a person carries about God are connected to the beliefs he or she carries about him or herself. If a person feels small and unworthy, then God's love can seem unattainable. Similarly, just thinking of God as the aloof Almighty, and not as the loving and close Friend, can create a further separation and reinforce feelings of unworthiness.

Several years ago I had lunch with a woman who had gone to India and met some of my teachers. She made an interesting comment. "We are afraid to come close to spiritually evolved people," she said, "in case they see our imperfections. The last thing we want is for them to look behind our masks and see us as we are."

"The same is true of us in relation to God," I thought. What stops us from coming close is the fear that God will see us in our imperfect state. Such a fear stems from a belief in an angry, vengeful God, One who will punish us for our weaknesses and wrong doings. God may be Almighty, All-knowing and All-powerful, but as souls we are the children of God, and in relationship to us God is a kind, loving, and compassionate Parent. Our weaknesses may be visible to ourselves and others, but in God's eyes each child is more beautiful than the next.

Some people do not like to think of God as a benevolent Parent. They allow their negative experiences at the human level to cloud their perceptions of the Divine. But this relationship with God cannot be compared to a human relationship or judged by human standards. The bond between souls and God is natural and eternal. As souls we are beings of light, made in God's image. Just as God is Divine, souls are also divine. This is the thread that links us to our Divine Mother and Father.

A close relationship is based on trust and understanding. There is a deep inner feeling that says, "I belong to you, and you belong to Me." As the Mother, God loves all souls and claims each one as Her own. Hers is not a possessive love, but a love that nurtures and sustains, that does not hurt or diminish any child in any way. God is the Merciful, the Compassionate, and Benevolent One. There is no one as caring as God, as wise as God, as Truthful as God. To the extent we come to know and accept God's personality, our trust in the relationship grows.

From God's side, there is unconditional acceptance. No matter what condition a child is in, or how many imperfections he or she has, from my experience God sees beyond all of that. God accepts us as we are, whatever we are, and is willing to be accepted by us in any capacity in which we have need, whether as a Mother or Friend, Protector or Companion. If we place God on a pedestal, He will love us from afar; if we accept Her hand of friendship, God will draw us near. God gives with an open heart. It is our choice how much to take and what we make of the relationship.

When I leaf through the pages of my life, I am able to see the myriad ways God has made Her mark. Her writing is distinctive -- sometimes bold, other times unassuming, but always there. God has come to me more often than I have turned to the Divine. And while I place some comfort in this, there were many occasions when I lacked faith and held back from receiving all that I could.

One day, around eight years ago, I sat in meditation trying to figure out this inconsistency. "At times, I feel Your love keenly. At other times, I don't feel it at all. What's going on?" I asked God.

The answer came immediately, "Remember your birth." I shook my head, "Huh?" I hadn't thought about my birth in years. But suddenly an old image flooded my mind. I saw God cradling me in Her arms, bringing light into the dark room, giving me breath, hope, life. Then I saw my reaction, the look of rejection on my face. "Why did I turn away from You?" I cried out. "You gave me life."

Suddenly, I felt sick. It was a yellow gnawing sickness filled with fear -- a dread so ancient I hardly recognized it, so rooted in my being I couldn't ignore it. Then I knew. This was my deepest wound -- the primal wound that afflicted all souls when we first moved away from the Divine.

This separation story goes back far in time. The moment we forgot that we are souls, we distanced ourselves from God and forgot our Home of light. Forgetting led to loss and feelings of abandonment. But it is we who let go of God and not God who abandoned us.

When hearts become distanced they close down and harden to protect themselves against the wound of separation. And even if God pours out endless love, our shells are too thick for us to receive that love. Yet, despite our defensiveness God continues to love us. But until we make effort to restore this relationship, we will continue to feel incomplete, torn apart, and lacking in some way.

Where to begin?

1. *Claim God as your own.*
Make God belong to you, create the feeling that you belong to God. Reflect on the thought, "God loves me and accepts me as I am. I am a beloved child of the Divine." Consciously pull toward you God's presence, guidance, and love. You deserve it. Begin each day, saying, "Dear, God, I accept You into my life. I am worthy to receive Your love."

2. *Release your old beliefs and create new ones.*
Reaching a deep acceptance of God takes time. It involves a mental reprogramming. Write down all your old beliefs about God. Create a list with your new beliefs. Watch for any resistances that might emerge as you generate your new list. Your old beliefs will try to cling to you. Release them with love.

3. *Write a letter to yourself from God.*
Try to visualize how God sees you. If God were to speak to you directly, what would God say? Compose a letter to yourself from God, as if God were addressing a dear child or a special friend. You may want to begin and end this exercise with meditation. When you are finished, read the letter to yourself out loud, or ask a friend to read it. Maintain the consciousness that this letter is coming to you from God. Open yourself to receive these precious words. Allow yourself to accept the vision God has of you.

4. *Concentrate on developing faith.*
Faith is certainty. It is the unquestioning confidence and belief in God's reality and goodness. And because God is Good, all that God does brings benefit. Create the awareness that God is with you, from the time you wake up until you go to sleep. Whenever you start to doubt God's support for you, create the thought, "My God is with me. My faith is strong." Don't just say these words like an affirmation. Get behind the words, feel their strength, feel your faith to be your backbone, subtle and strong.

5. *Create a closeness with God.*
Give time to God every day. Select a special time when you can be together. Make God the focus of your meditations. Begin by contemplating the nature of God's personality and qualities. An analogy that is helpful is to think of God as an Ocean, endless and deep. Meditate on God as an Ocean of Peace, or an Ocean of Love and allow yourself to be submersed in these qualities. During the rest of the day, keep God as your Friend. Talk to God,

listen to God. Maintain the awareness that God is so close, you can feel the love in His heart beating for you.

Once, years ago, a beautiful image flooded my mind during meditation. I saw a bridge and all the souls of the world were walking across that bridge, back to God. The bridge was like a golden thread, very fine, but also strong. It connected every soul of the world to their Mother and Father, their Beloved and best Friend.

You see, without this bridge, without this golden thread of love, there can be no greatness in the twenty-first century. All of our spirituality, all of our fulfillment, depends on this return to God.

SOMETIMES PUSH,
SOMETIMES PULL

The Father says: I remember those who remember Me. Where there is love from the heart, and a relationship of deep love and closeness, it is difficult to forget.

ONCE, WHEN I WAS a three-month-old practitioner of Raja Yoga, I made a bargain with God -- not for money or anything material, but a bargain for love. I entered the small meditation room and sat with a firm thought, "I'm not getting up from here until You give me an experience of Your love."

It seemed to me that God was smiling, but I was serious. It took all of my courage to speak to God that way. I was desperate in that moment to feel divine love. Somehow, I had understood that this relationship was worth standing up for. If I was God's child, I had a right to Divine love. Doesn't every child have a right to his or her parents' time, attention, and love?

At first I sat with a little fear in my heart. What if God wouldn't respond? What if in reality I wasn't worthy to receive Divine love? What if God didn't care?

Within the space of an hour, I had looked at my watch at least ten times. My backside was sore, but in stubborn determination I sat myself even harder on the floor. It would be a long night. I said, "I'm not getting up from here, God. I told you I wouldn't. Not until You show me Your love."

Another hour went by. I rubbed my eyes to keep myself alert, and all the while my mind kept saying, "I'm here, I'm here." My mind felt as tense as a tightly wound ball of string. Slowly, surely, before an endless night I was teaching myself how to unravel it. I was learning to let go and let God. Then, when I least expected it, a long hand reached out and opened the door to my heart. There it lay, trembling and exposed, my vulnerable heart melting under an extraordinary heat, softening before the intensity of God's touch. Like a transmitter, God was beaming His energy down on me, pouring His love over me. He turned the intensity up, higher and higher, stronger and stronger, until I could not hold it any longer.

"Stop!" I told God. "Please, stop." It was rude. But I had to let Him know. There was only so much love I could take...

Having a relationship with God is a two-way street. You make effort, God responds. God reaches out, you respond. Sometimes it's a push, sometimes a pull. Sometimes you can spend hours talking to God and feel you aren't getting as close as you would like. Other times, out of the blue, He reveals Himself to you, makes you feel special, as if no one else is as precious to Him as you are.

This happened to me a few months ago. I was sitting in my bedroom cross-legged on the bed. I was minding my own business, not even thinking of God, writing a letter to a friend. Suddenly, a pure, silky energy descended on me and covered me with a warm glow. I knew it was Divine energy. It had that soft, luminous quality to it, that unmistakable firmness and strength. Wrapped in God's blanket of love, I felt protected. Not that I needed protection at that moment, or even love. God was making a silent offering, a gift of His presence.

At times like this, I am grateful for God's grace. I ask, "How can I receive so much tenderness when the loving is not initiated by me? Does God consciously choose to reach out when He feels like it? Or is it simply that, at certain peaceful moments when I have no tension in my mind, I am more in tune with His energy and can feel His presence? Or maybe these moments are a return for the efforts I have made earlier to forge my link and make my connection with Him strong?"

Whatever the case, this phenomenon of God taking an active role in our relationship astounds me. I cannot explain it fully. All I know is that God has His ways of doing things. So, I've learned not to question God's timing or reasoning, but to enjoy His magnetic pull whenever it happens.

There are times on the mystic path, however, when the pull is conditional upon our state of soul as well as our own desire for union. God is like a Magnet seeking out the needle of the soul. But if the soul isn't ready, or if it is covered by the rust of restlessness and negativity, then the pull cannot happen so easily. Internally, each of us is aware of the heaviness within and the reasons why there are moments when we are not attentive or attracted to the Divine.

While God does not stop loving us, we have to be conscious how to draw His love toward us. Attracting the Divine into our lives requires a clear mind and a clean heart. Dadi Janki, my spiritual mentor, once said, "Make your heart clean for God to sit in. Where do you keep God? In the temples and mosques, or in a clean heart? If you keep the world's garbage inside you, God's love won't be able to enter your heart."

So think about making your heart a temple, and invite God in. Each time you meditate, prepare yourself with love. Sit with freshness, as if you are connecting to God for the first time. Do not think about the experience you had yesterday, or the one you might have tomorrow.

No two meditations are the same. You cannot recreate the time when you sat on a rock by the sea, the dry wind caressing your face, and light streaming out of your hair. You can remember the sweetness of God pulling you into silence, but if you impose that scene on your meditation today, hoping to retrieve that same sweetness, that same silence, then you will miss out on the magic of the here and now.

Be open to the present. Each moment is like a seed waiting to flower. Each opportunity to connect with God demands all your attention. Go deep into God. There is no limit to what God offers, no limit either to the steps you can take toward the Divine.

The desire for intimacy is reciprocal. God sees the effort that you are making and gives you a million times return for each tentative step. It's His way of training you to take responsibility for this relationship.

If you keep God in front of your eyes, He won't let you out of His sight.

REFLECTIONS ON
SPIRITUAL KNOWLEDGE

Reflective Questions

1. How well do you know yourself? What steps have you taken so far to explore your inner world?
2. How has the knowledge that you are a soul changed the way you perceive yourself?
3. What aspects of body consciousness are limiting your spiritual growth? For instance, do you base your identity on your age, physical appearance, gender, job description, wealth, or position in society?
4. How close do you feel to God? If you feel far from God, what old beliefs are preventing you from forming a relationship? Make a list.

Exercises for Spiritual Practice

1. To connect to your seat of spiritual power, have the awareness that you are a soul. Deep within lies a treasure store of many virtues: patience, tolerance, happiness, contentment, courage, wisdom, etc. Spend five to ten minutes each day contemplating these inner qualities. Think about the times when you experienced these qualities and remember how you felt. Now meditate deeply on each quality so that you radiate it out from your whole being.

2. Think about the qualities of God that attract you. God is the Ocean of Love and Peace, Happiness, and Truth. Visualize the Divine as a fountain of light and that these qualities are rays pouring down on you and filling you.

3. Consider the relationship that you would like to develop with God. Do you like the idea of God as your Mother or Father, Teacher, Beloved, or Friend? Have a conversation with God in the context of that relationship. You can talk about your hopes and fears, your life plans and spiritual efforts.

4. At the beginning and end of each meditation, take time to realize that you have the right to be in relationship with God and to receive all the Goodness that God has to offer. Practice having gratitude for what you receive.

Meditation on Peace

Turn your attention inward. Find your place of focus on the still point within. Become aware of your thoughts. Start by creating thoughts of peace. Allow each thought to be filled with peace, and then fill each space between your thoughts with peace. Become aware that peace is your original quality of being. You are totally at peace with yourself. Your mind is a vehicle of peace. Your body is a temple of peace. You are so peaceful that outside events and circumstances do not disturb your peace. Say to yourself, "I am a beautiful soul filled with the power of peace."

Peaceful feelings now flow from your thoughts of peace. Notice that your energy has changed. Internally, you feel stronger, more alive, more concentrated. Now turn your attention to the Supreme. Feel that God, the Ocean of Peace, is beckoning to you. From the world of silence, God is calling you to His Home, your Home. You stand before God as if you were standing at the shore of the Ocean. Waves of God's peace lap against you, filling your mind, filling your whole being. You are held by peace, supported by peace, nurtured by the peace of God.

STAGE THREE

SPIRITUAL PRACTICE

*Now it is time to sit quiet, face to face with thee,
and to sing dedication of life in this silent and
overflowing leisure.*

– Rabindranath Tagore –

SILENCE

The loveliest thing in the world is silence. Have you experienced the greatness of the power of silence?

WHEN I WAS EIGHTEEN, I didn't like to be still. I was active, curious, and intense. In reality, I was scared of being alone. A group of us used to meet regularly in the afternoons at Denny's Den, the university bar. My friends drank Molsons Canadian, while I ate popcorn and drank coffee. The guys talked about football and ice hockey, I dreamed of being a journalist.

Then one day, out of the blue, I walked out of Denny's Den and didn't go back for a week. I don't know what made me do this, but something deep down told me that I needed to confront my fear of being alone. I had to become free from the need of external stimulation and of being in the company of others to feel good.

For the first two evenings, I studied Beaudelaire's poem about the white albatross killed by sailors on a ship. I read Sartre, Unesco, and Jean Genet. The European existentialists and absurdists made sense to me. Their nihilistic concepts paralleled my own darkening gloom. My thoughts turned to my friends, and I imagined them in the Den laughing and having a good time.

By the third evening I was depressed. The books remained unopened on the dining room table. The TV got switched on and off, maybe three or four times. I was desperate to escape my tumultuous mind.

On the fourth evening, I sat quietly on the sofa with a cup of coffee in my hand and listened. At first I heard only the sounds of neighbors in the apartment above, then an ambulance siren, then nothing. I started to count the cracks on the ceiling, and then stared at the whitewashed walls, suppressing the urge to switch on some music. I kept waiting for something to happen, for feelings within me to change, for this storm of insecurity to pass.

Soon I became aware of the quiet of my own gentle breathing. I felt beautiful breath nourishing each cell of my body, the softness of my own existence creeping like the sea over a naked shore, holy and fresh. As I became quieter, more aware of myself inwardly, my mind stopped questioning. It was as if my walnut brain had suddenly cracked open and I was still, at peace. There was no longer the pull to my friends, nor to the familiarity of clinking glasses. All that existed was this timeless, sacred moment when fear had left me and silence had come.

This was not a silence outside of myself; it emerged from within. I was deeply silent. The experience was similar to what Thomas Merton calls, in his book *The Springs of Contemplation*, "A true silence which is alive and which carries a loving presence."

I like this idea of an alive and loving silence. A silence such as this is not empty, but full and overflowing. Silence is not a blankness of thought or a vacuous feeling inside. It is the kernel of existence, a place inside as safe as home.

If you trace the entire expansion of human consciousness back to its place of origin, you will find silence. If you gather all the qualities that exist in the soul and distil them to their essence, you will find silence. Just as white is the common base of all the rainbow colors, similarly, silence is the essence of soul. If you want to know yourself, then go into silence. In your silent state you are beyond external distraction, free from agitation and disturbance.

Learn to be silent
let your
quiet mind
listen
and absorb
– Pythagorus

When I had my first 'breakthrough' into silence, I was not a meditator. I possessed no clear understanding of my own internal functionings, nor any method to guide me. I was just someone who wanted to face a deep-rooted fear of being alone. To avoid being with myself, I had filled my life with all kinds of social activities. When I stopped those activities, I had no place to run, no person with whom to engage, no entertainment to distract me. My mind went into shock. I felt vulnerable, lost, and alone.

After the initial shock, my mind gradually calmed down. It began to look inward rather than outward for a place of focus. Then, without any direction on my part, as if by instinct, my mind pushed through its own wall of resistance, that crushing fear of loneliness, and discovered the loving silence. "This is it," I cried. "This is what I am."

Many of us are frightened of breaking through the noise of our own delusions. We use actions as a diversion and means to validate our existence. The common assumption is that through multi-tasking and jam-packed timetables we will achieve happiness and fulfillment. In reality, this over-activity is stressing us out and taking away our peace.

About nine years ago, I was in San Francisco attending a meeting of community leaders. It was four-thirty in the afternoon. Many of the people kept looking at their watches. I could feel tension mounting in the room as the time came for the meeting to end. One official explained, "This is my fifth meeting today. I've another one at five with the AIDS group, and another at six-thirty with the Shelter for the Homeless." As he spoke he inched his way toward the door, sweat pouring from his chin, spotting his already red-spotted tie.

We've all been there. Modern life is a roller coaster of tasks and responsibilities that rarely affords any of us the peace and quiet that we desperately need even if our well-being is seriously at risk. We think, "I work to pay the bills and look after my family. I give time to my community. I don't have time for silence." It's not that we don't have time, it's simply we don't want to make time. Being overly active is a lifestyle choice. "How are you?" "Really busy, thanks." The choice is made partly out of habit, partly out of fear. Many of us are not used to stilling our bodies, let alone our minds. The idea of sitting quietly and going deeply into silence is a frightening undertaking. It's like going to a country where no one speaks our language. In today's world, silence has become a foreign language and being still a forgotten art.

Part of the problem, I believe, is that we live in a society disconnected from spirit. Silence isn't valued in our culture. Spirit is ignored. In ignoring spirit we have opened up a deep chasm that cuts across the surface of our existence separating ourselves from our true selves. This chasm has turned us into human machines, performing functions and tasks, deprived of our spiritual needs.

Silence is the forgotten key that can help us to connect again to soul. Silence doesn't take us away from the world, but gives us the strength to be in the world and give something back. Silence is the nurturing force that empowers us, making all that we do vibrant and meaningful.

Some people resist meditation because they think of it in terms of renunciation. It is true that in the past, and even today, yogis and mystics left their homes, families, and responsibilities, and shut themselves away to seek enlightenment. In many ways they were losing the most fertile ground for spiritual development. For modern mystics the best place to grow spiritually is at home, at school, at work. These places will provide you with the best conditions to explore "your self." Nowhere will you be more fully tested in your application of spiritual principles than in real life situations among the people with whom you are in close connection and those whom you dearly love.

Think of silence as your backbone. With it you will be able to enter life more fully, rendering it more beautiful and sane. Spiritual development is about learning to live in the hustle and bustle of the world, and yet being able to go beyond the effect of negative situations and surroundings. Dadi Prakashmani, my other spiritual mentor, once asked members of the general public who had come to hear her talk, "Do you have peace of mind? Ask yourself this question every day. Some of us have the tendency to live life just for the sake of it. Others really want to know life. Through meditation we are able to realize the real power that lies within ourselves. Silence is the power that can take us beyond all negative experiences, and give us the strength to live life positively."

There are a number of ways you can develop the power of silence:

1. *Begin by valuing silence.*
Make time during the day to be in silence. Make a conscious choice to not fill your space with noise. Turn off the television, the radio, the CD player. Get used to being *in silence.*

2. *Commit yourself to exploring and experiencing silence.*
Stop all your activities, find a quiet place, still your body, still your mind, and connect to yourself as a soul. Know that at the deepest level of your being, you are silent. Silence is not the absence of thoughts. It the state of being fully self-aware, not thought-less, but full of thought power.

3. *Learn to bring the power of silence into your words and actions.*
Carry on with your normal activities, but talk less, use less energy. *Infuse the power of silence* into your relationships and activities. Think of silence as

the power of soul filling each action, each connection, with a loving and peaceful presence. Then instead of rushing through life to get things done, you will perform actions that shine, not as deeds of necessity, but as acts of grace. The German mystic Meister Eckhart once said, "The very best and utmost of attainment in this life is to remain still and let God act and speak through you."

Take the first step of courage. Decide to create for yourself a life of balance, one that is active and reflective, expressive and silent. Making a commitment to silence applies to beginners on the mystic path as well as to those already established in their practice. Even a practitioner of twenty or thirty-year's standing can experience moments of resistance, when the pull to noise is greater than the pull to silence. No matter how much you may love silence, there may still be the temptation to move away from it. Yet if you step into silence, all that you need will come to your door.

A retired judge once told me the secret of his success. He said, "Every night I spend an hour alone in my study. I call it my quiet time. If there is any decision I need to make, I think about it in this quiet hour, and I always receive the right answer."

Similar advice is given in the story from the Desert Fathers, a group of ascetic monks who lived around the fourth century AD in the Middle East. Once a brother went to visit an Abbot in Scete to ask him for some advice on a problem he was facing. The Abbot said to him: "Go, sit in your cell, and your cell will teach you everything" (*The Wisdom of the Desert*, translated by Thomas Merton).

In today's modern world, you do not have to sit in a cell to gain insight, but you do have to sit quietly -- by a lakeshore, on a sofa, at a meditation center.

Sit in silence and silence will teach you everything.

MEDITATION -
THE LOVING WAY

*As are your thoughts, so will your world be created. Create happy
thoughts and in a second you will experience happiness. Create determined thoughts and obstacles will disappear like magic.*

I FIRST STARTED MEDITATING more than twenty-three years
ago at a time when I was emotionally out of control. I was nineteen years
old and in an intense relationship that took me to great highs but also
plunged me into dreadfully painful lows. I would often get upset and cry,
then feel exhausted or ashamed about my behavior.

One late afternoon in May while driving with my boyfriend across the
Arizona desert, I watched myself bobbing like a yo-yo, laughing one
minute, crying the next. I witnessed the same cycle repeat itself two or three
times within the space of several hours. I remember thinking, "Why is he
doing this to me?"

As the sun sprayed a trail of red paint over the mountains, I shouted
at him, "That's it, we're finished." I was about to jump out of the truck and
walk back to Canada, which would have taken a month or more. But the
desert lulled me into silence. In the vastness of her solitary cradle I found
respite from the madness.

Then, out of the silence came a zigzag flash. A white thunderbolt --
like the ones you see in comic books -- shot through my brain. I thought
I'd been pierced by a spark from Apollo's fiery chariot as he chased the sun
over the far-distant horizon; in reality, I was having a "realization." It was
not a big one, by many people's accounts, but to me it was bigger than the
desert sky. What I realized all of a sudden is that human experience is governed by choice. As individuals, we are not victims of circumstance; we can

make choices about the way we think and feel and behave.

Exercising my own freedom of choice meant that I could either go emotionally insane before reaching our destination or I could stop the insanity. This was not the road to Damascus, nor was I experiencing a conversion. But my emotional crisis had led me as far as Interstate 40, and several hundred miles outside of Las Vegas, Nevada, I whispered, "Dear God, help me to change."

In Buddhist iconography, the thunderbolt is an important symbol. It represents the spiritual ability to shatter illusion. It takes a huge jolt to break through the sturdy walls of self-deception that cover the truth and keep our shortcomings hidden from us. When this metaphorical thunderbolt hit me in the Arizona desert, I saw my situation clearly. Even though I was blaming my boyfriend for my wild fluctuations, I was the one who was out of control. This realization was so powerful that it shut me up. We didn't argue for the rest of the trip.

As soon as I returned home to Calgary, I took up a friend's offer to teach me Transcendental Meditation. Around the same time I began reading books on positive thinking. They taught me that the mind creates our reality. "You are what you think," I read. "Positive thoughts create a positive self-image." It soon became clear to me that I lacked self-esteem and this was the cause of my mood swings. Because I didn't have sufficient self-love, I turned to others to have my needs met. And when those needs weren't met, I fluctuated emotionally. It was an old pattern that had become outdated. If I wanted to become emotionally stable and strong, I would have to become more inwardly calm and loving toward myself.

I decided to meditate twice a day, once in the morning and again at night. Within a few months, I had fewer mood swings and felt more balanced within myself. Five years later I came across Raja Yoga meditation that would take me to even deeper levels of understanding.

People meeting me today laugh when I tell them about this experience. "But you're so calm," they protest. They find it hard to believe that I used to be volatile. Yet my story is not unusual. People take up meditation for the most humane reasons. Tired of the stresses of life they want to give themselves a break. Through meditation they find relief by bringing their thoughts and emotions under control. However, learning to manage the self takes time. Meditation is not a band-aid for patching up the parts of ourselves that we do not like. It's about accepting those parts that we wish to change and then releasing them with love.

There are many different ways to meditate, and they all involve the use of the mind in some way. In some practices, such as Transcendental Meditation, a mantra, or a special word, is repeated internally to slow down the mind; in other practices, prayers are said with loving intent to make the mind still and receptive to the Divine. Other methods use the mind to observe the breath in order to arrive at a sense of stillness. In the meditation that I practice, the mind is trained to be calm so that the soul can connect to God. Much of spiritual practice, therefore, depends on cultivating a positive and peaceful state of mind.

Just as artists take care of their brushes and writers their pens, meditators look after their minds. Become a mother to your mind. Feed it good nourishing thoughts. When your mind is full and glowing with peace, you will be happy and at ease with yourself and the world.

Some people have the tendency to be hard on themselves. They criticize and put themselves down. Or they feel guilty and ashamed at the slightest thing. By having negative thoughts they lash out against themselves again and again. With force, not love, they think, "I have to change. I must control my mind. I should get rid of my anger."

The desire to change is necessary, but if it is motivated by dislike for the self rather than compassion, the effect on the self is damaging. The mind is sensitive. Under duress it folds up and shuts down. A closed mind is of no benefit to the self or others. The Buddhists say the mind is like a parachute, it works best when open. If you want your mind to work for you rather than against you, be loving, be kind. Learn to meditate with compassion rather than compulsion.

What I do in my own meditation is gently pull the focus of my attention away from externals and concentrate on the still point within. To increase concentration, all meditations involve a place or an object of focus. Some are external, such as a candle flame or a serene scene in nature. Others are internal, such as the contemplation of an idea or symbol. For me, the point of focus is the seat of the self, namely the soul. I have found that focusing on myself as a soul in meditation not only increases my concentration power, it harnesses and balances my energy, empowering me with feelings of self-love.

Today, after years of spiritual practice, I am closer to my authentic self than ever before. I have learnt that a person cannot change out of compulsion, only through a genuine love and respect for truth.

So how can you embrace the loving way? How can you learn to be kind and gentle with yourself?

Begin by looking at how you think and feel. Thoughts and emotions are deeply connected. Your thoughts lay the foundation for your emotions. If your emotions run wild, it's because your thoughts are out of control. Hence the need to still your mind. You can start by reducing the speed of your thoughts. When they become peaceful and deliberate, instead of wild and uncertain, your mind returns to its naturally tranquil state. A tranquil mind does not erupt or react to things, rather it has the capacity to observe.

Try this: sit quietly for a moment and observe your thoughts. Watch them as you would the currents of a river. See where they take you. Thoughts keep on traveling, sometimes they veer to the right, sometimes to the left, they even go round in circles. The mind is like a factory; it cannot stop producing thoughts. Thoughts are produced even in sleep. Wherever your thoughts go, you go too. The thoughts you create determine your state of mind. Both positive and negative thoughts affect your moods, contribute to your personality, and shape your entire worldview. You cannot eliminate thoughts -- they are your creation and the basis of your awareness. You can, however, observe them and then change them.

First of all, create a space. Create a tiny distance between you, the creator of thought, and the thought itself. Into that space, into that second of silence, insert a tiny pause. Now fill that pause with stillness and calm. And before you have the urge to think another thought, decide what you want to think. Don't just create just any thought, consciously select a positive thought that will make you feel good about yourself.

Just as a swimmer in a pool completes a lap one stroke at a time, similarly, you can learn to think positively one thought at a time. After each thought create a tiny pause, then fill that pause with stillness and calm. Imagine that you are typing -- dash, dot, dash, dot -- on your mental screen. In this way by filling the pause after each thought with silence, you will be able to slow down the speed of your mind. At the same time, ensure that you choose uplifting thoughts. Strong beautiful thoughts keep the mind stable. Anxious or sad thoughts cause the mind to race and go out of control. Let go of them.

Once during a meditation class I was conducting in Calgary, we had a discussion about monitoring our thoughts. A student named David said, "I see it more as shepherding thoughts. My thoughts are like sheep. I decide which ones are useful to me, and I let them through the gate. Negative thoughts are like the runts. They don't increase the value of my herd. So I stop those thoughts at the gate."

Meditation is a conscious choice to create quality thoughts. You will reach tranquil pastures by shepherding your thoughts.

Some people say that meditation is a selfish act. They think that time spent alone reduces the time that can be given to friends and family. This is only true in the case of people who use meditation as a means of self-absorption. To be constantly thinking about the self, about one's own needs and problems, is a form of self-obsession. It is a negative focus on the self, rather than the kind of positive focus that meditation encourages.

Dadi Prakashmani once said, "Only a powerful soul can offer love." What she meant is that only an empowered soul has the energy to give. When Dadi said that, years ago in a class, I began to pay more attention to myself. I noticed that when I had not meditated sufficiently, I was less loving toward myself, family, and friends. Without that flame of inner love, I was more demanding of others, less inclined to give. In that condition, my love for the world was greatly diminished.

As you continue on your journey, pay attention to this. When you become too self-absorbed, you will find it difficult to stay spiritually aware and will have little or no energy to give to others. Love, on the other hand, energizes the soul. When you generate loving feelings for yourself, others, and for God, that love expands and overflows.

MASTER OF MIND,
MASTER OF SELF

Just as in science you are able to switch something on or off in a second, in the same way, check whether you are able to control your mind for as long as you want in the way that you want.

FATHER, I AM AFRAID. Father, are you listening?"

The cool pine air mingles with the fragrance of cedar and eucalyptus from the sauna. I am laying on a wooden floor, next to the women's hot tub at the Japanese Spa in Santa Fe. I am oblivious to the women around me, who are bathing in the last rays of a November sun. It is my thoughts that are preoccupying me now, not my body.

"What are you afraid of, child?"

"That I can't do it all. That I can't run, write, cook, get my mind clear, be Your instrument. You know, all the usual stuff."

God takes a while to reply. "Your mind deceives you."

"Okay, so I worry a lot."

"You are not in control of your thoughts."

"I can't help it sometimes."

"I have taught you how to be a master. Have you forgotten?"

I do not answer. I know God is right. When I am not in control of my mind, I allow thoughts that are not useful, even those that are harmful, to run riot. On those occasions when my mind is undisciplined, it's no wonder I sometimes feel anxious or afraid.

Someone once asked me, "Why is it easier to think negative thoughts than positive ones?" The answer is simple: habit. The mind is accustomed to be being wild and willful, and to doing exactly what it wants. Buddhists call this the Monkey Mind. In my practice, the mind is compared to a runaway horse. It runs and runs down a long sandy beach, and no matter which way you pull the reins or try to make it slow down, the mind keeps on racing.

People whose minds run fast, say, "Teach me to switch off my mind." They think they can gain control by stopping all thoughts. But just as the heart's job is to beat, the mind's job is to think. What's important, therefore, is to learn how to think, how to switch the mind on, not off. The mind is brought under control by turning away from the negative thoughts and staying focused on the positive. Qualitative thinking is the key to self-mastery. Just as in other pursuits of excellence, a person doesn't become a top pianist or chef overnight, similarly, mastering the mind, every day, under all circumstances, requires constant awareness, dedication and practice.

Many years ago when I was in Guatemala visiting friends, I fell sick, and had to be put on an intravenous drip. As I sat in the health clinic, I noticed that the solution in the drip was moving slowly. "Can't we make it go any faster?" I asked the nurse.

"Try to relax," she said, patting my right shoulder.

I stared out into the garden. It was the rainy season in Guatemala, one minute rain, the next minute sun. Cloudy skies would drag on for days, making the earth heavy and compressed. I thought, "I just don't want to be here. I want to leap out of this chair and run through the rain. I am supposed to be a meditator, but right now, I want to be a long-distance runner."

My thoughts were making me tense and slowing down the speed of the drip. I said to myself, "You'll be here all day if you don't become quiet and still." So I did what the nurse said. Instead of resisting the treatment, I settled into it, embraced it. I reminded myself that this treatment would make me strong. Instead of dwelling on the pain, I began to meditate. My eyes were open, and I was fully aware of my surroundings as I concentrated on the still point within. And there, from that place of stillness, I became the silent observer. I observed the drip, the needle, my throbbing vein, but I was no longer disturbed by any of it. Instead, I created such thoughts of peace that soon everything in me became calm.

Then I smiled to myself and thought, "Yes, it's good to relax."

Gaining self-mastery is one of the highest aims of meditation practice. A master is not controlled by his or her mind, but knows how the mind works and directs it appropriately. There are many examples of yogis in

India who walk barefoot over coals of fire and meditate naked in the snow. Zen masters in Japan are also known to deprive themselves of food and sleep for weeks with the aim of freeing the mind from the limitations imposed by the body. However, the kind of self-mastery that I practice does not involve these kinds of ascetic feats; it is more concerned with mastering the mind so as to be able to master one's entire personality.

The practice of Raja Yoga goes back thousands of years. Tradition says that God Himself taught the ancient Raja Yoga of India. 'Raja' means master or ruler. 'Yoga,' as you will remember, means link or union. This ancient yet modern practice involves the spiritualization of thoughts and feelings, behaviors and actions to achieve a transformation of self. Becoming a self-master depends upon the correct use of the mind, since thoughts are the primary agents used in meditation to connect the soul to God.

When I refer to the mind, I do not mean the physical organ known as the 'brain,' but the spiritual 'organ' contained within the soul. The mind has to be spiritual, not physical, in order to generate the subtle vibrations known as 'thoughts.' The soul operates the brain, using the mind to convey thought-messages to the body through the organ of the brain. Thoughts can be felt but not seen. What the brain does is simply to translate these vibrations of soul -- namely thoughts -- into chemical responses that circulate up and down the body, thus allowing us to function in the physical world.

Since the soul is invisible, its connection to the body is complex and subtle. Information received through the physical senses, through sight, touch, taste and hearing, is transmitted back to the brain and interpreted by the mind in the form of thoughts, feelings, and reactions that impact directly upon the soul. Whatever goes on in the soul at the level of thought or emotion ultimately affects our attitudes and behaviors, even our health, determining the way we live and navigate through life. Thus, there is a reciprocal relationship between the soul and its body, and the outside world.

To be able to interact positively in the world and not be pulled down by what we see, hear, sense, or touch, we need to harness our soul power, namely our spiritual energy. In the meditation that I practice the eyes are kept open. This helps to develop the necessary self-mastery to remain aware of surroundings and circumstances, and yet not to be affected by them. Uniquely, this is not a meditation done behind closed doors, away from the world when no one is looking. It is a meditation conducted in the moment, on the job, with our eyes open, bodies relaxed, minds focused and alert.

Being in this state of natural concentration is similar to being in the driver's seat of a car. One is totally aware as one drives down the highway of life, both hands on the wheel of the mind, directing the caliber of each thought. Mastering the self is a deeply internalized process. It begins and ends with the mind. The mind is the generator, experiencer, and clearing-house for all thoughts and feelings within the soul. Feelings are thoughts experienced in the mind at a deeper level. If, for instance, you create the thought, "I am afraid" in reaction to something that you see or hear, that thought of fear can also be experienced more deeply as a feeling of fear. If you respond again with fear to that same situation or to another, then that fear becomes even more deeply ingrained. Over time that imprint of fear will dominate you. You will even forget that fear began its life as a thought, and that your ability to transform it is merely a thought away.

A wise yogi once told me that all problems begin as the creations of a weak mind. When our minds are out of control, small situations can seem difficult or life threatening. But when our minds are strong, a crisis can be transformed into an opportunity because we perceive the situation differently.

Several years ago, I conducted a workshop in Quebec, Canada, on the power of the mind. Somewhere I had read that it takes six repetitions of a thought, whether negative or positive, for it to reach and influence the body on the cellular level. I was fascinated by the idea of repeating a thought six times and observing the results.

I decided that as part of the workshop we would conduct some experiments with the mind. In one of the experiments I told participants to think of an obstacle or problem that they were currently facing in their lives. I turned on some music, guided them into a relaxed state, then took them through the following exercise:

"Visualize yourself walking into a room. It is empty apart from two chairs in the middle. You come in and sit down on one of the chairs. Soon the door opens, and the obstacle or problem that you are facing in your life, walks in and sits down in the chair opposite you. Observe your obstacle for a few seconds in whatever form it has appeared in front of you. Now repeat the following thought, slowly and with conviction, 'Hey, problem, I am a powerful soul. I am more powerful than you are.'"

I allowed a short space of silence and then told the participants to repeat the words again, "Hey, problem, I am a powerful soul. I am more powerful than you are." I repeated these words six times with a silent pause between each repetition. At the end, I allowed the participants more silent time in which they could reflect on what had happened.

During the feedback following this visualization, one man told the group how his obstacle had appeared as a huge boulder that broke the chair when it sat down. At first he was afraid, but as he started repeating the words, the boulder started to get smaller and smaller until, by the final repetition, it had completely disappeared. I asked the man what the boulder symbolized. "Fear," he said. I asked him how he felt after doing the exercise. "Great," he replied. "Now I know the power of my own mind. If I create fear, I can also remove it."

I was happy that this man had achieved such a realization. So much depends on the mind. The mind is that powerful -- it creates our reality on the basis of how we think.

Over the years Dadi Janki has taught me a lot about the mind. She once spoke about a wise teacher who had been like a spiritual mother to her. She called her Mama. Dadi said, "Mama spoke very little and thought very little. She became wise not by thinking a lot, but by thinking very little." Then Dadi gave me this advice: "Think very little, but think in absolutely the right manner." When facing a difficult situation, try this. Say to yourself, "I will find a solution that is right for me. Whatever happens will be for the best."

Every day make a habit of creating strong, determined thoughts

HIGHER CONSCIOUSNESS

Only create those thoughts that bring success.
Let there be greater result with less effort.

EACH MORNING while in Santa Fe I climb the shrub-dotted hills of the Estancia Primera estate where I am staying to clear my mind. It is important to begin the day with some fresh thinking. The sun is out and I find my usual spot, sheltered from the wind, behind a brick wall. From here, I can look out across the scattering of brown adobe houses and cedar trees, as far as the Sangre de Cristo mountains.

Here, in solitude, I can concentrate on creating thoughts that will lead me into higher consciousness. Instead of thinking about Chinese stir-fry for lunch, brown earth on my blue jeans, or the sun on my face, I can focus inwardly on myself as a soul and go deeply into a particular thought. The thoughts that I use as the basis for my contemplation are carefully selected ones, especially designed to raise my energy levels.

It's not always easy to live in the world and be spiritual. There are many forces that conspire to pull down our energy. When energy levels drop -- due to stress, tiredness, or over-thinking -- many of us find it difficult to meditate. Then instead of progressing in our practice, we spend time struggling to regain lost energy. What is needed is a simple method to boost spiritual energy and keep it high. Just as a plane requires fuel to take off and fly, similarly, we require fuel for the soul. Powerful thoughts generated purposefully each day elevate consciousness so that we can connect with God and stay connected for a long time.

For the past nine years I have paid careful attention to this practice. Each day, I choose one or several thoughts that excite and inspire me. I have experimented enough with my own meditations to know which ones set me ablaze with happiness and joy. As soon as I think them, I feel spiritually charged. I consider these thoughts to be power generators that boost, energize, and strengthen the soul.

It takes a conscious effort to redirect my thoughts so that they can elevate me, rather than limit me. This is why I have come to sit behind the wall. In this tranquil place I contemplate the beauty of my inner being and my light-filled connection with God. These thoughts take me out of an ordinary state of awareness and into another realm. It is as if I become a surfer riding the waves of a great ocean of energy to higher consciousness.

Dr Stanislov Grof, one of the primary founders of Transpersonal Psychology, talks about the experiences people have when they shift from ordinary to non-ordinary states of consciousness. "In non-ordinary states," he says in an interview (the particulars of which are no longer in my possession), "people describe the world as a dynamic process, where there are no solid structures and everything is a flow of energy."

In higher consciousness there is an automatic flow of pure energy from God to the soul. In this higher state, the soul is filled with divine power. As the soul is energized, it becomes stronger, capable of receiving more energy. The effect of this energizing over time is transformational. A meditator's thoughts, attitudes and behaviors are filled with such a divine force that higher consciousness becomes a reality of his or her existence, and not just an experience acquired only during concentrated meditations.

To enter into higher consciousness requires some purposeful and directed meditations. These need to be based on the understanding that thought creates reality. Take a thought such as, "I am a powerful soul, full of spiritual power." Begin by creating this thought in your mind. Allow it to sit there for a few seconds as you digest it fully. Repeat the thought again so that you can settle more deeply into it. Consciously allow yourself to accept this thought, "Yes, I am a powerful soul." Believe that this thought is true, and that, despite any weaknesses you might have, this is the reality of your original state of being. Once you access your soul power, you are truly powerful.

Now, a part of you might reject this thought. People tend to resist thoughts of higher consciousness because of feelings of unworthiness. So repeat the thought again. "I am a powerful soul, full of spiritual power."

Allow yourself time to dwell on this thought. This indwelling or reflection is known in most spiritual traditions as 'contemplation.' As you stay focused on this singular thought, allow feelings behind the thought to emerge, "Yes, I am a powerful soul, I can feel my spiritual energy rising." This action of contemplation in a purposeful manner empowers the soul directly. It is an entirely distinct activity from the use of affirmations or the repetition of words and mantras. The distinction lies in the conscious awareness that contemplation leads to experience. A thought produces feelings and the combination of thought and feelings leads to experience.

As soon as you experience that you are a powerful soul -- and palpably feel the fullness of your spiritual energy -- that experience is imprinted as a memory in your subconscious mind. It becomes a new reality that you can access at will. Over time, and with regular reinforcement, this subconscious imprint will begin to impact upon the activity of your conscious mind. Soon "I am a powerful soul" will color your attitudes, perceptions, and beliefs. In other words, the more you generate thoughts of higher consciousness, the more this reality will become first nature to you. You are a powerful soul.

There are many thoughts of higher consciousness. It is important that you identify the ones with which you resonate. Either generate your own list of powerful thoughts, or experiment with some of my favorites below:

I am a pure being of light.
I am a divine child of God/the Divine.
I am a peaceful and loving soul.
God is my Companion and is always with me.
God, the Ocean of Love, fills me with love.
I, the soul, love and respect myself.
I am a powerful soul, full of spiritual power.

Now use the following steps to raise your spiritual energy and connect with God. Like climbing a spiral staircase, it is a process of going both inward and upward:

1. *Select one thought of higher consciousness.*
It should be so meaningful to you that when you think it, a buzz of happiness or excitement is generated inside. You love this thought.

2. *Turn your attention inward* and find your focus on the still point within. Hold the awareness that you are a soul, a beautiful being of light.

3. *Take your selected thought of higher consciousness* and put the full force of your determined thinking behind it. For the thought to become powerful, feel it, accept it, believe it. Feel the reality of experience behind the thought.

4. *Now watch your energy level change.*
Observe how within yourself you are becoming more energized. What you have just done is to use a thought of higher consciousness to generate high spiritual energy within yourself. Energy is power and spiritual power is needed for concentration in meditation. If you are lacking in energy, you won't have the ability to concentrate, connect, and stay connected.

5. *As you begin to feel spiritually uplifted,* take your awareness upward beyond this physical domain. Use the power of visualization to see yourself moving, not physically but metaphysically, beyond the earth, sky, and universe, and into a beautiful dimension of light. This is where God resides. By using your special thought to become energized, you will be able to reach this dimension in a second or seconds. The energy generated from this thought of higher consciousness will also strengthen you internally and increase your capacity to receive from God

6. *As a soul, in this dimension of light,* place yourself before God, the Supreme Soul. Feel that you are spiritually connected. Open yourself to receive God's power, light, and love. Open yourself wide. Feel the subtlety and power of God's energy flowing to you. Feel that you are being filled with divine power from a Higher Source. This is the highest, purest energy you can ever experience. Bask in its glory. Know the glory of God.

The meditation I have just described is a directed meditation. Experiencing it will make you strong. The accumulative effect of receiving power from God will seal the bond between you. Eventually, you will be able to come to God spontaneously without the need of a 'method' meditation, simply because your heart is attached to God and God's heart longs for you as well.

In the mystical tradition, the image of a stairway or ladder is used to describe the inward and upward 'flight' to God. I prefer the image of a spiral stairway for it more succinctly conveys the necessity of journeying inward as well as upward to experience the Divine. Gregory the Great, a Pope in the sixth century, described this process as the soul climbing into itself, "whereby in ascending from outward things it may pass into itself, and from itself may tend unto its maker."

From the perspective of my own practice connecting to soul is the first step on the inward journey. Creating thoughts of higher consciousness then leads the soul upward. The next turn inward on the spiral staircase is developing the deeper realization and experience of higher consciousness. Taking one's consciousness beyond this physical world and into God's domain lifts the soul onto the next level. Turning inward again, the soul focuses on its connection with God. Receiving God's power lifts it higher still. Basking in God's power moves the soul more deeply inward. Being filled with God's power lifts it higher. And so the journey continues.

Although there are a number of ways to practice 'ascent,' according to the various spiritual traditions, there are few explanations of how 'grace' is received. Grace describes the moments when God does all of the work and pulls the soul up several flights of stairs without any effort on its part. In these moments of undirected meditation, the soul is in uncharted territory. God is in control and the soul is the lucky recipient of whatever treasure God wishes to bestow upon it.

In moments like these give thanks and let go.

PRACTICE MAKES PERFECT

Those who listen to others, who speak of others, can be deceived.
But someone who has experienced something for him or herself can
never be deceived.

WHEN I WAS YOUNG I trained myself to play tennis. I used to come home from school, grab my racket, and hit a ball for hours against the granite wall of our house. Even in winter, I used to play under the drizzle of rain until it was too dark to see the ball. I remember my father poking his head outside the window to call me in for dinner. I didn't care about eating, sleeping, or playing with friends. All I wanted was to feel my body dancing through space and to hear the ping of a clean ball springing off the center of my racket. I was in love with movement, rhythm, artistry, with perfection of the mind when it is focused on a singular effort.

Later in life, when I coached tennis to pay my way through university, I could easily recognize the students who were keen. They were the ones who practiced in between lessons. They held their rackets as if they were going somewhere. They bent their knees and chased down every ball. These students didn't just love tennis so they could win tournaments and be better than anyone else; they loved tennis, period.

When I began to take my meditation practice seriously, I had an interesting thought. I said to myself, "If you could dedicate yourself as much to meditation as you have to tennis, you could achieve a real level of spiritual proficiency." In the beginning this thought of loving my meditation practice as much as I loved tennis -- even more -- fuelled my spiritual efforts. I didn't miss a day, didn't miss a beat. I was as regular and punctual as clockwork. And the discipline of consistent meditation made me strong.

These days there is a lot of talk about being spiritual. While much can be gained from reading books and moving in spiritual circles, spirituality is deepened by putting spiritual principles into practice. The proof of spirituality is apparent through one's actions and is visible on one's face. The Chinese say, "Talk doesn't cook rice." Similarly, you can talk all you like about meditation, but if you want to be spiritual, you will need to practice meditation, or contemplative prayer, or some other form of internal silencing.

I once tried to teach a woman to meditate. She wanted to learn, but not to practice what she had learned. Everything I told her she said she already knew. The real reason she came to the center each week was because she wanted to be validated. She wanted someone to affirm that what she believed in was true. I told the woman, "You have a great love of spirituality. But until you make time each day to experience the truth of it for yourself, your knowledge will be incomplete."

A teacher or a book cannot take the concepts you have in your head and make them sit in your heart. They cannot graft a love of meditation onto you, if you are not willing to develop your own love for meditating. Since spiritual experiences are born and nurtured from within, you need to be willing to participate in your own spiritual process.

If you want to experience God, then come to God. If you want to meditate, then meditate. Meditate because you love to do so, not because you think you should or because someone else has told you to meditate. As you claim your life, claim this spiritual practice as your own. Meditate because you recognize its value, knowing that the act of turning within will ultimately lead you to God's door.

For a long time I have been fascinated by the life of St Teresa of Avila. There is much to be learnt from her spiritual process, which she described in her autobiography, *Life*. At the beginning of her journey, St Teresa admitted that she vacillated between her commitment to God and her love of worldly affairs. So intense was this inner struggle that it seriously affected her health. She became paralyzed for three years. Even after her cure, Teresa got caught up again in her old habits. She loved being the center of attention at the convent parlor, which was more like a salon for people wishing to discuss spiritual matters along with the local gossip.

For an entire year, Teresa was unable to engage in any type of spiritual practice. She couldn't bring herself to pray. She described her conflict like this: "I derived no joy from God and no pleasure from the world…A battle like this is so painful that I do not know how I managed to endure it for a month, still less for many years."

After nearly twenty years in spiritual hiatus, at the age of thirty-nine,

Teresa experienced a dramatic awakening or 'conversion' that secured her steps on the mystic path. Later, as the great teacher she became, Teresa warned her students of the difficulties encountered on the path. She wrote about the dangers of laziness and carelessness, and the consequences of neglecting practice. She revealed how some mystics lose their determination in the face of obstacles and wish to leave their journey half way. Teresa wrote her warnings four hundred years ago, yet they aptly apply to the spiritual journey today.

When you begin your journey, begin it well. Just as the foundations of a building need to be strong, similarly consider laying a firm foundation for your spiritual practice. In today's world, lives are so full that it is easy to become distracted. But if you are serious about your spirituality, you will create a suitable timetable for yourself in which you make sufficient time for practice.

Like other meditators of my tradition, I meditate at the same time each day. I get up early in the morning and mediate before going to work, then again in the evening before starting to teach. I also have the practice of creating 'peace moments' for myself during the day. This is when I take short five-minute breaks and go beyond all thoughts of the world. I forget about doing, and just allow myself to be.

Each day is different. Some days, I don't meditate well, nor is my heart as engaged as I would like it to be. I have experienced bouts of laziness in my life, periods of weakness and backsliding. At times, I have reduced the time that I dedicate to my meditation. But I have always maintained my practice. There has not been a day in more than twenty-three years when I have not meditated. I tell people, "You wouldn't think of leaving your house without brushing your teeth or combing your hair. In the same way, I personally can't imagine going out of the door without first having focused my energy." Combining meditation practice with an active business, family and community life is a priority for me. I love being in the world, but I also love being peaceful.

Strangely enough, one of the most challenging tasks I face as a teacher of meditation is convincing people to meditate. Many enjoy learning about meditation, and love coming to a center to experience peace, but they are hesitant to create their own moments of silence. I could tell you all the reasons for their resistance, such as fear, a lack of commitment, a lack of faith in themselves, etc, but I doubt that knowing these reasons will really help.

In fact, forget what I have just said. Sit down right now and practice. Go within. Be with yourself. My words can't help you now...

About four years ago a desperate man came to one of our centers. He was a spiritual counselor. "Why would someone like him need our help?" I wondered. Then Jerry told me his story. He was a spiritual guide for thousands of people. He said he could read auras, tell the future, and guide people in overcoming their problems. Creatively, he was a genius, working on many projects at the same time. He experienced regular 'spiritual highs,' but after each high he would spiral downward into drugs, alcohol and depression. He had gone through this cycle many times before. Lately, it had become once too many.

Jerry's whole body was shaking as he sat in front of me. He said, "If you don't help me, I will die." Looking at his wasted face, I knew he spoke the truth. Within a week he could easily be dead.

"I can't help you, Jerry," I said. "Only you can help yourself." Then I gently told him what I observed: that his spiritual high living was not established on firm footings. He would convince people that he was helping them, whereas he was using the energy of their praise to feel good about himself. He had no sustainable practice to call his own, and therefore no means of staying spiritually charged. On top of that, he was in an addictive cycle of self-abuse that he needed to be willing to face.

It took a lot of courage to speak the truth to this desperate man. At the time, it seemed the only way to break through his fog. I didn't teach Jerry to meditate. His mental state was such that he couldn't even begin to focus. Instead, I created a silent, supportive and healing space in which Jerry could learn to create one positive thought, "I am peace."

"You may not believe it right now," I said, "but if you repeat this thought ten times or twenty times a day, as you walk from your home to the train and from the train to the center, this thought will give you strength. It will give you hope. And peace will come to you."

Jerry nodded. When he left the center, he still looked depressed, and I was not sure if he would keep our next appointment. But the next day he did return and told me that he had done the practice we set. "After all," he said, "it's a matter of life or death." After a week of practice, Jerry's hands had stopped shaking, his head was held higher, and the dark cloud on his face appeared to be somewhat lifted. He had also enrolled himself in AA.

This story illustrates one simple fact: even the most basic practice can bring enormous benefit. For some people meditating every day seems an impossibility. If this is true for you, then start with some positive thinking. Create one strong, positive thought for yourself every day, several times a day. Observe the difference it makes in you. Once you are more strengthened, you will naturally feel inclined to go deeper into a spiritual practice that is comfortable for you.

When we first set up the meditation center in Vancouver, a young man in his early twenties visited us to see what we were teaching. He said to me, "I know all this spiritual stuff, but why can't I make my life spiritual?" I told the young man that if he continued to read more books and go to more lectures, he would become more confused than he already was. Somewhere imbedded in our North American culture is the notion of having success without putting in any effort. We accumulate as much knowledge as we can, yet neglect to put it into practice. It is easier to follow someone else marching through the forest than to forge a trail ourselves. The illusion of rewards without commitment is tempting, but also suspect. In life, there are no "freebies," nor are there any short cuts on the mystic trail.

Apparently, when the Buddha was about to leave this physical plane, he said to his disciples, "Work out your own salvation with diligence." Here was a man who had invested effort in his own enlightenment and helped others to do the same, but his last message was simply this: Do the work yourselves.

I like this. I like the honesty and cleanliness of spiritual truths.

A practice is different from a spiritual path. You follow a path, even follow the leaders of your tradition down this path, but you make a practice your own. You enter into silent space and claim it as yours. The beauty of sacred ground is discovered when you firmly plant your own feet there.

Here are some suggestions for creating and sustaining a spiritual practice.

1. *Choose a time to meditate*, preferably first thing in the morning, and again at night.

2. *Meditate at the same time each day* and for the same amount of time. Sit and connect, even on the days when you don't feel like it. The regularity of your practice will make you strong.

3. *Start with fifteen minutes twice a day.*
Then increase one of your meditations to half an hour. When you are ready, try meditating for a full hour. Longer meditations will allow you to break through the resistance of your own thinking and to experience the depth of

your own spiritual essence.

4. *Use thoughts of higher consciousness* to start off your meditations. They will give you a lift.

5. *Divide your meditations into segments* so that you can experience different spiritual concepts.

Sometimes people get bored in their meditations. You need to be inventive to prevent your meditations from going dry. For example, spend fifteen minutes contemplating one of your inner qualities, such as peace, happiness, or joy; fifteen minutes connecting to God and being filled by God's love; fifteen minutes conversing with God, telling God about your day, your plans, the things that are on your mind; fifteen minutes creating positive thoughts for others and the world.

Discover what really excites you in meditation. Then go for it. Meditation is all about spiritual passion. If you love your practice, it will love you, and the joy of it will radiate out from every part of your being.

THE GAME OF
REMEMBERING AND
FORGETTING

You don't remember Me because you are remembering everything else.

A MAN IN SANTA FE was given a drug during an operation. When he woke up he couldn't remember who he was, didn't recognize his partner, had no memory of his life before the operation. His mind was a complete blank. He felt disorientated and unsure of himself.

When I read his story in the paper, I thought, "What a strange thing to have happen. Imagine waking up one morning and not knowing yourself." Then I had a curious thought. "Spiritually, we face the same thing. We walk out of our homes each day, into the big wide world, and we forget. We forget who we really are, where we come from, what we are doing here. We want to remember, but our attention gets sidetracked. The distractions of the world outside pull us out of soul connection. Our forgetfulness increases; we lose sight of God.

This is no ordinary state of forgetting, but a slip of consciousness that has become habitual. At times, we remember, but most of the time we don't. In today's world actions have become all consuming. We cook, eat, drive to work, talk like crazy on the telephone, but all the while we are disconnected from the beauty inherent in each single act. Our hearts aren't with the action; they are lost to the pressure of getting the action done. We are people who have forgotten how to be.

The controversial early twentieth century philosopher Gurdjieff used to compare people to robots going through life in a daze, revealing only a small portion of their potential. Gurdjieff attributed this to laziness and to the tendency of human consciousness to 'drift.' He believed that most people tended to think about mundane things and act in mundane ways, except for rare bursts of creativity. This drifting, in Gurdjieff's view, came from a lack of paying attention.

Gurdjieff devised all kinds of psychological means to try and free his students from their automaton state and release their creativity. He encouraged a technique of self-remembering by focusing the arrow of thoughts inward to intensify awareness. What mattered to him above all else was freedom from limitation.

Even meditators with the best intentions in the world drift throughout the day. They concentrate well during meditation, but once the meditation is over, their energy scatters. To stay connected to soul while engaged in action, and to be mindful of that action, requires constant attention. Yet that attention can be as simple as allowing a forgotten memory to return.

Stop what you are doing right now. I know it is hard to stop in mid sentence, but I would like you to experiment with spiritual memory. Remember the days of your childhood when you first learned to ride a bike, or kick a ball, or climb a tree. Don't strain yourself to remember. Allow the memory to surface on its own. Remember the freedom you felt, the excitement of something new, the happiness of expressing yourself.

Now go back to a time when you were completely at peace. Remember how as a soul you once lived in a world of light. This was your life before you came to this plane. You can remember if you choose. The memory of your divine light is indelibly recorded within you. Allow that memory to surface. The cloud of forgetfulness may have temporarily obscured your vision, but it cannot remove the truth of who you are. You are a being of light, a silent, peaceful soul. As you bring this memory from the back to the front of your conscious mind, you will naturally remember who you are.

An office manager in San Francisco once told me that she was so busy at work she couldn't stay centered. I told her, "You take coffee breaks, why not spiritual breaks?" Then I suggested that she designate three times during the day when she would stop all activities, turn within, and remember that she was an eternal soul, free from all limitations. "You only have to become soul conscious for a few minutes to gather your energy," I said, "and then when you come back to your tasks energized, everything will be easy for you. You will be present with your actions and not burdened by them."

What I asked her to do is an exercise that I've been taught. This exercise can also help you to develop soul consciousness and stay more present in the here and now.

Time past and time future
Allow but a little consciousness.
To be conscious is not to be in time.

So wrote T. S. Eliot in his poem "Burnt Norton." Eliot was a mystic who understood that eternity lies at the heart of the mystical experience. Beyond the restrictions of time and space the soul just is. There is no pull to the past or the future; rather past, present and future are experienced as an 'eternal now.' Why do we yearn to be in this state? It is, I believe, for reasons of sanity. We feel sane when we are in the here and now, incapacitated and often depressed when we are not. In the soul-consciousness present we are colorfully alive, connected to all that we do, and totally at peace.

Try this: Practice being aware of yourself as an eternal soul while in action. As you walk down the street, go to the shops, wait to see the bank manager, remember who you are. Remember you have come from a world of light and that you are here to bring light into each and every situation. Through your physical eyes look out at the world, but with your internal sight see the light within. The writer Anais Nin once said, "I do not see the world as it is, but as I am." Remembering your true self gives you the power to see the world in a new light. There can be no greater force for change than this.

As you practice soul consciousness, you will notice a shift in your attitudes and thinking. Your energy levels will change -- become subtler in the sense of being more refined -- and your powers of concentration will increase. Situations around you will begin to change, to lighten up. The vibrations that you emit will no longer be scattered or chaotic; they will be gentle and loving, able to create an atmosphere of well-being around you.

Spiritual practice is both a solitary and a communal activity. It requires a balance between time spent alone in silence and time given to others. Even when the call to action is there, our practice demands that we do what needs to be done peacefully and with compassion. The proof of our spirituality is that we remember and do not forget.

God also likes it when we remember Him. He likes it when we forget everything else and concentrate on Him alone.

"What is the cause of unhappiness," I asked God one day in meditation.

"Children forget Me. They do not know how to make Me present in their lives."

"It's true," I replied. "When I forget You my life seems dry."

Sometimes God likes to play with me. God is my Friend as well as my Teacher. He teaches me to love Him by encouraging me to remember Him more and more each day. Sometimes when I am in the middle of something important, such as writing this chapter, He demands my full attention. For instance, just now my hands were flying across the keyboard trying to keep up with the words filling my mind. All of sudden I sense that my Friend is calling me, telling me, "Stop!"

I don't want to stop. I am engrossed with my writing, with the speed of my hands at work. But this is a game of remembering and forgetting, and God is checking how I play. Do I care more about writing or about being with Him when He calls? It takes a few moments for my mind to slow down, for my thoughts to take me Home. I return to the world of light beyond and become still in front of God. God is resplendent before me, an Ocean of Love. He is as eager to give as I am to receive. He wants to fill me with as much as I can take. And when I've had enough, God lets me go.

Like a yo-yo released from a taut string, I bounce back to the awareness of the room, to the hum of the computer on my lap. "You can work now," I seem to hear God say. I sit for a moment in total silence, aware of how His powerful energy still envelops me. Whether God pulls me to Himself, or I consciously choose to remember the Divine, an amazing thing occurs. Our connection releases a surge of creative energy and all that I do afterward is colored by the beauty of His company. Even now, I sense that the room is sunnier, the computer lighter, and words appear in larger, brighter form.

In the Gita, one of India's most revered scriptures, there is an important spiritual directive: *Manmanabav.* Literally translated, this means, "Keep your mind on Me." In others words, "Remember Me alone." To pull away from action and single-mindedly concentrate on God alone -- with no one else and no other thing in between -- is an important yogic practice. Doing this several times a day, even for few minutes, brings immeasurable benefit.

Try this: At a time when you are busy suddenly pull your thoughts away from what you are doing. Direct your full attention toward God. Think of God as the Still Point of Light, radiating Love, Peace, and Happiness. Allow yourself to be immersed in God's company. Remember God as a child remembers his or her Friend. Not because you have to, because you want to.

Then consider this: The experience of God's love is already recorded within you. It's like a song on a CD just waiting to be played. Just turn on your memory machine and let God's music flood your being. You don't have to strain to remember. When you remember God, God remembers you. God receives the vibrations of your thoughts even before they are released in His direction and responds with a current of love. Even when you forget, God still remembers.

Some meditators say, "It's hard to experience God's love." Understand that communication between soul and the Supreme Being takes place at the level of vibrations. Love is the energy that God sends us, rather like the frequency emitted from a satellite in space. The soul is akin to a satellite dish that must be turned in the right direction to receive God's frequency, namely His love. When the mind is preoccupied with other matters, then reception is blurred. But when the mind is concentrated in a singular direction, receptivity is high. Then we leave the forest of forgetfulness and walk out into a field of light. Our lives expand. We become extraordinary.

Only when I am silent, can I hear you. Only when I no longer ask for things or question Your judgment can I receive the intentions of Your mind. My thoughts are steady and sure now; they do not spring up involuntarily like they used to. My mind is still. Even though You speak no words, I hear what You say.

I understand Your meaning now. You no longer have to explain. You are; I am. Together, we are silent. I have no other desire but to fulfill Your wish. You are my dearest Friend.

I see everything clearly: what I have been, what You want me to become. You awaken within me memories of the vastness of my being. Am I really this large? Do my wings cover the whole sky?

In silence I walk with You, and sense the magnitude of a new life dawning

REFLECTIONS ON
SPIRITUAL PRACTICE

Reflective Questions

1. What are the merits of your spiritual practice and what can you do to improve it? If you haven't yet cultivated a regular practice, could it be fear, a lack of commitment or discipline that is holding you back?
2. Create a pie chart to illustrate your use of time. Divide it into the time spent at work; time given to family, friends, and community; time utilized for everyday aspects of living such as cooking, eating, traveling; time allotted to nurturing yourself spiritually, and within that time actually dedicated to remembering God. Is your chart balanced? If not, what can you do to bring your life more into balance?
3. In what ways are you loving toward yourself? In what ways do you give yourself a hard time? Which thoughts elevate you; which ones bring you down?

Exercises for Spiritual Practice

1. Select one of your qualities or strengths and work on cultivating it for a week. You can choose from a whole list: patience, tolerance, happiness, courage, determination, faith, integrity, honesty, simplicity, wisdom, contentment, etc. To practice, think about filling each action with this particular virtue. For instance, when you do your ironing, practice ironing with patience; cook with patience; conduct your business meetings with patience.
2. Get up early in the morning and let your first thought be of God. Before going to bed at night, go over your day and hand over your mistakes as well as your successes to God. Then wake up the next morning with a clean slate.
3. Three times a day, once in the morning, once at midday, and then in the afternoon, stop all activities and turn your attention toward God. Keep your mind like a compass focused in this one direction for three minutes. This practice will increase your power of concentration.
4. Consider deeply what the Hindu mystic Meera once said, "A moment without God is no moment."

Meditation on Freedom

I would like you to come for a walk with me. Imagine the sun is out and the beach is calling. It is early morning and we are alone, walking across the wet sands, scuffing the seaweed with our sneakers.

All of a sudden, you become aware of a vague scratching noise behind your back, and turning around you see an army of limpets itching against the black face of the rocks. A gun goes off. You whisk around and look up. Three or four white gulls are circling in the clear blue sky. Another bullet rips through the air. Your eyes focus on the stone jetty that stretches from the bank to the water's edge. One of the gulls dive bombs toward it and drops a clam from its beak with full force. Bang. The clam shatters on the stone.

You stop in your tracks near the edge of the sea and wonder which way to go. The sun has heated up and you feel its warmth on the back of your neck. You are aware of the pungent smell of seaweed that lies in strips of green and black, popping and belly-aching under the sun's strong rays. The sands start to heave, and you half expect a sea serpent to rise up before your eyes. But it is only the clams gurgling under your feet. You walk back along the beach toward the bank where some logs lie abandoned by the sea. You want to sit on a log and think.

Now that you are on the log, you feel secure. A gentle breeze caresses your face. From a distance you hear the low moan of a ferry as she rounds the coastline heading to harbor. Your eyes gaze at the calm azure waters, but at the same time your attention is drawn inward. Just as a tortoise withdraws its arms, legs and head, similarly you rein in your thoughts, feelings and emotions. You bring all your energy that was previously engaged with your physical senses back to a single point of focus, inside. This is the still point where you are silent and peaceful. You are now completely concentrated on the world within. The noise outside has stopped because you are not aware of hearing; images of nature blur because you are not aware of seeing; smells of the sea cease because you are not aware of taking them in. You breathe in quietly and deeply, but your breathing occupies only a fraction of your awareness.

You are now beyond the pull of your senses, free from the influence of your body and the limitations of time and space. What draws you deeper inward is a feeling of being at ease. You have no need of anything, nor are you lacking in any way. This feeling of freedom overwhelms you with joy. A bubble of joy bursts inside you and spills out all its contents. You are flying with the thought of being alive, immersed in the joy of being. You think to yourself, "I am free."

After a while you slowly turn your attention back to the sea and the sand, and to the creatures that inhabit the beach. You survey the scene with joy, as if you are seeing it for the first time. You are filled with a silent awareness that you are not in this world to take but to give.

STAGE FOUR

DARK NIGHT OF THE SOUL

One may not reach the dawn
save by the path of the night.

– Kahlil Gibran –

WALKING THE PATH

Become wise with the enlightenment of knowledge.

THE DAYS OF our spiritual childhood are wonderful and unique. We live with God, play with God, and experience the happiness of our spiritual awakening. The first few years of my spiritual childhood were among my most glorious. I was alive, alert, and brimming with energy. I remember thinking at the time, "God is with me, I am with God." I laughed a lot, and was truly happy. Wherever I looked, in the editing suite, on the subway walls, at the meditation center, I saw only God dancing before me.

This beginning period is referred to as the 'springtime of the spiritual journey.' It is often described as being 'easy,' 'rewarding,' 'insightful.' For many people -- though not for all -- this is a time when God is particularly close and loving, ever available to guide and care for the soul. One can be sitting on a park bench, on a bus, in an airport lounge, and all of a sudden be filled with a quiet knowing. God is near.

During these early years I didn't question the importance of contemplating spiritual teachings together with daily meditation. Somehow the wisdom of this discipline was intuitively lodged within me. Over time I also began to realize that contemplation and meditation were more than just tools for cultivating self- and God-awareness, they were the pillars of a spiritual framework. This framework was designed to encourage my growth and lead me to my destination. My journey had a course, a divine plan.

Within that plan God first pulled me to Himself and made me strong in loving Him. At the same time God taught me to love and appreciate myself. By meditating on my innate qualities -- those divine gifts of love, courage, and compassion -- I grew in confidence and faith. With this newfound strength came the power to look at myself objectively, and face the dark side of my personality.

Acknowledging this dark side was a new stage in my development. It was as if God held up a mirror before me, and said, "Look into your own heart. Tell Me what you see."

"I see aspects of my personality previously hidden from me," I replied. "Like blemishes on a pale skin these negative blotches obscure my inner beauty."

God smiled. He took my hand and led me forward. No longer a mollified child, suddenly I was a tiger pouncing after truth. I was an outrageous adolescent questioning myself, questioning God, and trying to come to terms with my own story. Soon I discovered there were weaknesses to acknowledge, strengths to cultivate, and a mountain of pain just waiting to erupt.

In moving from the beginner to intermediate stage of spiritual development, the many complexities of a mystic's nature are revealed. Beneath the layers of muddy masks and cover-ups lie our personal and sacred stories, just waiting to surface. They do not come out all at once. We would be overwhelmed or devastated if they did. Rather we discover our stories gently, one layer at a time.

Since the destination of our spiritual journey is to return to our original state of truth, all that obscures the truth and is superfluous to our growth must be gradually stripped away. Without the support of our spiritual framework many of us wouldn't have the moral or psychic strength to journey forward and discover the deepest parts of ourselves. But God, in His infinite wisdom, wraps us in a safe cocoon. In the comfort of His arms He takes us through the pains and illuminations of spiritual growth. We do not journey alone.

To every thing
there is a season,
and a time to every purpose
under the heaven
– Ecclesiastes 3.1

What has always fascinated me about the spiritual journey is its process. Walking the path is not simply about getting from point A to point B, or from one state of consciousness to another. It is how the traveler gets from A to B, and the lessons that are learned along the way. Spiritual process is the curious but specific unfolding of each person's journey. Each twist and turn, each significant up and down, each synchronistic signal points to where the traveler needs to go in order to learn what is essential for his or her development. In this school of life, the curriculum is universal, but classes are tailored for the individual. This is why I love spiritual process. I trust in its design.

According to divine plan, the issues that you need to address will come to you in the form of specific lessons. Becoming fully conscious of them is what makes the journey interesting. Even the most challenging situations are lessons in disguise. These lessons will be repeated, appearing in different forms and guises, until you have finally learnt them. For example, if you had difficulty dealing with the issue of authority as a child, you will continue to attract authoritative figures into your life. Until you work through this issue and change your response, teachers, partners, work colleagues, even fellow travelers on your path will appear controlling and domineering. Once *you* change, authoritative figures may continue to exist in your life but they will no longer adversely affect you.

The Spanish poet Antonio Machado wrote, "Traveler, there is no road. The road is made as one walks." As soon as you have mastered one lesson another one awaits you. Whatever is necessary for you to grow will come to you at the right time, when the right people and circumstances are in place. No two journeys are the same. Part of human nature is to make comparisons. People often measure themselves according to others' growth and achievements, and consider another's journey to be better than their own. Comparisons such as these weaken spiritual development rather than encourage it. Instead learn to marvel at your own journey. Trust in its wondrous unfolding.

See the world as a stage. You are an actor with your special part to play. You come onto the stage of life with your unique personality and features, with the ability to make of life what you will. Though we all share similar human experiences, the miracle of life is that each of us is different. The difference is created according to the uniqueness of our spiritual DNA that we bring with us into this world. This spiritual core influences the development of our beliefs, attitudes, personalities and actions. Despite what psychologists say about social and family conditioning, no two people are alike or react to life in the same manner. People who grow up in the same family and share the same social and economic conditions often chose totally different approaches to life. Whether they take the left fork in the road or the right fork, whether they walk with happiness or drag their feet in sorrow, is a matter of inclination and choice and is determined by their spiritual core.

Some travelers are optimistic whereas others question each and every turn. In times of difficulty, they ask, "Why is this happening to me?" They do not see the connection between their outer and inner landscapes. They believe that situations happen to them, not because of them. By thinking of themselves as victims of a cruel fate, they do not accept responsibility for their journey.

Life on the road has many challenges. The best way to journey is with an attitude of learning. See yourself as a student of life. Don't expect to wake up one day and say, "Well, I can stop learning now." Some of my spiritual elders have been on their spiritual journey for more than sixty-five years. Yet they still consider themselves to be students. They have taught me that to walk the path means to journey until the end. And in the next life there is always more to discover.

To facilitate your journey, consider the following four spiritual laws. These laws are universal. Understanding them will help you to unravel your story.

1. *The law of manifestation.*

Thought precedes action. Thought creates form. Every thought we have has a consequence in the physical world. We need to be careful of our thoughts because what we think eventually happens. If we think something good will take place, we pull that event toward ourselves. Literally, we will manifest it. But if we think something bad will happen, it is only a question of when. For example, after six months of repeatedly thinking I would be injured while in Paris, I had the car accident described earlier. Without much difficulty, I manifested my fears and have the scars to prove it.

2. *The law of cause and effect* -- also known as the law of karma or action. This law states that each action has an effect, which, in turn, is the cause of something else. Sir Isaac Newton observed that "for every action there is an equal and opposite reaction." In other words each action has an impact and brings an equivalent return. As we sow, so we reap. Actions are like seeds that once planted bear fruit, either immediately or at some future date. An act of kindness to a neighbor is returned with a similar kind act at a time of need or when least expected, either by the same neighbor or by a total stranger. A deliberate attempt to hurt a friend, colleague, or family member shows up later as an unexpected mental, emotional, or physical injury against our person.

Like a boomerang thrown into the air, our thoughts and actions return to us. There is a consequence to everything we think and do. To accept this law and live by it means to take responsibility for everything that we put out into the world. Many times situations arise for which there are no immediate identifiable causes. Such scenarios are often the result of actions carried out earlier for which the soul is accountable. The delay between cause and effect is often the reason for our bewilderment, especially when situations seem beyond our comprehension or control. The best approach is to accept these situations, learn from them, and move on.

3. *Consciousness creates reality,* individually and collectively.

A person can consciously create either a happy life or a life filled with sorrow. The fact that we live in a world of pain and sorrow is equally our collective creation and responsibility. The world is shaped according to how and what we think and can only be made beautiful again through a dramatic shift of human consciousness that involves each one of us. As the Buddha said, "What we are today comes from our thoughts of yesterday and our present thoughts build our life of tomorrow. Our life is the creation of our mind."

4. *Outer realities reflect inner realities.*

External circumstances mirror the state of the soul. Just as inner realities take on physical form, similarly, the events in a person's life are often symbolic reflections of his or her inner processes. At a global level, the state of the world powerfully mirrors humanity's spiritual condition. The horrors and catastrophes that currently plague our world are in fact symptoms of negative consciousness. By learning to view our life and world events symbolically, it is possible for each of us to pinpoint what our critical issues and lessons are.

An opera singer called Claudette once told me how each time she performs an opera she is confronted by the dramas in her own life that need to be worked out. In her personal relationships, especially among family members, Claudette had to deal with issues of trust and betrayal. When we met, she was playing the role of a woman who was betrayed by her sister and almost sacrificed for the sake of the father's ambition. By seeing the connection between the roles she was playing in opera and those she was playing in real life, Claudette gained a deeper insight into her own spiritual process.

The laws that I have just outlined are spiritual guidelines for living life well. Be mindful of them as you walk your path. It is easy to forget. Though many of us understand the law of karma, often we forget to pay attention to our thoughts, words, and deeds. Almost without our being aware we project a lot of negativity into the world. Through inattention not only do we hurt others, we end up hurting ourselves even more. As one woman said to me, "I didn't realize the power of my thoughts. I can bring about harm or good just by how I think."

As you embrace these universal laws, you will be taking responsibility for your journey. At the same time, use them as touchstones to unravel the myriad threads of the ancient tapestry that is your own unique story. It was the German mystic Meister Eckhart who said, "A man has many skins in himself, covering the depths of his heart. Man knows so many things; he does not know himself. Why, thirty or forty skins or hides, just like an ox's or bear's, so thick and hard, cover the soul."

And his advice to the aspiring mystic? "Go into your own ground and learn to know yourself there."

THE FALL

People write of the Rise and Fall. You know that at the start you were in Heaven. People remember Heaven as the land of happiness.

AS A CHILD I READ VORACIOUSLY. History books were my favorite, so too were books on legends and myths. I saw history as a compilation of stories about real people and events based on accepted fact. In my young mind, I understood myths to be more or less the same thing, except that they were more embellished and fanciful. Until I began my postgraduate research, I didn't realize where a love of history and mythology would lead me. It opened the door to my subconscious world and allowed me to explore crucial questions that people have reflected on down through the ages.

"Where do I come from? What am I on earth to do? What is the meaning of my life? Where is my destiny taking me?" Most of us have asked these questions at some point in our lives. If we ever receive any answers, we consider ourselves fortunate. In my case, the answers that I needed didn't come all at once but in spurts, through a synchronistic convergence of knowledge from a variety of sources.

In October 1981, I started a masters degree program at the Sorbonne in Paris. I chose "Journeys to the Otherworld: Visions of Heaven and Hell in Medieval Literature" as the subject of my thesis. I was passionate about my work and spent hours poring over ancient manuscripts at the Bibliotheque Nationale. My research led me to study two important universal myths: the story of a lost Golden Age, and the Fall that brought that enchanted world to an end.

I was amazed to discover a wealth of medieval literature, particularly from the lives of saints, about journeys undertaken in search of Paradise. I was especially interested in the sea voyage of St Brendan, a sixth-century Irish monk, who set out to discover Heaven and ended up, some scholars believe, landing in North America before the Vikings. The medieval texts describing St Brendan's voyage were Christian reworkings of Celtic adventure stories about the Otherworld. They contained elements similar to the Greek, Babylonian, and Indian paradisal myths.

Heaven was a major obsession for people in the Middle Ages but not for religious reasons alone. I believe their love affair with the enchanted garden was an equally astonishing expression of 'collective memory' born out of a universal longing to return to that lost land and experience its beauty and pleasure. If Eden had existed, the medieval saints probably reasoned, surely it would be possible to go there again, or at the least to have a vision of it. Monks such as Brendan set out in pursuit of heaven believing that it was a place of ultimate salvation, or perhaps it was also because they had a memory of it and were trying to find their way back.

Over the years scholars have been divided on the interpretation of myths. Some take the view that myths are exaggerated tales of historical events. These events must be rooted in reality, they argue, in order for them to have been handed down as stories from generation to generation by most of the world's ancient peoples. As Vallet de Viriville wrote, "Whenever you see a legend, you can be sure, if you go into the very bottom of things, that you will find history." Other scholars, most notably C. G. Jung and Joseph Campbell, tended to view myths as allegories for spiritual processes, symbolically real but not actually true.

I prefer to interpret myths from both viewpoints. Myths are important because they contain symbolic as well as historic elements. While this perspective might seem paradoxical at first, it can be reconciled spiritually through an understanding of our journey as souls across many lifetimes.

As souls we are beings of pure energy. We use the vehicle of our bodies to express and interact in the physical world and naturally succumb to the laws of change. Any change of energy that is experienced internally will ultimately affect us physically. Literally our thoughts affect the very atoms and electromagnetic fields of our bodies as well as the world in which we live. Similarly, any change that we experience in our physical surroundings or circumstances influences the way we think, feel, and view the world. Energy is information and the information keeps changing daily. As the old saying goes, "The only thing that is certain is change itself." In this way, there is a reciprocal exchange between us, as souls, and the world in which we live.

Over the course of my journey as a soul, I have come to see life as one big game of change. Just as day turns to night and night turns to day, and the seas rise and fall upon the earth, human consciousness moves from high tides to low tides, from light to dark and back to light again. Cosmic patterns shape the destiny of nature and chart the soul's course. Hold a mirror to the soul and see the cyclical movements of nature reflected. Look at nature and see the intricate dynamics of human consciousness mirrored back. Birth and death, growth and decay, transformation and renewal -- these are patterns we all know well. They shape our world spiritually and physically, personally and globally.

Myths are important. As symbolic representations of the changes in human consciousness, they shed light on what we would not otherwise know how to interpret. Because there was an inability to talk directly about the subtleties of consciousness our ancestors told stories instead. Just as we do today, they used allegories, metaphors, and symbols to communicate the patterns of change as they experienced them.

Thus, for example, when they went through dark times they would depict negativity as a monster. The monster would represent the darkness in the world and also any dark phase of the soul. Personal and global stories would inevitably intersect. Take the legend of St George and the dragon -- a story historically believed to be about a martyred Christian in the third century who stood up for his faith against the Roman Emperor. On one level, the saint can be seen as a symbol of the soul and the dragon as a monster within. By slaying the dragon, the soul transcends its weaknesses -- fear, doubt, uncertainty -- and is restored to a state of strength. On another level, due to his beliefs the saint is a man going through a very real spiritual battle. In defeating the dragon, St George achieves a personal victory of faith.

It was later in the Middle Ages that St George's story became popular in Britain and he was adopted as patron saint. His victory over the dragon can be seen at yet another level as a defining moment in history -- depending on how one wishes to interpret the event -- for the strengthened position of Christianity in the Western world at that time signaled the end of the influence of pagan practices and thus the end of those so-called dark ages.

What I have learnt from studying myths is that our personal and global stories dovetail. The personal is global and the global is personal. Myths record the shifts in human consciousness that occur over time, as well as the inevitable impact of a changed collective consciousness on the world. In this way, the story of the change in human consciousness can be viewed from the perspective of both reality and myth. Both inform us. Reality is what actually happens to us as human souls going through a human experience in the physical world. Myth is our human attempt to describe symbolically these changes of consciousness, as well as the events that take place as a result of them.

To further illustrate this point, let us consider the following story as a possible 'history of soul':

In the beginning, we souls live with God in the world of light. In our original state we are powerful and pure, full of divine energy. Our journey begins when we leave our Home of light, come down on earth, and adopt physical forms. The world is our playground. We live in total harmony with each other and with all creatures of the earth. Our inner beauty is reflected in the beauty and lushness of nature. Sickness and sorrow do not exist; it is a world abounding with happiness and peace.

But gradually, over time, as we interact with our bodies, surroundings, and each other a change occurs. This change is experienced as an almost imperceptible loss of energy from within. Just as the afternoon sky is gradually drained of its light, in a similar manner, we experience a tiny dimming of our inner light.

This loss of energy makes us susceptible to external influences. Gradually, the physical world becomes more and more the focus of our existence and identity. The result is a shift of consciousness. Instead of seeing ourselves as souls now we begin to identify ourselves with our bodies. As the experience of soul consciousness diminishes, our attachment to the physical pulls us into lower consciousness. Our divine qualities lose their strength tarnished by this negative overlay. A similar erosion begins to take places in the world. Intolerance, injustice and suffering now begin to afflict the human condition. We experience the shift as a fall from grace, a terrible feeling of separation from God.

The garden is gone, Paradise lost.

Captured on the film of collective memory, this event became immortalized in myth as the Fall from the Garden of Eden. Practically every religion, from Hinduism, to Judaism, to Christianity, to Islam; every indigenous group, from the North American Hopis to the Aborigines of Australia; and every ancient civilization, from the Greeks to the Chinese, speak of a Golden Age of humanity, an Age of Truth or Perfect Virtue. Even those of us who may not want to believe such a world existed, must be struck at least by the recurrence of the paradisal theme in all the world's mythologies and religious texts.

Yet, strangely enough, it is not the story of a perfect world that troubles us. Rather the story of our Fall is vastly more disturbing. Why? The event left its mark. Each day, we humans face the consequences of our imperfections and feel the pain of countless transgressions. Ours is a fragmented world, torn apart by poverty, sickness, corruption, and war. The levels of human suffering are so intolerable for some that we might as well consider ourselves to be in Hell. Indeed, we have come a long way from Heaven.

People ask: "Why is there so much suffering in the world?" Such a question can only be raised when there is the belief that things *were* or *can* be different.

However, the real question is: Are we destined to remain fallen forever? A friend once told me that she had never liked religion because of the Fall. She was concerned by the lack of stories about our human recovery. My friend has a point. The Fall doesn't make sense if humanity is left dangling. Even sorrow and suffering have a limited duration.

The Recovery story exists, but it is buried within a rich body of prophetic literature. Most religions and traditions speak about a return to Paradise. But there is little in the literature on how this return might be achieved. However, significant material exists detailing the transformation of the old order that will precede the renewal of the world. These events have been prophesied as a time in which the forces of good will battle the forces of evil, and win.

The idea of a restored Paradise, a return to a previous harmonious world order, is recorded in both Eastern and Western prophecies. The Hindus talk about the end of Kali Yuga, the Dark Age, and a return to Sat Yuga, the Age of Truth. In the divine poem, the *Voluspa*, Viking prophecy speaks of Heaven emerging after the flames and waters have subsided, "Now do I see the earth anew, rise all green from the waves again." A similar vision is described by John in Revelation 21.1, "Then I saw a new heaven and a new earth." There is also the Scandinavian myth of Yggdrasil, the cosmic tree, which remains standing after the earth is covered by ice. From the trunk of this great tree comes a regeneration of the earth, seas, and human life.

But how is this story of Paradise lost and Paradise regained useful to our lives today? How can the Recovery story be understood within the context of our spiritual development? Since our journey as souls is not linear, but multi-dimensional and layered, it is useful to turn to current events for the answer. Today, across the world, people are awakening as if from a deep sleep. There is a powerful desire to heal and be healed. It is as if the earth itself is clamoring to be restored. Many people are taking up spiritual practices in an attempt to 'recover soul.'

For each of us and for humanity collectively, soul-recovery is an instinctively driven healing process. It involves cleansing and transforming all that is old and unnecessary to our growth. Understanding the Paradise myth gives us the confidence to heal. It is easier to return to a state of wholeness, knowing that destination is already a part of our history.

To begin your healing process, evoke memories of your original and divine state of soul. Remember how you felt when you were full of light and spiritual power, free from all negativity. Hold this vision. Know that it is the blueprint of your true essence. As a being of light you have the experience of divinity recorded within you. Let the memories return.

At the same time, learn to accept and embrace the Fall, those moments when you did not think or act in a conscious way. Each and every situation in life carries a lesson. Look behind the challenging events in your life and see their significance. External situations reflect inner processes. Instead of questioning why things happen to you, allow them to reveal the wounded places inside you that are still waiting to be made whole.

The Recovery story may be a myth; but it is happening right now in this new millennial age. The passion for healing is leading to a transformation of individual and collective consciousness. The more we turn to God for this healing power, the more the vibrations of our healing will affect the planet and all living creatures. As we change, the world changes. As we heal, the world is also healed.

When we regain soul power, our original divine state, Paradise will return. It's written in our myths. It's our history in the making.

THE ALCHEMY TALE

God has such attraction that you can cling to Him completely.
However until the rust of your negativity is removed this attraction
cannot be experienced fully.

FROM THE TIME OF the early Egyptian civilization right through
to the late Middle Ages, philosophers, scientists, and esoteric practitioners
have searched for a substance called the Philosopher's Stone. This was
believed to be a magical elixir that would change base metal into gold. Only
a substance or force more powerful than gold, it was thought, could change
something into gold. Alchemy was the ancient art dedicated to the discovery of this rarefied substance. It was a physical art that had its origins in
mystical knowledge.

While the physical practice was concerned with discovering an agent
capable of transmuting an impure metal into its perfect equivalent, the
mystical practice was concerned with the secret of immortality and the
attainment of divine perfection.

Hazrat Inayat Khan *(Spiritual Dimensions of Psychology)* tells an old
Sufi tale of a king who desired to know the secret of alchemy. One day the
king heard that a wise old man possessed the knowledge and he ordered his
ministers to find him. The old man was dragged before the king but denied
any knowledge of it. The king flew into a rage and sent the sage to prison.

Still obsessed by his desire to obtain the secret of alchemy, the king
forged another plan. Every day he dressed himself up as a porter and visited the sage in prison to attend to his needs. But the old man revealed nothing. This went on for many years until finally one day the old man whispered the secret knowledge into the porter's ear. He did not tell the king the
secret, he told the humble porter.

There are many ways to interpret this story. What concerns us is its relevance to the mystical journey. Sacred knowledge cannot be revealed to

someone just because he or she desires it. A person has to be ready to receive it. By serving the sage, the king went through a deep inner transformation, a spiritual alchemy. In becoming the humble porter he lost his arrogance and attained all that he hoped for.

Spiritual alchemy is a profound process. It involves transforming negative human characteristics into qualities as pure as gold, changing what is negative in the soul back into positive. The process is intrinsically linked to the secret of immortality, namely that the immortal soul does not die but is reborn. Through a journey of many births the soul's original golden qualities become tarnished and a burden of suffering accrues from within. Spiritual alchemy cleanses the soul of its burdens, restoring it to its original pure state.

At the center of this spiritual recovery lies the Source of all knowledge and power. Only God is the powerful purifying Agent -- the Philosopher Stone -- capable of transforming an imperfect human being back into a divine one. The power and knowledge received from God in meditation form a magical elixir strong enough to penetrate and 'burn' the unwanted impurities within the soul to reveal the residue of once golden splendor.

O Alchemist of my soul, essence of all truth,
once your cure appeared
everything else lost its meaning.
– Rumi

People ask, "If my original state is pure, where do my negativities come from?" I tell them, "First understand your depth and history of soul. You are not just the product of one birth. As a soul you have journeyed through many lifetimes, living in different countries, surroundings, and circumstances, in both male and female forms. Through meditation you can receive insights of your previous births. The details are not essential. It is enough to know that your past experiences shape who you are today. Not everyone can accept this concept of past lives, but the depth of the soul cannot be fully realized without it."

The soul functions like a record with many different tracks. Within the soul lies the conscious and subconscious mind. I have learnt that everything we have ever thought, felt, said, or done is recorded as imprints or grooves within the subconscious of the soul. Amazingly, we keep the entire essence of all our lives on record. As these imprints in the form of mental or emotional patterns filter into our conscious mind from the subconscious, they affect our attitudes and responses to life in the present moment. Therefore, much of what we think, feel, and do today is determined by what we thought, felt, and did before. Some grooves in the soul are deeper than others. It depends on the extent to which they are reinforced. For example, if a person performs an act of kindness and as a result feels good about it, there is every likelihood that he or she will behave again in the same manner. Similarly, if someone acts negatively by lying or cheating, and has no regret, then that person's subsequent behaviors will be influenced by the earlier pattern. Positive behaviors generate positive feelings toward the self whereas behaviors that reinforce the negative groove create feelings of low self-esteem. Both behavior patterns and how a person feels about him or herself eventually become so ingrained they form the whole personality and way of being.

Indeed, we are the products of patterns arising out of the imprints accumulated and deepened over many births. We are today the sum total of what we created yesterday. What we create now is what we will live with in the future. Each thought, each action, has its own effect and brings its own return. Our entire 'history of soul' is accessible if we but care to look.

I sometimes compare the soul to a cactus plant that has grown spikes around its soft nourishing center. These spikes are our defenses created from patterns of low self-esteem, fear, and other negative imprints. The spikes cloud our vision of our true nature. Instead of seeing the beauty of the cactus heart, we are pricked by what we see first -- our negativities. This increases our fear, disillusionment, and feelings of unworthiness. As a consequence of seeing these negativities, we fail to acknowledge our own beauty and the beauty of others. As these spikes harden and grow, they prevent the cactus heart from interacting positively in the world. Or as Rumi once said, "If you find the mirror of the heart dull, the rust has not been cleared from its face."

Recognizing our negativities does not mean that we should dwell on them. It is important to forgive ourselves for our faults and release any hidden guilt. What helps is to return to the soft core of our being, that God-given place of inner beauty. From there we can look out dispassionately at our negativities which no longer seem to be so fearsome. Instead, an illumination occurs. Quite literally, we will light up with realization, "Oh, I get it. This is where my anger comes from. This is why I get depressed. This is how I lost my humility."

Facing the self in a real way is what differentiates spiritual growth from personal development. Whereas personal development is more concerned with change for the sake of individual enhancement and success, spiritual growth embraces the entire complexity of the soul. Facing the truth hurts but it also liberates.

In my own practice I have found that the assimilation of knowledge combined with power received from God in meditation works like a medicine to cleanse the soul of false attitudes, beliefs, and patterns. This process on the soul level is similar to what happens on the cellular level when flower remedies are taken to address specific physical ailments in alternative healing. Drops from these highly concentrated flower essences work subtly on the body's systems, tracing and healing symptoms in the order in which they last occurred, back to the original cause. Spiritually, our whole practice of receiving knowledge and having communion with God is a medicine for the soul. Drop by drop the intake of knowledge and power works on the grossest level of sickness to the most subtle, from the most obvious stain to the tiniest seed of blocked energy that has tarnished the soul and taken away its spiritual health.

Just as in alternative healing old symptoms come to the surface, similarly as we begin to heal spiritually old negativities erupt. In both instances, eruptions are part of the healing process and need not cause undue alarm.

Spiritual alchemy is a mystical process that involves a simultaneous purification and illumination. During this time the soul is uplifted by the grace of God's love. In restoring the soul, God has two tasks: He both purifies and illuminates. During illumination there is the experience of God casting the light of Divine knowledge on the soul, allowing us to see ourselves clearly. Divine light shines through the imperfect overlay to reveal the beauty within. Light attracts light. The more our pure essence is revealed, the more keenly we feel God's presence and become free from the unconscious hold our negativities have on us.

At the same time, God's power purifies the soul, burning through the dross of darkness. Purification involves a healing and eventual transforming of all our negative patterns. It is the cleansing from our very being of all hurt, guilt, and foreign matter. As those negativities fall away, we are drawn toward the Light and to the experience of our own divine perfection.

In the *Tao of Physics*, Fritjof Capra says that process of enlightenment "consists merely in becoming what we already are from the beginning." No matter which tradition or spiritual path they follow, most people have the belief and desire to become whole.

How each of us is transformed by God, and when, is dependent on our own efforts. Without the guiding hand of God there can be no return to wholeness. Anyone who thinks it is possible to journey alone has not yet discovered the power of the Philosopher's Stone.

"Where do I begin?"

"Start with a vision of your pure essence. What do you see?"

"I see a strong diamond light, pointed to perfection. I see the many facets of my divine nature, rainbow qualities reflecting the light. I sense the color of my feelings, the softness of abundant energy rippling out from my core."

"What do you feel?"

"I feel an immense love, an overwhelming gratitude to the Beautiful One. You have cast Your light through my dark shadows allowing me to see that I am made in Your image, a being of rare and distinct beauty."

You smile. "Now what do you see?"

"I see myself as a full-winged tiger butterfly, unbound and free."

THE DARK NIGHT

Instead of becoming afraid of adverse situations, learn a lesson from them, and become a powerful soul who moves forward.

I WOKE UP IN BED the other day thinking, "When I leave this body, all that I will take with me is what is contained within 'I,' the soul. I can't take my books, the river across the road, the mountains in Vancouver, the friends who phone or send email messages... I can't take a thing, except what lies within."

This was a great realization. The soul is immortal, the body perishable. Then I thought, "What is my strength of character? What state would I like to reach before leaving this life? How would I like to come before God?"

It was a strange way to wake up. The day before I awoke with these thoughts, I had been walking down by the river, fighting with myself. The conflict I was experiencing was not new. I have been struggling with it all my life. It is my desire for permanency in a physically impermanent world. For years, I have known that when a soul leaves its body -- for that lifetime at least -- everything is said and done. All that a soul can take with it are the accounts of its good and bad actions, weaknesses and strengths, memories and impressions, its love and faith in God -- the total package of its spiritual endeavors on earth. People facing death know this well. I have known this, yet I have not really known it. A part of me has resisted the truth.

In today's competitive world many of us are driven by our ambitions and desperate need for success. And yet when it is time to leave this life, only the intentions that were behind our actions will be useful to us in the next. Only those positive qualities that we cultivated and shared with others will carry us forward. Forgiveness, understanding, loyalty, honesty, caring, humility, respect -- these qualities are useful for our journey. We cannot rely on anything external for our safe passage, nor can we take any monuments of achievement with us.

In the seventh grade I read a poem about a king who created a memorial to himself in the middle of the desert. But over time the winds and sands washed over his memorial and erased it from human view. I loved that poem because it spoke the truth, the same truth I felt early Thursday morning when I awoke knowing with absolute certainty that I am an eternal soul, and that everything physical I have an attachment to, including this body, is not mine to keep and cannot come with me.

One of the illusions of life is that everything physical is in a state of permanency whereas in reality the human condition and even the world itself is in a constant state of fluctuation. We consider that there is security in the permanency of money, achievement, fame, and sometimes even relationships. But in a changing world anyone of these things can be lost in a moment.

In Eastern spiritual traditions, attachment is understood to be one of the major causes of unhappiness. We can have attachment to a person, material possessions, status, or recognition from others. Attachment is the desire for reciprocity: to receive a return of love from the person or a return of gratification from the object of our affection. In pursuing these attachments we lose our freedom to operate independently from their hold over us. Our unhappiness arises from the anxiety that we might lose them.

Attachment, fear, desire, and many other negativities are the cause of our struggle and suffering. The Christians speak of seven deadly sins; the Buddhists refer to six main stains. On my spiritual path we recognize there are the five core vices of anger, greed, attachment, desire, and ego out of which all the other negativities emerge.

Each vice has a power and influence that cannot be underestimated. Like an infectious virus it infiltrates our thoughts, words, and actions. As a collective, the vices have spun a toxic web of negativities throughout our whole system, producing arrogance, jealousy, possessiveness, dependency, laziness, hatred, and selfishness, to name but a few. These negativities have to be faced and transformed at their root.

Pale sunlight
pale the wall.
Love moves away.
The light changes.
I need more grace
than I thought.
– Rumi

Virtue and vice are two sides of the same coin, representing the pure and impure energies of the soul. For your negativities to be transformed a simultaneous bolstering of your virtues has to occur. Go deep into your virtues and you will be filled and strengthened by them. In meditation, experience, "I am peace. I am love. I am happiness. I am pure energy. I am spiritual power."

In her eighteen steps of *Conversion and Penitence*, Angela of Foligna described being filled with the intensity of Divine Love, and then later going through a tremendous physical suffering. This illness was the start of an amazing process of healing and purification in which, she said, "Every vice was re-awakened within me." Angela's insights shed light on the spiritual process and have been a great encouragement to me on my own journey. She talked of the fear she had of being stripped of all her false pretences and of facing temptations she had never known before. "When I was in that darkness of spirit, I thought I would have chosen rather to be roasted than to endure such pains," she wrote.

So deep and profound is this experience of the soul facing its dark side that the great Spanish mystic St John of the Cross called it "dark night of the soul." At the same time, he referred to it as "happy chance." The purer the soul becomes, the more happily it is drawn into closer relationship with God. Just as the dark night ushers in the dawn, the reward of going through this cleansing of negativity is the joy of being more consistently illuminated by God's presence and grace.

In his literary masterpiece *Dark Night of the Soul*, St John outlined two levels of purification through which God leads the soul. The first is a cleansing of imperfections related to seven sins of "pride, avarice, luxury, wrath, gluttony, envy, and sloth," which he called "dark night of the sense." In his treatment of these imperfections, St John gave examples of the frailties associated with each one and how they block spiritual progress and keep a soul from God.

Translated into modern-day practice, this first dark night is about reforming our most basic human weaknesses. Becoming impatient, intolerant, or critical of people are negative traits associated with anger. Comparing one's spiritual progress to others, wanting praise or validation are traits associated with ego. Being jealous, coveting someone else's position or possessions is greed. Expecting results from one's actions or fixating on relationships and possessions is attachment. Manipulating or seeking control over others or situations are expressions of desire.

This initial phase of the dark night is about recognizing, facing, and eventually transforming these imperfections to the extent they are no longer visible externally in our behaviors. This does not signify their total disappearance from our being. We can still experience anger mentally and emotionally though we no longer express it through our words or actions. Our desire for recognition may not be manifest in overt attempts to pull people's praise and attention, yet it can continue to fester inwardly as dissatisfaction.

St John called the second phase of purification "dark night of the spirit." At this more advanced stage a mystic confronts the more subtle traces of his or her negativities. According to St John, these are "like roots, to which the purgation of the sense was unable to penetrate." Whereas the first level is concerned with more recently acquired negative traits (the fresher imprints), the second level is about transforming those that are more long standing. The dark night of the spirit also addresses the vanities that often accompany spiritual progress. For example, even after achieving a high spiritual state a mystic can still fall victim to the arrogance of his or own goodness, taking pride in his or her virtues, considering him or herself to be an excellent meditator perhaps, or even a great teacher. To be cleansed of the more subtle forms of arrogance means to surrender one's virtues, talents, and achievements to God. What is Divinely given ultimately needs to be accredited to the Source.

And so what do these dark nights look like? What is their relevance to your journey? The moment you commit to spiritual growth, you will inevitably set in motion a series of events that will bring your hidden negativities to the surface. All negativities, like the sicknesses they are, have to erupt before they can be transformed. Assume that you will be tested by just about anyone or anything. Either your negativities will come up in the form of internal conflicts or they will manifest externally as unexpected challenging life scenarios, or both.

For instance, imperfections that you didn't know existed will suddenly be right in your face. Whereas before this dark night you considered yourself a caring person, suddenly a spotlight falls on a hidden part of you. Now you see that by helping others you were only fulfilling your own need to be needed. Whereas before this dark night, you considered yourself to be a good team player, now when someone else dominates the meeting, you feel the heat of jealousy rising. The spotlight of illumination will shed light on the places where previously you were afraid to look.

Obstacles also appear in different forms and guises. Whereas before this dark night you thought your life was in order, suddenly it will be thrown into chaos. For instance, you may lose the job you love as a test of whether your self-esteem is based on what you do rather than who you are. Or a friend or a colleague ignores your success as a test of whether you are still attached to receiving praise and recognition. Or you wake up one morning and find a lump on your breast, as a friend of mine did last week, and you are suddenly confronted by your fear of illness.

Each manifestation of the dark night comes to show you what needs to be transformed within you. And because you desire to be cleansed, consciously or unconsciously you will pull toward you the issues that you need to resolve from this life and previous lifetimes. The dark night is a healing of the past on a grand scale.

People react differently to their dark nights. Some see it as grace, others as a necessary but unpleasant part of spiritual growth. Some mystics are shocked to discover they aren't as virtuous as they originally thought; others begin to think they aren't virtuous at all. There is a tendency on the part of some to become paralyzed by fear when they first witness their imperfections. Others don't want to admit to being imperfect and blame other people believing them to be the cause of their dark nights. I once met a man who blamed his teenage son's behavior for his unhappiness at home. He took up meditation because he wanted peace of mind. The man's inability to admit that his own expectations of the boy may have been the cause of his growing anxiety prevented him from moving forward spiritually. Eventually he stopped meditating.

Some people become afraid when they see negativities return that they thought they had already overcome. One advertising executive said to me, "What's happening to me? I must be backsliding." He had been a meditator for four years and was experiencing new levels of inner peace. Then the old anger, which had plagued him before he began his path, suddenly erupted with a vengeance. He was shocked. I told him, "Don't think you're going backward. This dark night is a sign that you are moving ahead. A wise yogi once told me that when climbing a mountain the path doesn't lead straight to the summit. It goes up, then down. It flattens out for a bit, then goes up again. In spiritual life the downs as well as ups lead to the summit. Or think of it another way. As Dogen, founder of the Soto branch of Zen Buddhism, once said, 'When you walk in the mist, you get wet.'"

I have met people who have tried to rush through their dark nights anxious to skip over the unsavory parts of their personality. They wanted to reach the light before they had walked without fear in the dark. I have also met people who were afraid to go past the beginner's stage of growth and have faith where God was leading them.

Just as a child sleeps with a small night-light on, trust is your light through the night to reach the dawn. Trust in the dark night.

A few years back, I had a conversation with a young Australian. We were standing on the roof of a three-story building in India enjoying the sun. Kerry was an athlete who had spent one year biking all over Australia. The next year, he had biked from Vancouver to Alaska. He knew about endurance, determination, and courage. He knew how to trust the road, his bike, and himself, but he was afraid to trust God. I took him to the edge of the roof and we looked down at the concrete road below.

"Go on, jump!" I said. He looked at me as if I had gone crazy.

"Just jump," I repeated.

"What, now?" he said.

"Now!" I replied. It took a minute or so before a smile spread slowly across his face. "I've jumped out of airplanes before," he said, "and so I know about the fear of letting go and trusting that you will be safe."

"Jump into God's arms," I said "and you will be safe." He looked at me intently for a while, and said, "OK."

Then spiritually he jumped.

SPIRITUAL WARRIOR

This battle is against the five vices. You conquer these vices with the power of yoga.

THERE IS A TENDENCY IN HUMAN NATURE to want to take the easy way out. When life goes well, we smile and say to ourselves, "Yes, well, I've paid my dues. I deserve this." But when life becomes tough and situations go differently from how we would expect, we say to God, "Get me out of here." We want to get out of a situation before we even get into it or before we even realize there may be some benefit in it.

Mary, a businesswoman I know, was going through a bad financial year. Her business was failing, her partner was refusing to take any responsibility for the work, and her husband and children were resenting the extra hours she spent in the office. Where once life had been sweet and successful, now she was struggling to balance both the business problems and demands made by her family. She felt she was walking a tightrope and that at any moment she could fall. As the pressures mounted Mary felt overworked, stressed, and unappreciated.

In a moment of desperation, she said to me, "I've reached a crisis in my life. I just wish God would make it all go away." I nodded. "These challenges have come to strengthen you. They are showing you where to change and are related to your inner work."

"I know," Mary said, letting out a little groan. "I just wish there was an easier way."

Like Mary, many of us on the spiritual path expect to become free from our anxieties and problems. We want peace and happiness, lives that go well, and spiritual attainment in all of its magnificent forms. We want all of this without having to go through the necessary inner work. It's not the struggle we are so against, but more the uncertainty of the shape our lessons will take and whether or not we are sufficiently capable of rising to the challenge. Behind the fear of change is the feeling of not being good enough, powerful enough, or adaptable enough to go through the rigors of the journey. Frequently the extent of our inner resources is forgotten, and it is only after we have been through a crisis and come out the other side that we can view the situation differently. A friend once said to me, "Funny how things that we see as discouragements and setbacks can be the very things we need to go forward in a more complete way."

In turning to God to get us out of unfavorable circumstances, it should not surprise us that God will lead us right into the heart of our discomfort. For it is here in facing our fears that we are illuminated. The beauty of going through our dark nights is the joy of coming out of them more full of light. In fact, the journey to reach the light is a hero's adventure, full of inner struggle and self-doubt, until ultimate self-mastery is achieved.

Mary is a good example of a modern-day heroine. The crisis she went through brought to the surface many of her life issues: a lack of clarity about her priorities, relying on the status of her business for her self-esteem, her fear of failure as a wife and mother, and the betrayal she felt when her business partner let her down. To overcome these challenges, Mary would have to go deep into herself.

In *Hero with the Thousand Faces*, Joseph Campbell gives a clear analysis of the elements involved in a typical hero's adventure and which are found in many of the world's mythologies. These include: "a separation from the world, a penetration to some source of power, and a life-enhancing return." Drawing on this analysis, Mary's journey into the dark night involved a separation from her familiar experience of success, a descent into crisis, followed by a battle with her inner monsters. She would have to overcome her fear of failure that was based on ego and turn inward to reclaim her true source of self-esteem and power. This would allow her to set clear priorities and restore balance and happiness to her life.

The hero's adventure is centered on spiritual recovery. Each of us has to go within and heal our inner conflicts. Like Mary many of us resist the process. It was Carl Jung who acknowledged the fear that most people have of facing the dark side or 'shadow' of their personality. He stated, "The shadow is a moral problem that challenges the whole ego personality, for no one can become conscious of the shadow without considerable moral effort" *(Aion)*.

Several years before I even acknowledged my dark side or understood the heroism implied in spiritual transformation, I had a conversation with Sister Jayanti, my first meditation teacher, and another student called Paul.

We were driving somewhere in the car, discussing the nature of illusion, *Maya*. Illusion is an important concept in Eastern philosophy but one that is easily misunderstood. Illusion is the false perception of the nature of our being and is the opposite of truth. Anything in the soul that is negative or harmful is illusionary, not because it does not exist, rather because it veils the truth of who we really are. Maya cloaks the luminous being within.

Vices and deception are all forms of Maya. Maya can surface as an internal weakness and also as an external negative force. People ask, "Is this what the devil is?" I tell them, "The devil is just a symbolic name and form given to the negative forces we cannot always understand. All negativity starts from within."

Another face of Maya is that it pretends to be something that it is not. Fairy stories and legends are rich with warnings about the deceptive nature of illusion. There's the wolf that tried to trick Little Red Riding Hood dressed up in her grandmother's clothes. Or the wicked queen who, disguised as an old woman, succeeded in giving the beautiful but poisoned apple to Snow White. Due to its deceptive nature Maya dresses up human frailties presenting them as something they are not, making us believe we cannot live without them. In fact, the deception can be so great that many of us continue to use pride to bolster our self-worth and greed as an excuse to accumulate.

Right from the start of my spiritual journey I was warned about Maya. Though I didn't experience it in any dramatic way during spiritual childhood, just knowing that it existed helped me to prepare for any future encounter.

On the day we went driving together, it was clear that Paul didn't see Maya that way. He turned to Sister Jayanti and said, "Why does everyone keep talking about illusion? Whatever it is, I'm sure it won't come to me." Sister Jayanti said nothing. But her eyes smiled as if to say sweetly, "Yes it will, Paul. Deception comes to everyone." I remember the warning in her eyes. I thought to myself, "I won't ever say that something will or won't come to me. Who am I to know what challenges I must face?" I didn't realize it then but that thought was like an armor. Instinctively, I was gearing myself up to be the future spiritual warrior. Eventually, I faced not one battle but many battles.

Later on, I reflected, "It's strange how spiritual people, who are committed to principles of non-violence, love and peace, use metaphors of war to explain the internal struggles faced on the spiritual path." Of course, the metaphor of war is there to remind us how real Maya is. Time and time again our negativities deceive us. The deception can be so illusive that rather than face our negativities we choose to deny them.

Part of this denial is a reluctance to deal with the shadow side. Out of context, our shadow appears repugnant and dark, a side of ourselves we would rather keep hidden. In context, it is part of the landscape that can lead us home. Truth is reached by facing illusion, by walking through the dark and leaving it behind. In Frederick Pierce's *Dreams and Personality*, a distinguished opera singer related a curious dream in which she chose to walk down some muddy, sewer-filled streets of a town, rather than the clean paved ones. In interpreting her dream, she said, "Perhaps some of us have to go through dark and devious ways before we can find the river of peace or the highroad to the soul's destination."

All mystics have to face their shadow. You are not the first to confront your dark side and you won't be the last. Think of it like this: You are a spiritual warrior setting out on a hero's adventure to tame and transform your negativities. Mythology is full of tales of heroes fighting monsters and overcoming great obstacles. Jason dodged a fierce dragon, retrieved the Golden Fleece, and returned home to claim his kingdom in Greece. Beowulf, hero of the old English epic of the same name, fought the monster Grendell who had been devastating the land. Later he dived into a deep lake for three days and nights to wrestle with and kill Grendell's monster mother. Theseus, another hero, ventured into the great labyrinth of Crete to kill the Minotaur, and came out alive with the help of Ariadne's thread.

From the religious traditions there are equally sacred stories of the spiritual warrior who has to struggle against negativity. Jesus spent forty days and nights in the desert where he was tempted by the devil and given many opportunities to renounce his spiritual throne in favor of false power. There's the legend of Buddha's Great Struggle under the Bo Tree when he was attacked by Kama-Mara, the god of love and death, wielding weapons in his thousand hands. *The Bhagawad Gita*, one of India's main scriptures, tells the story of the Mahabharat War in which Lord Krishna (one of the Hindu gods) appears and gives advice to Arjuna. The young warrior is on the battlefield and afraid of fighting because he is facing his kinsmen. The dialogue between Lord Krishna and Arjuna is a literary masterpiece in the form of spiritual metaphor. "Think thou also of thy duty and do not waver. There is no greater good for a warrior than to fight a righteous war," Lord Krishna tells Arjuna.

So what wars were being played out on the battlefield of Arjuna's mind? No different than the ones we all face today. Ultimately, Arjuna had to find the strength to overcome his attachment to his relatives who had turned against him, and claim self-mastery. Jesus rose above Satan's temptations to understand and fulfill his destiny. The Buddha remained non-attached to the disturbances that crept into his mind and achieved enlightenment.

This battle with negativity is real. It comes to all mystics who are doing their work. What is important is the attitude with which we enter into the dark night. If the battle is perceived as a huge struggle, it *will be* a huge struggle. But if it is viewed as a hero's adventure, as a normal part of the mystic's journey, then the battle will seem more like a game. Or, in Joseph Campbell's words, it will appear as "a labor not of attainment but of re-attainment, not discovery but rediscovery." This is because the power or enlightenment that the hero gains has been within him or her all along. The battle is just an exercise in reclaiming lost spiritual power. "The hero," as Campbell says, "is symbolic of that divine creative and redemptive image which is hidden within us all, only waiting to be known and rendered into life."

Here are some important guidelines to help you become a courageous spiritual warrior:

1. *Be aware of the presence of illusion.*

Weaknesses, vices, imperfections, internal conflicts, and inner demons exist. They are powerful and life threatening. Make a list of the things that disturb you. Accept them knowing that they are your own creation. By drawing on God's healing power, you can transform them.

Once you acknowledge your weaknesses and imperfections, don't hang on to what you see. They are just an illusion. At the highest level of truth, they do not exist. In your original divine state you are free from negativity. Don't let illusion deceive you by making you believe you are something that you are not. Become like Perseus, the Greek hero. He cut off Medusa's snake-infested head, not by looking at her face directly, but by using his shield turned toward the sun as a mirror to reflect her image. In the same way, don't see your weaknesses and believe them to be the truth. You may experience guilt, fear, and unhappiness, but they are not your truth. Love, peace, happiness, purity of soul are your truth.

2. *Validate the reality of your existence.*

Say to yourself, "I am not anger. I am not peacelessness. I am not my addictive patterns." They may be there right now. But they do not reflect who I am. So who am I? I am the stillness of my silent point. I am a love that heals all wounds. I am content and full of peace. Meditate on these qualities. See yourself as a golden chalice brimming and overflowing with the nectar of your pure qualities.

The more you validate the reality of your pure essence through meditation, the more the hold that the illusion of your negativities has over you will diminish. Stay focused on the light within. Just as one small candle can give light to a darkened room, similarly the light of your inner being can dispel the darkness within. Keep hold of the light. It illuminates the path during the dark night.

3. Learn to love not hate your weaknesses.

Sometimes just seeing your negativities can make you feel dislike for yourself. Such a reaction only serves to strengthen your negativities. Love is a great healing power. It is a stronger force for change than any negative emotion. Love is warm and soothing, love nurtures and restores. Learn to love yourself. By understanding and accepting your negativities you will release the necessary energy to transform them. As Mahatma Gandhi once said, "When you are confronted by the enemy, conquer him with love."

4. Recognize it, accept it, embrace it, release it.

I developed this formula nine years ago to help myself deal with my negativities. Take fear, for instance. First of all, recognize when you have fear. Feel it in the pit of your stomach. Accept that you are afraid. Don't deny your fear, or your denial will keep the illusion in place. Embrace your fear as you would a frightened child, for that is what your negativities are -- frightened children. I know that this may seem difficult to do, but you can train yourself to embrace your dark side. Positive life-enforcing energy has the power to transform. Finally let your fear go. Release your attachment to it. Your fear is not you.

Be like the Buddhist monk who was confronted by a monster with ferocious teeth. Instead of being afraid or believing in the illusion, he put his head in the monster's mouth and immediately the monster disappeared.

When walking through your dark night, become like an Aikido master who does not resist the on-coming forces but moves with them.

5. Let go of sorrow.

When Dadi Janki once told me, "Let go of your attachment to sorrow," it took me a long time to understand what she meant. Think about it. When you feel pain, or see others in pain, what do you do? If you are like most people, you will probably harbor that pain in the form of sorrow. It will be recorded at the soul level and even in the cells of your body. Holding on to this pain will make you attached to sorrow. Too much sorrow causes a person to be over-sensitive. That sensitivity prevents you from facing your negativities or seeing others go through pain without becoming adversely affected.

It is important to know how to grieve in situations of loss. Admit the loss, but then let go of it. Sorrow often arises when there is a lack of forgiveness for mistakes or transgressions made by the self and others. By dwelling on such situations, they magnify and grow out of all proportion. Begin by acknowledging the mistake or transgression. Tell yourself, "It is now in the past. I have learnt from this situation. I forgive myself. I forgive others. Now I need to move on."

Becoming free from your attachment to sorrow will release inside a great feeling of happiness.

6. *Hand over your problems, transgressions, and negativities to God.*

Get into the habit of giving all these things to the Divine. Don't think that because you have imperfections you have to keep them all to yourself. God is a mighty Ocean of Love. Tell God, "Here is my problem. It's Yours. My pain is no longer of any use to me." And just as water is the universal solvent, God, the Ocean of Love, can dissolve all pain. As a Mother, she takes it all into Her big healing lap. The waves of God's love are so powerful She can accommodate all the sorrow of the world.

If you hand over your problems, anxieties, and mistakes of the past to God, the Ocean of Love will wash over you, cleanse you and make you whole.

THE HANDLESS MAIDEN

Check to what extent your intellect is drawn to an individual or a possession, and to what extent there is a leakage of power.

IN THE SOUL POWER SEMINAR that I run I ask participants, "What drains your energy and what restores it?" Then I give them this example, "Just as one negative thought of low self-esteem can pull you down, one positive thought of love can energize you. There are many different ways in which energy can be lost or gained."

Later in the seminar I ask participants, "To whom or to what do you give your energy? Where do you excessively focus your attention? It could be a person, a habit, an attitude, a recurring thought, or a false belief. Think about a situation where you become tired, drained, and out of balance. Ask yourself, 'What has taken away my energy?' Write down your answer. You have just identified your Power Drainer."

Then I tell participants to reflect on a second question, "When your energy is down, what restores it? Think about a time when you needed to restore your strength, happiness, and inner power. Ask yourself, 'What revitalized and restored my energy?' This could be an activity, attitude, belief, thought, or spiritual practice. Write down your answer. You have just identified your Power Restorer."

Just by reflecting on these questions you, the reader, will also become more aware of how you manage your energy. Consider this: If your energy is low, this indicates that something or someone has become the focus of your attention. Perhaps by giving too much time to a heavy work schedule you have neglected your family life. Or perhaps you've become so busy looking after family and friends that you have neglected to take care of yourself. Thinking too much about a situation you regret or one that still traumatizes you also drains your energy. In other words, wherever your attention goes, your energy follows. And if your energy goes too far in one direction, you will be pulled out of balance. You will know when this happens because suddenly for no apparent reason you will feel out of sorts, troubled, tired, even depressed. When a disruption of your energy occurs, you will feel inwardly conflicted, disempowered.

In terms of energy use, I consider that there are four main aspects of the self that need to be in balance: spiritual and physical, inner and outer, heart and head, feminine and masculine. All these aspects are inter-related and need to be in harmony to attain optimum well-being in life. If one aspect of the self becomes more dominant than another this will cause an energy disruption leading to some kind of energy conflict. The art of managing all these energies and restoring them to balance is part of the journey to wholeness.

Pat was a woman who despite her meditation practice fluctuated between moments of extreme happiness and bouts of painful depression. She found it difficult to balance the inner and outer expressions of her energy. On the one hand she'd happily immerse herself in many activities, then become depressed when she no longer had time for herself. Pat would then go to the opposite extreme, stop being active, and spend a lot of time alone. Initially, she loved being in solitude but after some time she would long for human interaction. "I don't know what's wrong with me," Pat told me on the phone. "I'm not happy whatever I do." After I meditated on Pat's situation, it became clear that she was caught in a classic energy conflict, polarized by the opposite and extreme uses of her energy. Either she had to be active or reflective, she couldn't be both. What she needed to do was to set a timetable for the week that would nurture her active side, while setting aside blocks of time in which to be alone.

Many of the dark nights experienced by a mystic are directly related to issues resulting from the misuse and imbalance of energy. Leila is an academic and meditator whose dark night consisted of a conflict between her head and heart. She is an emotional person but keeps her emotions under control by burying herself in her work. It's not that Leila isn't a kind and loving person; it's just that by favoring her head she is emotionally restricted. Being unable to acknowledge her feelings and express them to others may account for her being frequently misunderstood. At the moment Leila is trying to get in touch with her emotions and cultivate a language for expressing them.

My own energy conflicts became apparent when after seven years on my spiritual path I began to feel dissatisfied. I thought, "I've done all the right practices, so what's wrong with me?" This anxiety prompted me to turn within and look at the way I was managing my energy. For a long time I'd understood that as souls we house both male and female energies. These represent the masculine and feminine aspects of our nature. In our original state of wholeness these energies are in balance and we are adept at managing them in such a way that no one side suppresses the other. However, through a gradual misuse and draining of our energy that natural balance is disturbed. To compensate, one side begins to dominate the other.

In Chinese philosophy a balance of the receptive feminine principle, yin, and the active male principle, yang, is considered essential for good health. The active masculine principle tends to express itself through external and rational-oriented activities, whereas the receptive principle tends to express itself through more reflective and emotional activities. Most of us -- men and women -- use our active masculine energy to get things done. We use our feminine receptive energy magnetically to pull toward us what we need for learning and survival purposes. Whereas masculine energy makes things happen, feminine energy allows them to happen.

As I began to examine myself I saw that as a personality type, I was more active than contemplative. Yes, I meditated, but I was a person who was used to making things happen. I didn't have the patience to allow things to take their natural course. Like many people operating in a results-oriented world, I relied on my active masculine energy to achieve important goals. Not that this approach was wrong for me at the time. But by favoring this 'go-getter' side of my personality, I had suppressed the softer, more intuitive, and receptive side of myself.

Much of what I am writing now started to crystallize some years back when Jacqueline, a writer friend from the Netherlands, sent me a short story to read called "The Handless Maiden." It is an old European folk tale about a young girl whose father makes a pact with the devil and loses what is most precious to him: his daughter. The devil proceeds to chop off the girl's hands. Humiliated, she leaves her father's home to find solitude in the forest. Eventually she comes to a pear orchard. Since she is hungry, but cannot use her hands, the girl begins to eat one of the dangling pears using only her mouth. Unbeknown to the maiden, the orchard belongs to the king. He discovers that his fruit is disappearing and hides himself in the orchard to catch the thief. When the king sees the handless maiden reaching for a pear with her mouth, he feels pity for her. He also falls hopelessly in love and wants to marry her. But the maiden is concerned. How can a king have a queen who has no hands?

The king decides to make his queen some beautiful silver hands. They are so beautiful everyone at court admires them. At first the queen is satisfied with her false hands. But after a while she becomes discontent. Even the birth of a son does not alleviate her growing sadness. Eventually, the queen decides to steal out of the palace with her baby and returns to the forest. As she approaches a river the queen accidentally drops the child into the water. She cries out in anguish, "Help! Someone please help me." She is a long way from court and so her cries go unheard. The queen has to rely on herself to save her son. Bravely she plunges her arms into the river, and miraculously, her original hands of flesh and blood are restored to her.

Upon reading this story I felt a stab of emotion. In it I saw my own story reflected and was touched by the rich symbolism. Drawing on some of Robert Johnson's analysis *(The Fisher King/The Handless Maiden)* an interpretation might go like this: The maiden symbolizes the feminine energy within all of us, whether we are in male or female forms. The girl is betrayed by her father who represents the male energy that exists within all of us. The cutting off of the girl's hands by the Devil symbolizes the damage that is done to the positive and creative expression of feminine energy when it is blocked or suppressed by the domineering aspects of male energy. The maiden goes into the forest, a place traditionally associated with solitude and healing. In the orchard she tries to restore her energy by eating the pears, a symbol of femininity. But the king, male energy, rescues her and gives her false silver hands. These hands represent the falsehood of male domination.

Even though she is now queen the maiden is desperately unhappy. She is not functioning in her own right. She leaves again for the forest to find the necessary solitude to heal. Her hands are restored to her when she must activate her feminine energy to retrieve from the river her son who is a symbol of pure male energy. In this way, the maiden is healed when her male and female energies are brought back into harmony and balance.

About a month after reading the Handless Maiden story, I had the following dream. I was high up in the Rocky Mountains on cross-country skis. A man with whom I used to work professionally was standing in front of me. I could tell it was him from his body, yet his face belonged to that of my brother Guy. We were in a ski competition. As the gun fired the signal to start the race, he pushed ahead. He raced past me, although I had now taken on the appearance of Carrie, an artist friend, who was dressed up in a red ski suit. I was both the observer of the dream and also the main protagonist in the form of Carrie.

Seeing the man on skis overtake her, Carrie burst into action. She pushed down on her poles to go faster but slipped and fell over. I panicked, "She's going to lose the race." Carrie picked herself up. Then with all of her determination she raced to the top of a high slope. Over she went into a free-fall. As Carrie crashed down, a blade from her ski fell onto her right hand and cut it off. A pool of red blood covered the white snow. I cried out, "My hand, my hand! How will I ever sew it back on again?" I woke up from the dream in a panic.

Later, after much reflection and meditation I realized that having my hand cut off symbolized a dangerous mutilation of my feminine and creative energy. How could I have allowed my feminine side to become so badly suppressed that in order to survive it was forced to compete? And in competing, it suffered more damage. This revelation was shocking to me. The competition between Carrie and the man represented a disturbing inner conflict about the use of my energy. Like many people, I had used action to validate my existence and to create a feeling of personal power. This had distracted me from my real spiritual work. The need to be active was so strong that my feminine receptive energy was completely cut off. I was not in balance. I was not whole. A similar imbalance could have occurred had I been suppressing my active masculine energy, as some people do, in favor of my feminine energy. Instead my lesson was to learn to respect and cultivate the more receptive, nurturing side of myself.

Spiritually we can learn to validate the feminine principle by letting go of the need to control our lives and allowing events to unfold naturally. Then instead of questioning our inner conflicts, we learn to accept whatever comes to us as a gift of learning. Through the power of silence, we magnetically pull toward us the answers to our problems. Answers will arrive, magically, symbolically, in a dream, in a book, in meditation. All the tools that we need for our spiritual recovery become available to us when we slow down and connect to that receptive part of ourselves.

Each person has a special way to heal his or her energy imbalances. Some people like to work through their issues by reading books, others talk to friends or keep a daily journal. All of these methods help. But to heal the damage of our energy imbalances requires an intense focus. When we are energetically injured we need to place ourselves in healing environments. And yet so often, in spite of our best intentions, many of us get sidetracked. Like the handless maiden, we marry the king, stuff our emotions and issues, and continue to feel desperately unhappy.

Many people use the arena of human relationships to try and balance out their energies. When they feel incomplete in themselves they turn to others in an attempt to become whole. For instance, if a man turns to a woman, he is searching to replenish the feminine aspects absent in himself. When a woman turns to a man, it is to find the masculine aspects that she herself is lacking. This quest applies in same-sex relationships as well. One's aim is to get filled up. In a Barbara Walters interview several years ago, a famous actress said about the latest man in her life, "He fills me up. He fulfills that part of me that I could not fill."

If human relationships lack mutual understanding and trust and are used for selfish purposes, there will often be a price for filling up in this way. A twenty-seven-year-old woman I know admits that while being in a relationship can enhance a person's best tendencies, it can also bring out the worst. She is currently working through some of the "dark stuff" that her relationship seems to have given rise to within her: fear, insecurity, low self-esteem, jealousy, the desire to control or to be controlled. In her letter to me, she wrote candidly, "I realize that I am repeating patterns that are destructive and make me unhappy, yet I persist in them. This is partly because I am so conditioned to believe in the possibility of a union with another person; a union that can answer all my needs. I might know intellectually that this is unrealistic, but emotionally I yearn for it to be true. I think it would solve all my problems, because I'd find my missing half."

As a healer, Barbara Brennan has done research on the energy fields surrounding the human form. In her book, *Light Emerging*, Brennan uses illustrations to demonstrate how people's energy fields take up offensive and defensive positions according to how they relate to others. From the illustrations, one can see clearly how different human responses affect a person's auric field. Positive ways of interacting reveal an expansion in the aura. Negative ways of interacting and manipulating people show up as a chaotic disruption in the energy field.

Unhealthy relationships have the potential to become a focal point for our energies. In *Anatomy of Spirit*, Caroline Myss calls the people and objects we are drawn to 'power-targets.' We connect to these targets, she says, so that we might draw their energy into ourselves. The down side is that by connecting to them, some of our own energy gets drawn into the target. And while at first this might feel good, especially at the beginning of a relationship, eventually it leads to a loss of energy. The way I see it, where our attention goes, our energy follows. In my seminars I find that participants tend to identity other people as their main Power Drainers.

Some people describe being in a relationship with a person who literally 'steals' their energy, draining them after every encounter. Other people are obsessive about their relationships. They become totally captivated by another person's looks, achievements, and personality. This obsessive attraction, however, dissipates their energy leaving them feeling disempowered. Often relationships between partners, friends, colleagues, and neighbors, break down because one person puts more into the relationship than the other does. This often reaches a point where the perceived 'giver' suffers a crisis, and is no longer able to go on divesting his or her energy.

One artist I know is at her breaking point. She loves her husband, but has come to realize that he is 'robbing' her of her energy. It took her twenty-five years to wake up and realize that the person she loves most in the world is making her sick. The worst part was realizing that she has allowed him to do it. He wouldn't have been able to drain her if she hadn't given him her quiet consent. At this point in her life, my friend's decision is to stay in the relationship, but to try and bring her spirituality into alignment by the way she manages her energy.

Most human beings have an intense desire to love and be loved. And while human love is natural and beautiful, it becomes unnatural and obsessive when we 'fall' for another human being. Ultimately, we pay the price for making someone our source of power. In taking another person's energy we actually lose our own. Our power is weakened as it becomes enmeshed with another's. The trouble with such false Power Sources, as I call them, is that they are attractive. They attract us so much we don't want to let them go.

Even on the spiritual path, many things have the potential to become our Power Sources. We use status, achievements, recognition, other people in an attempt to fill up and become whole. Part of going through the dark night is learning to recognize what falsely attracts our energy. The most insidious of all attractions is the desire for spiritual recognition, which can unconsciously become the main motivator for all that we do. Often it manifests in the desire to have one's spiritual efforts applauded by others on the path, or to be hero-worshipped by people who might consider us their teacher. Or it can be played out in the attempt to claim associative power by being seen in the company of the spiritual 'power brokers' of our own tradition. It is an illusion to think one is spiritually advanced simply because one keeps the company of spiritually powerful leaders. Seeking recognition from our teachers, or from anyone else for that matter, takes away a soul's self-respect and reduces its spiritual power. With a loss of power comes a feeling of alienation from the self and God. That's why our unconscious and false Power Sources can be so spiritually damaging.

So, the next time you find yourself attracted to someone or something, ask yourself: "What am I looking for? Is it love? Is it happiness? Perhaps comfort, or support? Maybe I need someone or something to depend on. Or maybe I require a special energy-boost when my spirits are low." Whatever the case, it's good to be aware of your motivations.

All souls want peace and eventually turn to God for that reason. God is the perfect balance of male and female qualities. As the Supreme, God doesn't require any external energy for replenishment. And because God is eternally energized, He/She is the perfect Source of each soul's fulfillment.

In the dark night, there are a thousand ways we lose our energy. But there is only One way to fill up.

God.

Here I am before You again with my divided self. My ego has created two empires. I am two people: the one who is active and fearless, who knows no limits or boundaries, who prides herself in her talents and accomplishments; and the other half who is frail and uncertain, who hides in small places, and tries not to be seen.

You see the whole picture. What I see is a canvas torn in two. "Where is this resistance coming from? This wall in my heart?"

You do not speak. You only hold me close. "What? No answers? No revelations? I don't need to be treated like a child. I want to know. I want..."

The silence of the room echoes the silence of Your mind. You take everything in, see every part of me with Your safe, all-encompassing eyes. You know how hard it is for me to let go. In holding me, You hold my pain. You take the pain of the whole world into Your big generous lap, Mother.

In Your eyes I see my future reflected. You see that a day will come when I will be free from all my sorrow. But until then, You hold me softly against You.

REFLECTIONS ON THE DARK
NIGHT OF THE SOUL

Reflective Questions

1. What are your soul issues? You can recognize them from the internal conflicts and struggles that keep manifesting in your life.

2. What destructive addictions, patterns, and beliefs are hindering your spiritual development right now? Trace them back to the five main vices: anger, greed, attachment, ego, and desire.

3. With whom or with what do you energetically connect? What is your Power Source? Other people? Position and job status? External identifications? Nature? Internal references? God?

4. How close do you feel to God? If you feel far from the Divine, what is blocking your relationship?

Exercises for Spiritual Practice

1. Think about letting go of the past. Make a list of all the painful events in your life, then imagine each event as a balloon that you are freely releasing. You may have to do this several times, since pain does not always get released all at once. Just being aware of what you would like to be freed from, and having the desire to let these things go, is an important first step.

2. Accompany this releasing of past events with a short prayer, "Dear God, from today on, I release to you all the burdens of my past. I hand everything over to You, and I become free."

3. Make a list of your weaknesses and imperfections. Stand back and observe them for what they are. Your weaknesses are not the real you. You have the power to transform them.

4. Virtue is the bedrock of the soul. Reflect on your original, divine qualities. Say to yourself, "I am peace. I am purity. I am happiness. I am love. I am power." By going into the depth of experience of these qualities you will find a change, not only in your understanding of love, but also in the way every day you live this love.

Meditation on the Healing Power of Love:

Visualize yourself sitting under a spiritual fountain of God's healing love. Speak these words out loud, and allow their power to penetrate your whole being: "Love is my true essence. I am born of love. I exist for love. I am connected to the Source of Love. In the silent, loving presence of the Divine, I feel myself being filled with a special healing light and power. Gently my pain dissolves into an Ocean of Light. God's love heals my wounds, liberating me from the burden of negativity. In this moment I am free from the past, free to live in the present. I step forward and embrace a life of love."

STAGE FIVE

ILLUMINATION

From delusion lead me to Truth.
From darkness lead me to Light.
From death lead me to Immortality.

– Upanishads –

SILENT WITNESS

You have come from immense darkness into immense light.

ZEN BUDDHISTS refer to moments of enlightenment as *satori* or *kensho* -- literally 'seeing into the essence of things.' In *Still Point: Reflections on Zen and Christian Mysticism*, William Johnston describes how Master Teshan received enlightenment by watching Master Lung-tian blow out a candle flame, and how Master Hakuin received it by hearing the sound of the temple gong.

While enlightenment is often described as the final stage of the spiritual journey, we can all experience moments of being illuminated along the way. Some illuminations come unexpectedly, when the fusion of seemingly unassociated thoughts and experiences suddenly produce flashes of insight. These insights can be about ourselves, or others, even about creative ideas. For instance, scientists struggling to solve difficult problems are known to experience 'eureka' or 'aha' moments. This is when solutions come to them magically, intuitively, in an instant of profound knowing. Darryl Reanney describes in *Music of the Mind* the case of French mathematician Poincare who, frustrated during the course of his rational deliberations, decided to go for a bus ride, "At the moment when I put my foot on the step, the idea came to me, without anything in my former thoughts seeming to have paved the way for it..."

Spiritually induced flashes are even more profound because they lead to an experience of certain spiritual truths. This light of realization is often followed by an outpouring of emotion -- extreme exhilaration and joy in the case of a fresh discovery, or tears and the release of pain when illusion is shattered.

I once experienced this shattering of illusion, standing in the parking lot in the rain, as I opened the door of my car. Suddenly, all of the joy I had been suppressing exploded in front of me. Like a wild rose, this joy shot up pink from the ground and demanded my full attention. It was as if I had passed it every day by the side of the road, its lonely beauty distinct against the hedges and long grass. Until today I just hadn't noticed it. Now I wanted to fling myself down on the wet cement and weep. Weep for all the joyful moments I had let pass by, feeling myself unworthy to receive them. I couldn't bring back those moments of unlived happiness but the illumination that they were mine for the taking had changed me, awakened me to future possibilities.

Dewdrop, let me cleanse
in your brief
sweet waters...
These dark hands of life.
– Basho

Some illuminations are softer, quieter somehow, but equally dramatic. They steal over us when, in moments of deep contemplation, our consciousness focuses down on a particular thought or feeling until we arrive at its essence. There, at the core of feeling, we experience a silent 'knowing' -- "Ah! I've been here before." And in knowing the essence of something, we come to know all there is. This seeing into the essence of things stretches us spiritually, making us bigger than we think we are. Consciousness, when it is focused, expands. It moves beyond the confines of everyday perception, and connects us to the whole of ourselves, and the whole of creation. It is as if through some invisible eye, we are able to take in the interdependence of all things, and realize the unique threads of our own parts contained within this great pattern.

In October of last year, I ran a seminar on Managing Change for business executives in Jordan. We held the seminar at a resort by the Dead Sea. In the evening I slipped away from the group and sat on a flat rooftop to watch the sun fade over the hills leading to Jerusalem. I was sitting in an ancient land. It seemed to me then as if each stone had been a witness to the movement of tribes and nations as they criss-crossed the hills, valley, and deserts of this hard terrain, these biblical lands. The past was an intricate tableau spread out before me, an ethereal presence scenting the evening air with an exotic fragrance. Suddenly I became aware of the entirety of my life. Not just this one lifetime but all of my lives, past and future, as they melted into one glorious sea of red, one complete vista. It was as if a hand from my past had reached out and clasped the hand of my future, joining in soulful prayer.

In silence I watched the sacred unfold. I felt memories blending with scenes of a future landscape that were only now in the process of shaping. The businessmen and women with whom I had just spent the day were leaders in their field. They were eager to master the dynamics of personal and global change. During the seminar we had examined their desire to balance professional and family life, and to be role models who could contribute to their communities and their country. The group was small but influential. As they drew up their action plans I sensed the enormity of change that could be unleashed if these people were so inclined. The prospects had made my heart race.

Now here I was at the end of a working day -- a day suddenly made brilliant by the fact I had peeped through a crack in the wall and seen the significance of the scenes of my life passing before me. In one complete moment, I was a silent witness to all parts of myself, to the threads of my own story as it unfolded, interwoven with many historical movements. Then I knew at a level more deep than before: *What is personal is global and what is global is also personal.* They are one. There is one image, one motion, one reel of film that goes on and on, carrying our stories from the beginning to the end and back to the beginning again. We can tap into our own personal reel and get a sense of the whole. Then, at odd moments, we can be granted a glimpse of the cosmic reel -- the unlimited film that has captured and will continue to capture the scenes of all of our lives -- and somehow, inexplicably, through this illumination we will know ourselves better.

Life is a series of nature
and spontaneous changes.
Don't resist them -- that only creates sorrow.
Let reality be reality.
Let things flow naturally forward
in whatever ways they like.
– Lao-Tse

For a mystic, experiences of illumination are directly related to deepening the practice of observation. Observation works both inwardly and outwardly, adding colorful brushstrokes to our waking moments. By observing life and all its details, those details step out of the picture and become more alive. Through outward observation our senses are heightened and the object of our attention is magnified. On one occasion, when

I practiced this mindful observation, dark undulations stood out on the bark of a tree, the sweet aroma of pine became like drops of highly concentrated perfume, and leaves and branches shuddered under the thundering weight of an army of insects. As the silent observer, I could witness the magnificent contrasts of the forest, and yet remained unaffected and unattached. I was simply noticing, moment by moment, the forces of change going on around me.

When observation is turned inward, the senses cease to act, and the forest of your inner world becomes glaringly more alive. The art is to remain a neutral observer, unaffected, unattached to what you see. You just stand back and look at yourself with impersonal perception. Through this "inner sight" you begin to see yourself and situations from a different perspective. Then instead of shaping perceptions from the outside in, you form them from the inside out. I like to think of this internal action as the work of a silent witness. A silent witness does not judge or react but simply provides the necessary information. With a gentle nudging of new awareness, the silent witness lets you know, "This is what's going on. This is what I need. Here's where I've come off track."

I once read an article about the life and work of Jacques Lusseyran, a man who had been blind since the age of eight. A French Resistance fighter during World War Two, Lusseyran was betrayed to the Gestapo by a colleague. He survived Buchenwald, and much later emigrated to the United States and became a professor at Hawaii University. He wrote several books on perception, as well as an autobiography, *And There was Light*.

Lusseyran wrote beautifully about how observation works. He described how "every sound, every scent, and every shape is forever changing into light" on his "inner screen." He was able to perceive external objects, such as trees, gates, walls, and even people, according to the intensity of light or shadow they cast. He "saw" by differentiating between the variations of light or shade.

So how did Lusseyran develop this ability to "see?" Since he was blind, Lusseyran learned not to rush impatiently towards things. Instead, he found that by being still, things came to meet him. Any internal reaction or agitation on his part pushed things away; his impatience "displaced objects," his sadness "dimmed them." "By contrast," he noted, "joy illuminates everything." This perception made him sensitive to his own feelings and the feelings of others.

Just as Lusseyran found that inner calm helped him to heighten his skills of observation and perception, the act of becoming inwardly still heightens self-perception. Only when we are stabilized in peace, and free from the commotion of the mind, can we stand back and view ourselves with clarity and dispassion. This internal, impersonal perception is the ability of the third eye (the eye of the soul) to see past all falsehood and deception within the self and recognize the truth.

One Sunday evening in January 1998, when I was in Calgary, Alberta, to conduct a meditation workshop, I experienced a moment of such insight. The temperature outside had just risen from -35 to -15. As I trudged from the car park through the snow to the building on 11th Avenue, I felt a small tingling of joy, the kind of joy that comes from being calm and still in the here and now.

I remember standing on the steps of the building, the cold air jarring against my face. While my physical eyes looked up at the sky, with my third eye I became present in the mirror of my own inner sight. This action of being an observer made me feel bigger, more expansive in the way that I was thinking and feeling. All of a sudden I was struck by the smallness of my intentions. I had planned that night to repeat a workshop I had run earlier in New York -- it was easier for me to repeat what I had already done rather than create something new. All at once, the stillness of that insight brought on a rush of creative energy. "I have to expand, not contract," I thought. Impulsively I threw away my plans for the evening's workshop. My need to act on this illumination was bigger than myself.

Around twenty women and men had gathered for the workshop. "Imagine you are scientists entering you own personal laboratory to conduct some experiments," I told the group. "No experiment is more important than the next. No experiment fails. The results just are. Your job is to observe. After each experiment record the sequence of events, as well as your thoughts, and feelings." Some of the group laughed nervously. I sensed that maybe they hadn't attended an experimental workshop before.

In the first experiment, we practiced extending consciousness beyond the confines of the physical domain, into the supreme region of light. Once there, we found ourselves before God, and opened ourselves to receiving God's light and love. After the experiment, people spent five minutes writing down their observations. I then asked the group to share what they had written. "I saw light," said one man. "My mind was all over the place," piped up another. "I feel energized," said another voice. A woman named Hazel said, "I feel disappointed. Nothing happened."

I was glad this woman had spoken. She articulated what happens to many people who come to spiritual life with many expectations. Instead of remaining the observer, Hazel had invested her attention in what she thought should happen, rather than what actually did. When I asked Hazel to be more specific about her thoughts and feelings, she grimaced. "I felt a void," she said. "I know you wanted some kind of vision," I told her, "but that wasn't the point of the exercise." Hazel's face lightened. "The aim was for you to observe your thoughts and feelings, that's all. You did feel something -- maybe not what you wanted -- but it is important for you to articulate what you felt. Even feeling a void is valid."

We moved onto a second impromptu exercise, then a third one. Each time I encouraged participants to just observe themselves. "Whatever happens in your experiment is fine. Don't judge your experience as good or bad. It just is." By the end of the evening, people were more clear about their own inner dynamics. In becoming free from judgment and expectation, they were more able to look at themselves through the eyes of understanding and acceptance.

Hazel shared with me her realization. She said she had become more aware that her heart was blocked from receiving God's love. "I didn't trust God to be there for me," she said. "That's why I couldn't experience that love." Her ability to observe herself ultimately led to a revelation that brought her closer to an intimate truth. Hazel told me, "At some point, I must have loved God very much. Otherwise I wouldn't be so desperate to experience the Divine again."

Hazel's story illustrates the illumination that comes from being able to observe the self as a silent witness. When that self-observation is free from judgment it works like a spotlight to bring internal weaknesses into sharper focus. In seeing them without self-hatred, or shame, a person becomes free from the false perceptions that keep him or her in a loveless, fearful state. Once these weaknesses are illuminated, they lose their fearsome form. As Meister Eckhart once said, "True detachment is nothing other than this: the spirit stands as immovable in all the assaults of joy or sorrow, honor, disgrace or shame, as a mountain of lead stands immovable against a small wind."

And the beauty of this illumination is that in becoming non-attached and non-judgmental toward ourselves we actually become more loving.

ACHILLES HEEL

It's easy to look at others but it takes effort to look at yourself.

ALL OF OUR WEAKNESSES stem from one major flaw. This fatal flaw is our weak spot, our Achilles Heel. Achilles was the great Greek hero who was dipped by his mother, Thetis, in the Styx river to protect him from harm. But she neglected to dip the spot by which she held him -- his heel. During the Trojan War, Achilles' secret was discovered, and he was killed by a poison arrow shot through this vulnerable spot on his heel.

Spiritually speaking, even though we may have many virtues and talents, our weak spot, our Achilles Heel, brings us down, again and again. Any problem we face, any life issue that threatens us, can be traced back to this one fatal flaw. Until this fatal flaw is addressed it will continue to consume our conscious and unconscious attention, coming back to us in different forms and guises. Every time we worry, obsess, or complain to friends about our problems, we give it power. Our attention magnifies the flaw's hold over us. Though some people know of their flaw, they still remain in denial until unexpected events open them up to change.

Beth used to lead an active life in New York. She had many friends, but didn't feel herself to be worthy to receive love or the good things from life. When an important relationship broke up, she left New York to live in a small town. At first she was lonely and had difficulty coping with the solitude. But the vast country skies melted her resistance, cracked her open to the truth about herself. Prior to moving, Beth had recurring dreams of airplanes crashing. Later she read in a book that crashing planes symbolize a damaged spirit or spiritual way of life. "I spent ten years avoiding the real me," she told me on the phone. "I went through the spiritual motions but wasn't engaged authentically. I was too busy looking for people to love me."

"So what helped you change?" I asked.

"Spending time alone and reading. I became more aware of my

thoughts, my desires, and my recurring emotional patterns. I also realized my actions were motivated by low self-esteem. A month later I had another incredible dream. I was in an airplane flying way up high. Instead of the plane crashing, it landed safely."

"How did that happen?"

"Well, in the middle of the dream, I saw a dark thorn illuminated in my side. I knew the thorn was my lack of self-love. So I pulled it out. As soon as I pulled out the thorn, I felt a wave of God's love surrounding me. Then my plane landed safely."

Whereas Beth was eventually able to face her Achilles Heel, other people find there is a lot of mileage to be gained from hanging onto it. As Caroline Myss points out in *Why People Don't Heal and How They Can*, many people's intimate relationships are built around the support they seek and receive for their wounds. The addiction to the "power of the wound," as Myss calls it, creates a new language in our culture, which she has dubbed "woundology."

Similarly, people tend to become addicted to their fatal flaw since it is a major factor contributing to their personalities and life experiences. To let it go would mean losing a substantial part of themselves. They would be lost without their pain, without the identity and attention-seeking opportunities that their flaw provided.

One woman I know uses her illness as a tool to gain sympathy and to draw people's energy to herself. Her addiction to her ailments has reinforced the belief that she is a victim. This victim consciousness does not allow her to appreciate the comfortable surroundings in which she lives, the people who care, and all the other wonderful things that are happening in her life. Her Achilles heel is preventing her from healing.

In order to heal and become whole each person needs to track down the root of his or her negativities and pain. A friend once told me, "There are some negative and draining anxieties that I keep coming back to. It's almost like being addicted, or when you have a toothache and you can't stop touching the source of pain. I often feel like a hamster running around in a wheel and getting exhausted and going nowhere." I told her that these anxieties kept returning to her because she had not identified the main root from which they all stemmed. "You are diminishing your energy by scattering your thoughts in too many directions, by dwelling on each little negativity," I said. "Instead, why don't you look for the root cause. Once you have identified your Achilles Heel, then all your energy can go toward transforming it. By transforming this one main flaw, all your other anxieties and weaknesses will fall into alignment and be healed.

The soul gazes upon Truth without any veils of creatures
-- not in a mirror darkly, but in its pure simplicity
– Richard of St Victor

To discover your Achilles Heel adopt the art of observation. Learn to focus down until you discern the main cause of your weakness. As a demonstration of this concept, consider the following dialogue, which I have based on the Indian epic, the Mahabharata. In it, a young nobleman called Arjuna is being trained in archery by Yudhistra. The master asks his pupil what he sees,
"I see an eagle," replies Arjuna.
"What do you see?" asks the master.
" I see the eagle's head," says Arjuna.
"What do you see?" the master inquires again.
"I see the eagle's eye."
"What do you see?"
"I see the pupil of the eye," declares Arjuna finally.
"You have found your target," says the master.
Using the framework of this dialogue, consider the following questions. I have used them in my seminars to help participants discover their Achilles Heel. You may wish to ask a friend to read aloud these questions so that you can verbalize and listen to your own response. By answering spontaneously your first response will be closest to the truth. Try to answer these questions with just one word. Write down the first thought that comes into your mind.

1. Is there a negative thought that keeps re-occurring in your mind? What is that thought? What is the root of that thought?
2. Do you have a current obsession? What is the root of that obsession?
3. In which circumstances do you become upset or distressed? What is the cause of this emotion?
4. In which circumstances do you experience pain? What is the source of your pain?
5. What main weakness or negativity keeps re-occurring in your life? What is the root of that weakness/negativity?

Now look at the words that you or your friend have just written. Don't analyze, criticize, or make any judgment. Just observe your answers. Allow them to be. Let go of your attachment to them. Think of your answers as pieces of paper tied to a kite, and allow the kite to float away.

Now answer this question: What is the root of all the words you have just written?

Write your answer on another piece of paper. Again just notice it. Let the word be. Hold this word for a while, and see how the knowledge of it grows within you. If an answer doesn't come immediately, or if you still aren't sure, sit in silence. Tell God, "I need to know my fatal flaw, so that I can transform it." Then let go and trust the process. Rest in the knowledge that your flaw will be identified and healed.

Some people ask, "How do I know when I discover the root of all my pain?" Through inner sight, you will intuitively recognize it. You will just know.

Don't be in a rush to receive the answer. In its own time it will come to you, either when you're in the shower, walking on the beach, or driving down the highway. Do not become anxious. Just remain open, silent and receptive. When you are ready your Achilles Heel will be made known to you.

Once you have your answer, write it down on a piece of paper. Carry that paper with you in your pocket, or pin it on the wall above your bed. Rather than thinking a lot about it, allow it to exist, without judgment. This non-attachment will help you to understand your Achilles Heel. Soon connections will start to flow in your mind. You will begin to see and understand how many of your negativities are linked to this one major flaw.

Gradually, it will also become apparent, how you've been avoiding your Achilles Heel, by denying it, resisting it, even hating it. Keep hold of the word you have written. Eventually, the darkness around your Achilles Heel will subside, and behind it you will see light. Soon, you will realize that your fatal flaw hides your greatest strength, your most valuable virtue. This prize virtue is your specialty. It has sustained and carried you forward throughout your many births. This unique quality is the exact opposite of the Achilles Heel. Your flaw is an inverted use of your energy and thus a negative expression of your main virtue. That's why, if you prefer, you can discover your fatal flaw by first identifying your specialty, or greatest virtue.

This is what Bindu did. During one contemplation she looked back over her life and saw that she had always been a generous and kind person. She had great love for God and love for others. She identified love as her foremost strength. She told me, "But I also saw that I loved too much, and I gave too much to others. I didn't have boundaries. I became over indulgent with people I considered to be weaker than myself. I would try to do everything for them but this took away their self-reliance and made them dependent on me.

"At times, I felt so strong that I thought I could take over their problems. But this was a form of ego. What I should have done was given them some helpful advice, stand back, and let them work through their own problems. Being over indulgent to others led to hurt feelings. And because I felt unappreciated, I indulged myself. I started buying special foods to eat. I realized that too much love or love of the wrong kind leads to attachment. And my lesson? To remain compassionate, not controlling. This is the pure side of love when dealing with others."

What Bindu discovered is that while love was her specialty, attachment was her greatest flaw. It had led to an over indulgence of herself and others, as well as a weight problem. To transform her flaw, Bindu would have to focus on developing a love that combined non-attachment and compassion.

Now ask yourself: What is my greatest strength?

Give a one-word answer. Let the word sit with you. Let it nourish and inspire you. The gift of healing is to recognize and reclaim your greatest virtue. Now look at the ways that you have been misusing that virtue. What flaw lies behind its misuse?

In Bindu's case she gave love to receive appreciation from others and this was a form of attachment. Now ask yourself, if you are not using your virtue with the right motivation, what negativity lies behind your motivation? This process may help you to discover your Achilles Heel.

What may also help to shed some light are the short descriptions below of the five main human vices or flaws, together with their related negativities and the life issues that are associated with them. I have also included a short example of other people's experiences to illustrate the flaw, as well as the main virtue that illuminates it.

ANGER:
A strong emotion excited by a real or imagined injury that involves a desire for retaliation.
Related Negativities: Frustration, Impatience, Intolerance, Hatred.
Issues: Denial, Betrayal, Revenge, Hurt.
Story: As a child James was easy-going and loving. Yet as he became older

he developed great expectations for himself. When success didn't materialize, he became impatient and frustrated. His disappointment erupted in outbursts of criticism and anger toward others. He became increasingly cynical toward friends and colleagues and secretly blamed his superiors for overlooking his abilities.

VIRTUES: Love, Peace, Patience, Acceptance, Letting Go, Forgiveness.

ATTACHMENT:
To bind, fasten or join by either desire or affection.

Related Negativities: Possessiveness, Fear, Rigidity, Jealousy, Stubbornness.

Issues: Independence, Inter-dependence, Death, Impermanence, Entanglement.

Story: Marsha had trouble accepting that her mother was going to die. She knew that the soul who was her mother was leaving this lifetime and moving on to the next. Still, she was deeply afraid. Her fear was not about her mother dying; it was connected to that part of herself that made her feel safe and secure. Her mother's death meant losing a part of herself. Marsha's fear was of letting go. She was attached to the illusion of permanency.

VIRTUES: Non-attachment, Letting Go, Easiness, Self-sufficiency.

GREED:
Coveting, a fierce desire or longing to accumulate.

Related negativities: Selfishness, Desire, Discontent, Laziness.

Issues: Security, Power, Emptiness.

Story: Steve works fourteen-to-sixteen hour days on the stock exchange. He complains of tiredness, stress, and being unhappy with his job. He wants to get out, but is afraid to leave his job. The money he makes gives him a feeling of security. He thinks that if he works hard one more year, he will finally reach a position of financial security. Then he'll be happy. He's been saying this for six years, but is still working at his job and hating it. He knows that one day he'll burn out.

VIRTUES: Generosity, Contentment, Happiness, Bliss.

DESIRE:
To long for the possession of something or someone.

Related Negativities: Negative Power over someone, Lust.

Issues: Control/Domination, Wholeness, Intimacy, Depression, Co-dependency.

Story: Sarah is desperate for love. She likes being the center of attention, and uses it in a way to obtain love. Because she doesn't feel complete in herself, she relies on other people's attention to feel needed and to fill her void. Sarah craves love from others because she is withholding love from herself. She uses her body, talents, and personality to attract men into relationship, but still cannot find any solution.

VIRTUES: Love, Purity, Inner Power.

EGO:

The false perception of self.

Related Negativities: Pride, Arrogance, Low self-respect, Doubt, Criticism, Judgment, Conceit, Self-centeredness.

Issues: Victim/Savior consciousness, Inferiority/Superiority Complex, Identity, Approval, Validation, Comparison.

Story: As an immigrant to the United States Nasima had difficulty adjusting to her new life. In her country of origin she was an intellectual, with position and respect. In spite of this, at almost every phase of her life she had experienced loss. Nasima is frustrated in her new country because she cannot fully use her talents. Even when she started a business it failed. The more she was unable to use her talents, the more she started to compare herself with others, being jealous of their success and angry about her own loss. Without realizing it, she sabotages everything she sets out to do. She vacillates between feelings of superiority due to her talents, and that of a victim due to her inability to use them.

VIRTUES: Humility, Self-Respect, Love, Inner Power.

Dr Carl Jung once wrote *(Psychology and Biology)* that if the shadow side of a person "is repressed and isolated from consciousness, it will never get corrected." Facing our Achilles Heel is an ultimate act of kindness, no matter how painful a process it might be. To venture into the dark we need tremendous courage and a healthy degree of self-acceptance. Or as Jung put it, "we must summon all the powers of enlightenment that consciousness can offer" *(The Stages of Life)*.

EGO CRUNCH

There are many types of ego. Where there is arrogance there cannot be any satisfaction.

SOME FORTUNATE MYSTICS come to understand their major flaw early in their spiritual lives. They know that if they allow this fatal flaw to dominate them, they will not move forward on the spiritual path. So they deal with it quickly and intelligently. One such mystic is a teacher and friend of mine who lives in India called Brother Surya. When he was fourteen years old, he was warned by a friend at school to pay attention to his ego. "Ego will cause you a downfall," his friend told him. And because he didn't want this downfall to happen, Brother Surya became vigilant. "Whenever I had any thoughts of ego, I'd catch them and change them," he told me.

Not all mystics are as fortunate or masterful. Some choose a more labored and less aware approach. For this reason they are confronted by their Achilles Heel in more dramatic and devastating ways. It seems that many of us have to be knocked senseless before we can awaken to our darkest defect. "Disillusion me with truth," Teresa of Avila told her friend Garcia de Toledo in the sixteenth century. She wanted him to warn her in advance when she was falling into any illusion; her request of him was enlightened for it showed her willingness to face the truth.

Other people are awakened not so much by the vigilant pursuit of truth but by unexpected events whose sole purpose is to shake them out of their illusions. Thus, it is the circumstances or the people, those we love and those we do not, that become the perfect instruments to disillusion us with truth -- whether we want them to or not. All the signals can be there, pointing to what we need to change. But sometimes it takes a big 'wake-up call' to shift us out of our ignorance. In my own case, it was a combination of friends and circumstances that unwittingly conspired to make me confront my fatal flaw.

When I was a little girl I was told, "You are sensitive and delicate just like your grandmother." In my family this sensitive nature was considered virtuous. I guess it was my grandmother's delicacy that my grandfather loved for it made him feel strong. This sensitivity meant I could easily get hurt, had a low tolerance for personal pain, and also couldn't stand to see any human being or animal injured or hurt. And while this sensitivity gave me understanding and compassion toward others, I was not always so forgiving toward myself. I had a tendency to sting and punish myself if I thought I had done anything wrong, even when such punishment was unwarranted.

When I was sixteen, my family went through a financial crisis. It was a frightening time for us all since we did not know what the outcome would be. In the end, we lost our home, our money, our position in society, and our friends. The worst part was the splitting up of what had been a close-knit family. My parents divorced and my two brothers and I began to lead separate lives in different parts of the world. At the time, I was hurt and confused by what had happened. But at that young age, I had a lot of resilience and determination. At seventeen, I left England and went back to Canada to start my life again.

I had a strong sense of achievement and a desire to get ahead. I worked as a waitress and trained myself to be a tennis coach to pay my way through university, got a scholarship to the Sorbonne, and went on to work in journalism, which had been my dream. In rebuilding my life, I had cultivated what I thought was a healthy confidence in myself, a feeling that any goal that I set was achievable. I was easily able to transfer this attitude into my spiritual life. Any problem could be overcome simply by changing the way I thought about it. Nothing seemed impossible to me then and, therefore, nothing ever was. For many years, I had what seemed to be a charmed and successful personal and professional life.

Then it happened again, the loss of all that I knew and loved. I was thirty years old and heading up a team that was completing a large project at work. The project had taken over my life and become an almost all-consuming passion leaving me few thoughts for anything else. In my mind I saw the project bringing insight and benefit to many people. This vision fuelled my dedication, inspiring me to happily work long hours into the night. To my amazement in the middle of the project I discovered that some of my colleagues, who were also close friends, were quietly unhappy with the direction the work was taking. This led to a division within the team and it came as a shock when I was advised to step down.

It was the first big failure in my life. With so many past successes my ego rebelled. Without my work, I was lost. In response I felt rejected, abandoned, and betrayed by friends and colleagues in whom I had placed my faith and trust.

All of this triggered in me a deep sorrow and anguish. I had recurring nightmares of falling into a dark hole where frightening apparitions laughed at me. I would wake up in a cold sweat. I cried a lot, and kept asking myself, "Why did this happen to me?" I became angry and bitter. It seemed as if everything I had stood for had been violated: my faith, my trust, my belief in myself, my values, my work, and my friendships. All of my life was thrown into question. Without really understanding the full extent of what was going on, I collapsed mentally, emotionally, and physically. Everything I had known before no longer made any sense. I was not in control.

Some kind of strange force was at work. Brutally, it stripped away my supports: work, colleagues, friends, money, position, my reputation, even my health. I remember thinking, "I've got nothing left." It was true. Against such a force, nothing of the old me could remain intact. The walls that "I" had created, to isolate and protect "the false me" from my true self, fell as flat as the floor. Inside my head something snapped. I think it was I, the soul, saying, "I can't lie anymore." That unconscious release sent me into trauma as I plunged down, into the darkest of nights. It was the first time in my life that I had failed at anything important. It was the second time I had lost everything, but on this occasion I lacked the strength and inner resources to pick myself up and start again.

For years, I could not write about my fall. Every time I tried to write about it, I cried uncontrollably. This chapter, therefore, remained an empty page until my heart could be made clean. Over and over again I replayed the tape of that devastating event, looking for fragments of information that would give me insight into the cause of why this had happened. Slowly I began to piece together how my sensitive nature had distanced me from my colleagues. At times I was opinionated and didn't take on board their criticisms, and maybe this is why they had willingly embraced a new leadership. By the same token, my tendency to assume blame made me a willing scapegoat for the group. In my head I recreated that scene, giving others and myself different roles, different dialogues, trying to discover if there could have been another outcome. Finally, I reached the conclusion that this event was meant to be.

At some deep level, I, the pure soul, was yearning to be free from the artificial shackles that kept my ego in place. I had built up for myself a false identity based on an attachment to the professional role that I played, the relationships I enjoyed, and the results that I often achieved. It wasn't that I wore success as a medal or compared myself to others; I had a deep need to achieve the hard challenges that I set myself. My well-being depended on recognition from myself more than from others. This internally driven need to prove myself to myself propelled much of my ego consciousness. This is the reason I had a hard time forgiving myself for the mistakes that I made.

When this devastating event occurred I was totally unprepared to face my fatal flaw. Later, it became clear to me that my sensitivity was a construct of my ego. Now it all seems so obvious. But at that time, I held tight to my illusions and resisted this fall with all of my might. It was only inevitable that "I" should get crushed. When illusion falls, it carries a lot of weight.

In the middle of the journey of my life
I found myself in a dark wood
for I had lost the right path.
– Dante

Now, with a heart full of compassion, I know how frail human consciousness is, how little we really understand ourselves, and just how vulnerable we become when our support systems are taken away.

Many of the ancient mystics also warned of the dangers of the ego. St Augustine of Hippo faced considerable trials over his own cleverness, which he said at times separated him from God. He wrote, "By my swelling pride I was separated from Thee, and my puffed-up face closed up mine eyes!" Nine years after he converted to Christianity, St Augustine wrote *Confessions*, a fascinating account of his spiritual journey. In it, he detailed many of his inner struggles and how he experienced states of fluctuation between his attraction to God and the pull of his bodily senses, coupled with the weight of his own ego. He wrote, "I was caught up to Thee by Thy Beauty, and dragged back by my own weight; and fell once more with a groan to the world of the sense..." *(Confessions)*.

While the problems of the ego are common to all spiritual traditions, each path has its own definition. These definitions are often in contradiction to modern psychology, which defines ego as a strong sense of self and a necessity for human survival. In Raja Yoga, the ego is seen as a false perception of self, an assumed identity. It is considered to be the strongest and most persistent of the vices and therefore the most difficult to detect and transform. This is because the ego doesn't run up to you and say, "Hi, I'm your false self, your ego." Instead, it will say, "I'm who you are, I'm the real thing." Ego is the result of our body consciousness when we forget to see ourselves as souls and identify with our external masks.

In soul consciousness the ego does not exist. In soul consciousness we know who we are. In body consciousness we think we are something that we are not. Whereas our real identity lies in the internal qualities of soul, the false identity is the face that we show to the world through our talents and activities, the roles that we play, and the mechanisms that we use to deceive ourselves.

Since the ego is false, it leads to distortion. Ego compels us to focus on our own needs at the expense of the needs of others. This pulls us into an addictive cycle of selfishness, self-absorption, and self-centeredness. Behind each thought and action driven by the ego is the motivation, "What's in it for me?" Much of our modern culture promotes and sustains this kind of egocentricity. Television, films, and magazine advertisements all reinforce this fascination with the false self. They teach us that the thinner we are, the more successful we are, the easier it is to receive the attention, love, and respect that we so desperately crave. Ego says that we can get whatever we want, not by turning away from falsehood, but by indulging it instead. That's why the ego is so hard to renounce. It convinces us that it is totally necessary for our life and livelihood.

When I was sixteen, I got a summer job taking busloads of French tourists around the historic sites of the small island of Jersey where I lived at the time. One of the important stops on the east side of the island was Mount Orgueil -- Mount Pride -- Castle, a magnificent medieval monument built on high treacherous rocks above the sea. This castle was used over the centuries to defend the island against invading armies, pirates, and other unwelcome visitors.

Every time I visited the castle, I used to stand at the drawbridge and marvel at its construction. I'd think, "How were people of long ago able to lift such huge, thick slabs of granite up so high and piece them all together to make this fortress?" It was an extraordinary architectural feat. The walls were so thick and deep that not even canon balls could blast through them. The fortress seemed impenetrable.

Over the years, I keep returning to Mount Pride for the analogy she provides. When I think of ego, I see a massive stone wall protecting a soft center. The center is where the inhabitants of the castle live. If you have ever seen a medieval castle, then you will know the kind of walls I'm talking about. Ego is as thick and almost impenetrable as the walls of a medieval castle. Not only are walls built to defend against the enemy; they can also protect the enemy that is within.

Ego hides our weaknesses and then claims to the outside world that we have none. Of course, if we had no weaknesses, we would have no ego either. As long as ego maintains its position, subtle traces of weaknesses will remain in place. Ego and spiritual power are also connected. When a soul is full of spiritual energy, it is completely transparent. But when a soul loses its power, ego becomes its defense mechanism and a tool for doing damage control. Ego masks both the pain of loss and the loss itself. Ego is the replacement for soul power. It covers up our incompleteness and then pretends we never lost a thing.

Even though our Achilles Heel might be greed, attachment, or anger, ultimately, all our vices find their root in ego. In mystical terms, becoming free from ego is the final frontier.

When I realized the full extent of my own ego, I turned to Brother Surya for further insight. He said, "Early on, I realized I couldn't get contentment from physical achievements, or from other people's validation of me. I could only get it from God. So I decided to leave behind those temporary things, and focus instead on attaining peace and happiness from God. My intention was to build an inner peace so strong, it wouldn't be disturbed by anyone or anything. Nor did I want my happiness to be based on whether or not I was successful in my day-to-day work. Yes, I get lots of recognition for the things that I do, but it doesn't enter my consciousness. The desire to achieve recognition only causes a lack of peace. I wanted to make my life free from desire. I had this determination from the very beginning of my spiritual life."

Brother Surya is a contemplative mystic, in the best sense of the word. He is someone who learnt to view his weaknesses with quiet dispassion, not ever allowing himself to become disturbed by any unsettling internal or external events. "See your challenges as a game," he would say. "A master can overcome any weakness or obstacle."

When I complained to him about how others had treated me, he laughed and said, "I don't look at what others are doing. I just pay attention to myself, to what I need to change."

Learning to pay attention is a humble act. We become humble by heeding the little things: signals from friends, circumstances, our own internal investigations. These little things teach us what we need to change. Self-awareness is crucial at every stage on the spiritual path. A person who is self-aware embraces change willingly, rather than by force.

There are many levels at which the ego needs to be dissolved. What I went through was a crunching of the ego, an ego-death. This type of event takes care of the obvious, outer trappings of ego. The more insidious, less obvious traces have to be dealt with during an equally intense, but perhaps less dramatically painful, second dark night which St John of the Cross termed "dark night of the spirit." When St John of the Cross used this terminology, he was referring perhaps to the layers of falsehood hidden deep down in the soul that also have to be brought to the surface, purged, and healed.

Each mystic on the path is eventually called upon to confront and transform his or her ego. Not everyone goes through an ego-death event similar to the one I experienced. Mystics such as Brother Surya view self-transformation more as a game than a battle. They pace themselves through their dark nights, knowing that whatever comes will teach them, and that ultimately victory is guaranteed. Yet for many of us, it seems that the deepest enlightenment is often preceded by an unexpected crisis, some acute illness or humiliation that shocks us to the core. This shock sends us spiraling into the innermost caverns of our being, and there, in our darkest of moments, God awaits us.

At the bottom of the fathomless hole that my ego-death propelled me into was a pool of mud -- mud of the earth, mud of my mind. I had reached rock bottom. "Dear God, I can't get lower than this," I said in a hoarse voice. The thought appalled me, but in a strange kind of way, it gave me strength. Now that I was at the bottom I could look for a way to get out. I could jump, call for help, find a ladder. But the mud was thick. It held me close like a lover. I couldn't move.

I thought, "I'm going to die." It was a cold thought.

Then I was on my knees. The dying thought had forced me down even further. "Dear God," I begged, "Help me. If You don't do something, I will die." I pleaded with God over and over, "You've got to help me, please." As I cried out, all of me trembled. Was it the humiliation of the fall, or the fact that I was no longer suffering from the illusion of being in control?

Finally, there were no more solutions, no more thoughts, no courage, no breath. I had nothing. I turned my eyes upward and humbled myself in front of the Divine. Before I was a queen, now I was a beggar.

Then I cried. These were real tears, not tears of pain, but of recognition. I recognized that God is Great, and that I had fallen. I was a little child again, motionless in Her arms. God rocked me. Tenderly, God nursed me, lulled away the fear, the despair, the shattered bits of me.

Then, once I had gone all quiet, God whispered, "Africa. Go to Africa..."
When God said that, I didn't question, I didn't think.

I packed a bag and, within a week, I was gone.

TRUE HEART

The Lord is pleased with an honest heart. Those with an honest heart place news of the heart in front of the Father.

THIS WAS NOT THE GARDEN of my childhood, yet somehow it transported me back to that place. In Africa, I wanted to explore each flower and shrub, each leaf of green. I wanted not only to take pleasure from their fragrances, but to feel the juice of the mauve creeper at my fingertips, cup the cone-head of the yellow Moon flower in the palm of my hands, stroke the long beak of the bird of paradise with my cheek. Never before had I seen such finely sculpted flora.

When I was a child, I didn't like to touch things. Perhaps I didn't want to get my hands dirty, or maybe I was afraid of being cut or getting hurt. There were rules about playing outside: don't go beyond the confines of what you know, stay within safe perimeters. And yet Africa, I discovered, was not a safe place. It wasn't just that danger lurked on the streets or in the jungle. The danger lurked in Africa's beckoning me to herself with an urgency that demanded a visceral response. Africa had a way of ripping me open, tearing down my facades, exposing the softest, most vulnerable part of me. In this hazardous territory, I wasn't safe with my own emotions.

This danger was both traumatic and pleasurable at the same time. I was living on the edge, uncertain of how my heart might react. One day, my heart would hang loose, a large purple seed caught in the leaves of a banana tree. The next day, it would jump out of my mouth and glide with flamingo wings across the pink waters of Lake Nakuru.

Living in Africa I had no perimeters. There was no one to say to me "Yes!" and no one to say, "No!" I had free will to do whatever I wanted with my heart. Only I had to be true. I couldn't stay in my head and pretend I wasn't alert to the urgent details of staying alive. The dust and sweat of Nairobi air mingled with the drums and the dance of eagles as they sliced through a clear, blue sky, opened me up to infinite possibilities. It was like falling in love, not with a particular person or place, but with myself; with the simple, uncomplicated motion of stretching past internal barriers into the wild open space of an authentic 'me.' In Kenya, they call it "Africa sickness."

People talk about falling in love with Africa. Yet what we are really in love with is much deeper. It is the way we are in Africa, without malice, heartache or pretence. Africa has a way of making us real. She takes away our fancy clothes, important jobs, deadlines. In their place, she gives us sugar cane, beans, corn. She cooks, not with the future in mind, but with the present hanging from her apron. She says, "Eat, now." Forcing us to live in the here and now, Africa makes us dig into life. Today we are alive -- at this very moment we are in a flow with all that is around us -- and tomorrow? Who knows what tomorrow may bring?

So, I tell myself, "Slap bare feet down on the red murum earth. Shake hips, arms, legs, shake hair, brain, and teeth. Shake out the ghosts of the past, the burdens of misunderstanding, and the pain of a fragile, broken heart. Feel the red earth squishing between your toes and know that you cannot think beyond the measure of the beat. These African drums pull you into innocence, make you respond only to what is basic and true."

The trouble with spiritual life -- any spiritual life -- is that it is sometimes dry. In reality, it is not our spiritual knowledge that is dry, but rather the way we approach our practice with our dry, complicated minds. We take knowledge in through our heads, but do not allow it to melt into our hearts. This is because we do not deeply contemplate the divine truths that we receive and allow them to become part of the blood, tissues, and cells of our bodies, until these truths become our own. All too often knowledge remains separate from us. We talk spirituality, think spirituality, but only by experiencing spiritual truths is it possible to lead spiritually authentic lives.

Several years after returning to Canada from Africa, I gave a lecture on the importance of confronting one's ego. I spoke simply and honesty from the heart. During question-and-answer time, a man said something that made me pause. I do not remember his exact words, but he was repeating a phrase he had heard or read in a book. It was the way he said it that caught my attention, perfunctory, straight from the head without seemingly engaging his heart. The man shared what for him was a spiritual truth. But in his mouth, the words seemed dry and lifeless. My impression was that while he intellectually understood that particular truth, he hadn't experienced it.

I thanked the man for his comments and smiled, remembering my own condition when I left for Africa. I had a lot of knowledge but I wasn't living it fully from my heart. I had just gone through my ego-death and was in a shattered, fragile state. My heart was neither open nor closed. Like a wounded bird, with its heart barely beating, I didn't have the energy nor will to do anything except lie on my back, my wings tucked close to my side, little legs frozen in place. In that semi-unconscious state, I stumbled around Nairobi, went to meditation, spoke to a few people, and found tranquility in chopping vegetables in the kitchen. What I needed was distance from having to get things done, and the silence and space just to be.

In my mind I am back in Nairobi sitting at the kitchen table peeling potatoes. Yesterday, I peeled long stringy beans. The day before I chopped fat eggplant and zucchini. Nothing complicated. My heart can't take anything complicated. I crave simplicity like the Africans crave *ugali*, cornmeal. I don't want to think, analyze or remember; I only want to feel. Feel what I feel, sitting at the wooden bench, watching the knife move slowly through my hands.

I tell myself, "Feel the ache of the zucchini as you chop it into bits; feel the beat of the beans as you slice them in half; place your hand over the pulp of your crushed heart. Feel! Do not be afraid. Do not think about feeling. Do not dissect your ego any more. Just allow the pain to exist, all bloody and sore. Open your heart and let the pain surge through. Do not ask where this pain comes from. It has an ancient past. Embrace this pain so that it can go. You have no need of your pain. All you need is a true and loving heart."

The drums have been calling since yesterday. I go out of the gate, turn right onto Parklands Road, and find a group of twenty Africans, dancing, singing, laughing on the green island of the roundabout. They stretch out their hands. Strong black fingers grasp my small white ones. Without thinking, I melt at the sight of their moist, creased faces. Their songs, their worn-out bodies, and their ever so jubilant spirit teach me: "Sing, sister, sing. Rejoice in the Lord. Open your heart and let God's love in."

So, I clap, dance, and sing: "Praise the Lord. Hallelujah." The Lord of the Dance has come. The Lord has rescued my Anglo-heart. Now I am a joyful African in this swinging Salvation Army band.

So many deep emotions are buried within, blocked under layers of repressed memory. Attachment to the past keeps our pain in place. If we were to open the floodgates, a huge river of pain, as wide as the great Zambezi, would run through us. When there is too much pain, we cannot sit in our true power and experience our own energy of love; moreover, the fear of the love and the greatness that can be accomplished through its power prevents us from rising up to claim it. We fear our own greatness and this fear keeps us in a painfully restricted state.

Sometimes, during the dark night of the soul there is the experience of neither love nor pain, just nagging numbness and a heart that has folded in on itself. Learn to feel, either love or pain, and the numbness will pass. Ultimately, only the power of love, whether our own or God's, can help us to shift suppressed pain out of the subconscious and into conscious awareness. Love does not hold onto things, it liberates the past and gets blocked energy moving again. The Victoria Falls is as mighty, terrifying, and beautiful, as any force of nature that I have ever seen. Standing above and looking down on the Falls, reminded me of the power of love. I thought, "I never knew love could be so strong." I was humbled by its greatness. I decided then that I really wanted to learn how to love myself and surrender to God's love.

The Divine works in odd and mysterious ways. The Divine moves while I am walking, sleeping, eating *ugali*. My emotional storms can rage on, but the Divine is busy preparing the new day. After the heavy rains, the sun appears, bright and friendly, in a pale blue, clouded sky. Leaves, roots, even the bark of the palm trees smell sweet and clean. Nature is alive, tingling with expectation. Into this fresh, open space of awareness, the Divine exposes the rawness of my emotion -- all that my ego-death had shielded me from. In death, I was numb. Now I am alive.

I am standing in a cemetery, my bloody aftermath spilled before me on the wet grass. Now is the time to face it all, those ghostly scenes from a far distant past in all their shocking detail. If it were not for God's mercy, I would not have been able to look, and this illumination would have seemed worse than death itself. But light was there before the storm. Only I hadn't noticed it. This light from God, this breath of life, got my love flowing again. Now my spirituality lives and breathes, and bubbles up inside of me, because once again I have felt the breath of God.

A month after arriving in Africa, I asked God to close and heal the wounds sustained during my ego crunch. I wanted to reclaim truth and dignity, to recapture my self-respect. My heart had to be healed before it could become true.

Entering the oval meditation room at the Nairobi meditation center was like entering an oven. I remembered how the Native Americans sat in sweat lodges and sweated out their sicknesses. I remembered how other yogis I know sit in tapasya, intense meditation, to burn up their weaknesses. Now throughout the day, for eight days, I was going to sit in silence alone so that God could do His work.

It was time to come clean, to open the book of my past and reveal to God the accounts of my actions: the debits and credits. I was not proud of the recent events in my life and wanted forgiveness. I was like the blond four-year-old I saw at Coy's Clubhouse last week. She had spilled ginger ale down herself, wetting her blue dress. She kept crying, "I'm sorry, mummy. I'm sorry, mummy. I didn't mean to." Her mother bent to dry her tears and her blue dress. She said over and over, "It all right, Cassandra, it was an accident. It was only an accident." But the child kept sobbing. She was so quick to punish herself with tears that it wrenched my heart to watch her. Now I felt like I was four years old again, living my childhood shame. In the midst of my ego crisis, when I went to see Dadi Janki for some advice, she said, "To remove the burdens of the past, first forgive yourself, then ask God for forgiveness."

After my ego crunch, there was so much to forgive: a broken heart, the loss of friendship, the loss of my own internal power, my deviation from higher truth, all of my anger and bitterness. The list was a long one. I knew I had to forgive myself for all of these things before I could forgive others.

So, I began sending light and love to the people I had hurt, those dear ones who had hurt me as well. I placed myself — and them with me -- in a region of light, in a healing circle before God. We were wrapped up in a blanket of light. I sent each one a soft beam of light, filled with pure feelings and good intent. When their faces began to glow, I went round the circle and said to each one, "Forgive me."

But I couldn't let go and forgive them, not until the fire of God's love was sufficiently stoked up inside of me. So I went around the circle again. To each person sitting in the circle I said simply, "I forgive you." Then I came crunching down on a hard truth. There was nothing to forgive. There simply hadn't been enough love between any of us.

The power of God's love brought release. Prison bars opened, the past flew out, and mountains of pain melted under an extraordinary spiritual heat. A new, deep realization came out of this transforming oven like freshly baked bread. In that moment I knew that no person or thing can injure the soul. All pain is self-inflicted; the rest is an illusion. I had been a casualty of war with my own ego. Now I was in God's domain being healed.

Before me God was a mass of light. He was Power, Truth, Supreme. He lifted me to the level of His eyes and said, "Child, what do you want?" I said, "Father, forgive me. Help me to be true again."

In an oven-domed meditation room under a dark African sky, God, the Supreme Surgeon, performed a surgery on my heart. He didn't so much reconstruct it as give me a new one.

His gift was a miracle to receive.

FAITH

Together with having faith in the Father, have faith in yourself. The sign of having faith is that not even a little confusion will exist in the mind. There will be the feeling, "My Father is with me."

LOOKING BACK TO THE TIME of my ego-death it was my faith in God that saved me. Mine was a tenuous faith, like a baby's tooth hanging on by a single thread, but it got me through that dark night.

God shone a beam of light into my mind and gave me the strong directive, "Go to Africa." Because I had no solutions of my own I knew this intervention came from God. Only He could have thought of sending me to Africa. Immediately warm, healing vibrations soothed my heart and I pictured my feet sunk into rich earth. "That's it," I thought. "I will go where God leads me."

Somehow my simple faith in God gave me the courage to move forward. It was a slow process. In Africa I didn't have to think a lot, my only concern was with the most basic aspects of day-to-day living. God became my true Friend, my Companion. I was alive because of Him. As we walked and worked together, God was guiding me with His unseen hand. At the time, I was unaware of what He was doing; I simply had an intuitive feeling that His gentle hand was at work, rebuilding me for the future.

Even though I had retained a simple faith in God, my ego crisis had profoundly shaken my faith in myself. Often memories of the past would send me into a downward spiral, into dark places where, like a snake's head rejoining its own tail, I would come back to feelings of self-doubt and uncertainty. At times, my uncertainty held me in such a tight grip that I even despaired for my own recovery. Then, in quiet, unsuspecting moments, God would extend His hand of grace and give me comfort. God, the faithful One, was always there. But it was I, the unfaithful one, who left His side and traveled down troubled side-streets to meet the bogey man of my own creation. Gradually, over time, God's faith in me started to restore my faith in myself. Faith, the wind beneath my wings, became the means by which to fly.

> *Trust in the Lord with your heart*
> *And lean not on your own understanding*
> – *Proverbs 3:5*

I have learnt that if our dark nights are tough on us, that's God's problem, not ours. We have to accept our dark nights and place our trust in Him. If we fear too much, doubt too much, or dwell too long on the complexities of what is happening to us, we lose faith. Faith isn't just a fantasy that God will save us in times of need. It's the conviction that we are already held, taken care of, part of a Divine plan created for our benefit.

God knows the intimate workings of each heart. The Divine knows what each of us needs, and quietly gets on with the job of providing it. To understand God more fully, we need to be able to distinguish between His seen and unseen hand, the direct and indirect ways in which the Divine works. My going to Africa was the clear result of God's intervention, an experience of the benefit of His direct hand. In contrast, the unseen hand accounts for all of the indirect and invisible ways that God provides support. In our most vulnerable moments, at times when we are least aware, God is above us, beside us, beneath us, holding a space of grandeur that we can eventually grow into and claim as our own.

I admit that it is easier to have faith when God moves His seen hand, when we can feel and see what God has done, than it is when God moves His unseen hand and there are no visible signs or immediate results. During our dark nights we are quick to forget the support God has given in the past. Our concern is only with the moment. We are anxious that He should support us now in this hour of need. Faith is lost by wanting immediate results, thinking things should be resolved our way, forgetting that God has His way. God knows the solution for any situation and waits patiently for us to discover it, inviting us to draw nearer and find Him through deeper levels of consciousness.

At these times if we just show a modicum of faith our faith is strengthened tenfold. When I went to Nairobi I didn't know what if any miracle God would work on me. I just surrendered to a simple life, gave God my trust and plenty of space in which to work. Using His unseen hand God rebuilt me from the inside. It wasn't until many years later that I saw the result. God's love and power restored in me a spiritual confidence that had nothing to do with talents, the love of friends, or anything external. This was a confidence based on spiritual love and it became the rock upon which I grew in faith.

Last year I had a conversation with a student who was having a crisis of faith. I sensed that though he longed to be touched by God in a beautiful way he still wasn't ready to open himself up. "So what is faith?" he asked defiantly.

I thought for a while, then our conversation went something like the following: "Faith is having confidence in yourself, knowing who you are, what you are about, and living according to that. In Hebrew the word for faith is *emunah*, which means both faith and confidence. It comes from the root *amah* meaning to foster and nurture. To nurture the self with kindness and compassion kindles faith. As we learn to let go of the fears and doubts that we harbor about ourselves, a cheerful little internal voice of appreciation and understanding enters in.

"Faith grows on the basis of knowledge and experience. Spiritually we understand that there are three aspects of faith that are essential to life. First, faith in the self, second, faith in God, third, faith in life itself."

"My life is not going well right now," the student said. "I have some faith in myself but not a lot in God."

"Most people tend to have faith in one area more than another. Some people believe in themselves but do not feel that God is there for them. Others trust God but have no faith in the bounty of life. If one aspect of faith is missing we will fluctuate internally and experience life as a choppy sea of unwelcome change. When these three aspects of faith are in place, we achieve a complete, unshakeable faith."

The student smiled. "So are we born with faith? Or is it something we can develop."

"Both. Faith is an inherent quality of soul. Each soul possesses and expresses faith differently. Some people have a childlike faith stemming from their quiet, innocent love for God. Other people's faith is more complicated. They tend to intellectualize. Those who are analytical often struggle more. But even the yearning to be touched by God is also a form of faith. Though we are all different, with practice and experience we can deepen our faith."

"That may be true," he said, "But isn't God just a crutch for the weak?"

"I can only speak from personal experience. When I was alone and without the support of friends God's hand reached out and touched me in ways I couldn't have imagined. God is not a crutch in moments of weakness but a real, vibrant force that moves in our lives. We are like rough stones and God is the Ocean who flows over us, molding and shaping us, and leading us forward. This certitude in the presence and action of God is the foundation of our faith."

For a moment we were both silent. Then the student asked, "What do you do when you lose your faith? Can it be restored?"

"I have discovered that what weakens faith is uncertainty and doubt. Doubt stems from fear and creates inner conflicts and obstacles on our spiritual path. One student I taught had doubts in her meditation. She questioned everything, whether this was the correct yoga for her, whether she had the capacity to receive from God, whether she was using her talents in the right way. Faith is the illumination that comes from going through doubt and pain and not getting overtaken by negative emotions. It is the self-conquest to overcome those painful internal struggles that are not even visible to others, and thus arrive at a more complete kind of faith in the self, God, and the goodness of life."

"I can see all that," the student replied, "but what do you do if your life isn't on track?"

I smiled. "Perhaps it will help if I tell you the experience of my friend James. He discovered that his girlfriend had been unfaithful to him and that none of his friends had had the courage to tell him. James felt betrayed. And because he had no one to trust, he turned to God for guidance. He told me that he prayed all night for the right action to take. In the morning he felt a real change of emphasis in his thinking. A warm feeling came over him and he felt free from her betrayal and able to forgive. When God comes into our hearts, our hearts expand and release the necessary energy for positive change. Often in the depths of our despair we do not have the energy ourselves to make the right decisions. When we run out of our own resources, that's when God steps in."

Doubt is a pain too lonely to know
that faith is his twin brother
– Kahlil Gibran

When God speaks to me personally, as a Friend, He doesn't say much. In my private conversations with the Divine, God isn't verbose. His words come as waves of pure energy, in the form of vibrations. When I meditate and connect to God in a state of receptivity, these waves can be interpreted according to the qualities they emanate. Sometimes I experience waves of peace and joy, sometimes light and power.

Of course, God doesn't open his mouth to speak. There is no loud voice booming from the heavens, uttering words that only I can hear. God's language is silent. His waves emanate from a still, silent Point. They reach and touch me with what I most need to hear, filling me with a quiet knowing. St John of the Cross wrote, "The Father spoke one word from all eternity and He spoke it in silence, and it is in silence that we hear it."

Any seeker of truth needs to learn for himself or herself how to interpret God's language. How do we know when God is communicating with us? How do we interpret what He is saying or showing us? How do we know that this 'voice' we hear is coming from God and not just our own desire or imagination?

Here are some simple guidelines:

1. Deepen your relationship with God through faith.
Do not underestimate the importance of daily communion with God. By spending time with the One you love, a solid relationship is formed. To continue nurturing the relationship, imprint this thought into yourself, "My God is with me." Hold this thought close and tight to yourself and it will erase any doubt that you are alone. Reinforce this thought throughout the day. Stay strong and have the faith, "God is my eternal Support."
Each day learn to thank God for the little things. God does not need thanks or praise. But the simple act of gratitude will reinforce your faith.

2. Talk to God.
As your relationship matures, communication between you and God will become clearer. Talk to God every day knowing that He/She is your closest Friend. Just as you can spend hours on the telephone with a personal friend, divulging the deepest secrets of your heart, learn to tell God everything. Just as special friends don't let you down, but are always there for you, know that God will listen to you with all of His heart. Think that God is always available for you. As Al-Hallaj, the Sufi mystic, once said, "If God hides His presence from you, it is because He is listening to you."

3. Listen to God's unique voice.
If you are going through a challenging situation place it before God. Bring your body and mind into stillness. Let go of all negative, heavy or worrisome thoughts about this situation. Then with the power of pure thoughts

make your mind clear and receptive. "Dear God I am here before you, my heart open to receive Your guidance." Only in stillness will you be able to catch His response. Be patient for it may not happen at once. Keep the faith that God will give you an answer. At other times, you may not have any burdensome questions that you wish to resolve but are just seeking the company of God. Connect yourself powerfully to the Source and open your heart to receive.

4. *Be totally honest with yourself.*
Be honest with yourself and examine your own motivations. Learn to distinguish between what God desires for you and the desires of your own heart. Since God's perspective is unique, His response may not be what you expected. I have found that if I am attached to any thought, desire, need, or outcome, my ability to receive God's communication will be blocked. Letting go of my expectations and desires increases my chances of receiving a clear transmission. God speaks the truth and when He speaks I feel cleansed. God's guidance will not delude me or lead me in any situation that is not for my benefit.

In being honest with yourself, it is also necessary to discern the ways in which other people's opinions have influenced your thinking and how their guidance may have altered your ability to make decisions. Often there is a tendency to seek the advice of others rather than listen to the clear guidance of God. Listening too much to others weakens a person's faith in his or ability to make decisions. Faith is also weakened in God when God isn't consulted first. As the Sufi Jami said, "When it is possible to hear the Beloved speak Himself, why listen to second-hand reports?"

5. *Have an experienced teacher to guide you.*
For guidance in your practice, it is important to be in contact with teachers more senior to you on your path, whom you can trust. You will be able to know good teachers by the way they are doing their own work. They will not be shy about alerting you to false entrapments that are ego-based. Some people claim to hear spirit voices, receive visions, and experience extraordinary physical sensations that they over-exaggerate. They fall into the trap of seeking dramatic phenomena as a means of gaining attention and recognition. Teresa of Avila was particularly strong in her warnings about the dangers of false raptures. Ultimately communicating with God is a humble experience.

6. *Maintain the connection.*

If at any time you feel disconnected from God or that your communication is blocked, engage yourself in some worthwhile activity. Perform a pure act of charity, and dedicate it to God. Tell God, "This is for You. This is a holy offering from the bottom of my heart." Then don't worry about your connection. Just focus on the activity with love, be soul conscious and present as you act. You can sweep the floor, paint the kitchen, or chop vegetables. It really doesn't matter. From my experience, simple activities are best. Remembering God while doing these activities will unblock negative energy and allow the connection of love to start flowing again.

7. *Stay open.*

Indries Shah, in *Way of the Sufi*, tells a wonderful tale that goes like this: Salih of Qazwin taught his disciples, "Whoever knocks at the door continually, it will be opened to him." Rabi'a, hearing him one day, said: "How long will you say: 'It will be opened'? The door has never been shut."

SOUL POWER

Become stable in your own self-respect, then ego will automatically finish. The more you use your specialty in your thoughts, words and actions, the more it will increase.

THE FURTHER WE PROGRESS the more we discover how little we know. Just a few days ago, I was thinking about how certain life lessons repeat. Since we live in a culture that views progress as a linear development, there is a tendency to consider that once an issue is resolved we won't have to face it again. Yet, spiritual growth does not occur in straight lines. Somehow, our important life issues revisit us so that we may deepen our understanding of spiritual truths. In this way we re-enter more subtly into those things that we thought we already knew. There are ever-deeper levels at which spiritual truths need to be absorbed and applied. This is how we mature spiritually.

Last night I found myself saying to a group of students, "Karma is deep. It's deeper than we think. We say, 'Oh, yes, I get it.' But later we find out how superficial that comprehension was and how little we have really understood." I went on, "For example, it's not enough to understand the law of karma intellectually. Another side of you has to open up. It is important to embrace the law viscerally, circulate it through your entire spiritual system, accept and digest it into the subconscious part of you. Only then will it work for you, as a part of you."

Part of my spiritual recovery after my ego-death was learning greater levels of acceptance. By learning to engrave the law of karma on my heart, I began to reclaim my spiritual power. Karma teaches: "What goes around, comes around." Karmic law says that each of us is responsible for the actions we perform. Even the results or return of our actions are also our sole responsibility, no one else's. This principle is not so easy to accept when there is a delay between the time of action and the result of that action.

When some people make a mistake, they say, "I am innocent, I'm not to blame. If I had known better, I would have done better."

It's true. We all experience moments of ignorance and doubt. If we had had more information, maybe we would have acted differently. But we didn't. The law of karma doesn't teach us to hate ourselves for what we did; it teaches us to learn from our mistakes, forgive ourselves for them, and move on. And if others make mistakes, they too have their lessons to learn. It is not for us to pass judgment. This law of cause and effect underpins the whole of life, maintaining and nurturing it with a natural system of justice.

"Whatever you create will come back to you, in one form or another," I told the students. "If you create good thoughts and perform good actions, goodness will return. If you create negative thoughts, either about yourself or others, if you harbor jealousy, hatred, greed, and act out of any of those negative tendencies, negativity will return. If not now, then later. If not in this lifetime, then in another. The creation ultimately returns to the creator."

Lao-tzu, the famous Chinese philosopher once said, "Fortune and misfortune are the result of our actions. Reward and retribution follow us like a shadow." This is why nothing happens without a reason. Every event has significance and purpose. It comes to teach, restore, repay, and renew. This event occurred because it was meant to. You programmed it that way. You set up the scenes you are in. Whether you did it consciously or unconsciously, you chose the part you are playing.

If the return of your actions comes in the form of challenging situations, you have a choice how to respond: either you can indulge in self-pity, or you can meet the situation with willingness and take responsibility. Self-pity drains the soul of spiritual power. Taking responsibility increases soul power.

Even though I had done an enormous amount of healing several years after my ego-crunching experience I still felt raw. I hadn't yet fully accepted my own role within that unpleasant scene. Somehow, I was still searching for a person or a reason upon which to pin my pain. At one point, as I was trying to resolve this inner conflict, I said aloud, "But I chose this situation. I chose it to learn self-respect and humility." The moment those words popped out of my mouth, the emotion behind my denial kicked in. I couldn't believe I had been living under so much illusion. At some unconscious level, I was playing a victim and not taking responsibility. I still wanted to believe this crisis had simply 'happened' to me. But once I understood my lesson, I accepted that I was the creator and that my creation had just returned to me.

The ego creates many illusions. Playing the victim is just another of the ego's ploys to prevent us from seeing ourselves as we really are. Ego is not just the false self; it is also a false perception of self. Buddha said, "Attachment to an ego-personality leads people into delusions." A victim is deluded, perceiving him or herself as having no choice, no power, and no self-worth. Victim consciousness blocks the attainment of spiritual power.

A radical shift, both emotional and spiritual, has to occur before we can emerge out of delusion and into the light of spiritual power. We cannot experience self-realization until we accept the truth. The soul is not weak, stupid, or pitiful -- that is ego's illusion. The soul is strong, luminous, full of grace and grandeur. Now, that's the truth! The soul is so great, powerful, and beautiful, we hardly dare accept it. What ego fears most is our greatness.

O God
help me
to believe
the truth about myself
no matter
how beautiful it is!
– Macrina Wiederkehr

My friend Anna is an artist. She knows that settling the affairs of her business isn't the only solution to her problems. She must go deeper than that. In Anna's living room, in front of the fireplace, are two statues. I am amazed to see such powerful symbols representing Anna's spiritual dilemma. On the left of the fireplace is an Indian woman. On her head is a large heavy basket and in her hand is a broom. Her eyes are downcast and her face sad. On the right of the fireplace is an Asian goddess, eyes uplifted, arms open, legs flying. The goddess is dancing, celebrating the joy of life -- a dance of spiritual power.

I said to Anna, "Look. Here's your story. The woman on the left is who you are, the woman on the right who you want to be."

"You're right," she said, "I'm tired of carrying so many burdens. My spirit wants to be joyous, carefree." We stood quietly before the statues, taking in the enormity of Anna's unconscious world displayed so unexpectedly in front of us.

"Now look again," I said. "The woman on the right is really who you are. The woman on the left is who you choose to be. "

Again there was silence. Anna nodded. A big space opened up in my womb and I felt as if we were giving birth. In the afternoon sun, I swear, the goddess was laughing.

Actually, each of us knows the extent of our soul power. It's part of our spiritual DNA. Spiritual power is not the power you have over anyone else, it is the power that is complete in you. It is the full stock of spiritual energy accumulated in your being. With such vitality inside, no person can bring you down, no inner or outer force can destabilize you. This internal stability is your self-respect; with it you have no need to draw power from others. You are spiritually whole. You were that way from the beginning and you are becoming that again. Accept this reality. Reclaim your soul power.

Brother Surya once said, "Self-respect is the remedy for ego. Keep focusing on that." It was a mid-morning in February. We were sitting on the terrace outside the vegetable kitchen where he worked. I was interviewing him on the different stages of the mystic ascent and how to conquer ego. He was describing self-respect to me as the value a person has for his or her own being, based on the innate qualities of soul.

On the other hand, this self-respect -- this realization of soul power -- has to be tempered with humility, otherwise it can lead to a form of spiritual pride. Even as the soul grows closer to God, there is always the danger that pride will subtly creep in, "Look what I've accomplished. See how spiritual I am." In *Dark Night of the Soul*, St John of the Cross outlined the full spectrum of the subtlety of pride. Some people, he wrote, "dislike praising others and love to be praised themselves." Some of these, he continued, "make too little of their faults, and at other times become over-sad when they see themselves fall into them, thinking themselves to have been saints already..."

Pride doesn't increase soul power, it takes it away. Pride has two faces, and most of us, until we get stabilized, flip between the blown-up vision of ourselves, which is ego, and the deflated vision of ourselves, which is low self-worth.

"So how did you create a balance between self-respect and humility?" I asked Brother Surya. He laughed, "A turning point came in my life when I felt God telling me in meditation, 'Everything that you have is God's gift to you. Your talents, powers, virtues, everything comes to you from God.' These words were powerful and made me humble. They gave me such deep realization that I found the strength to transform my ego. Without God's power I had nothing. Because of God's power, I had everything."

After my conversation with Brother Surya, I remembered an important directive from the teachings of Raja Yoga, "Use your divine specialty. Then all other spiritual powers will come into you." As ego was my fatal flaw then self-respect, as the opposite of ego, was my greatest virtue. To respect myself meant that I could unconditionally accept, "I am a powerful soul," and that this soul power was God-given. Self-respect differs from self-esteem. Whereas in self-esteem the value placed on the self is more according to an appreciation of one's own talents and attributes, self-respect is the recognition and acceptance of the soul's innate qualities and that they come from God.

So I made self-respect my passion, my life work; I made it the focus for chats in the park, on the plane, in the workshops that I ran. For five years I concentrated on developing soul power on the basis of self-respect. And I learnt that when we use a virtue we love, it energizes us, and makes us more powerful. Then all other relevant virtues come into alignment around this specialty. Through self-respect, I had a doorway to cultivating humility, love, acceptance, non-judgment, and soul power. Through this inner work, I gained insight into many of the manifestations and deceptions of my ego. There were many hidden subtle traces that still needed to come to the surface in order to be transformed.

One day, as I was sitting on a park bench in Canada overlooking the Elbow river, an old feeling came back to haunt me. It floated up from some deep recess of my being, and translated into words that said, "You've made some stupid mistakes, messed up important decisions. Your life's gone all wrong." In the past I would have panicked, believing what I felt and heard, and dug deep into myself for corroborating evidence. This time, with all of the reinforcement of my spiritual power, I remained detached. I sat and observed. I recognized this as my 'victim's voice.' After so many years, it had come back to haunt me and usurp my spiritual power.

My first reaction was to get rid of this voice, banish it forever from my person. My next reaction was to try and understand it. If it had surfaced once more, it was for a good reason. Sitting in silence, the threads began to unravel. I could see the connection between this victim's voice and my strange unwillingness to accept responsibility for my life and my decisions. At some level I was rejecting the law of karma. This victim's voice was a profound cry of non-acceptance, a form of self-hatred, a lack of self-love. It was still there, like a virus, attacking my cells at a lower level of being.

To remove the virus, I decided to do a little ceremony, alone. I went back into my life, brought up each important event that had affected me, positively or negatively. Then without labeling the event as either 'good' or 'bad,' I allowed it to sit with me for a while. If remembered events had had a negative impact on me, I allowed my grief to surface, and, by emptying out the sorrow, I created a space for joy and gratitude. I empowered each scene as it went by, saying, "Thank you for teaching me." It was the same for any event that had impacted positively on my life, I blessed it and said with gratitude, "Thank you for teaching me." You may also want to experiment with this and see what happens.

Two hours later, I was positively swimming in light. This light was so expansive it empowered me with self-realization. I understood that I had chosen -- not to be weak, out of control, or powerless -- I had chosen to walk through the field of my own existence, and not feel diminished by being alive. I was a powerful soul. Each life event confirmed my soul power. Even the moments of weakness were only masks to hide my real spiritual power. These experiences confirmed my self-respect as a soul.

Finally, the little voice left. It had no place inside my being to call home.

Ego has many voices, many guises. Hiding behind the mask of other people's actions, in the shadow of our own stubborn responses, the patterns of ego that we need to transform will keep on showing up. Life will test us again and again to see how powerful we have become. The proof that we are powerful souls is in the way that we rise up and respond to these challenges.

Dawn lives in a little wooded area in the south of the United States. When her landlord started making changes in her home while she was at work, she blew up at him and then felt guilty about it. Dawn explained to me, "He made me feel out of control, not consulted or respected."

"Can't you see that it's just a test?" I asked.

"What do you mean?" she replied.

"The landlord was meant to act like that. It was a test of your self-respect. A test to see if you could respect yourself, even if he didn't."

A year later, Dawn's boss confronted her at work over a minor incident, saying that she had "a conflicting personality." He was already prejudiced by another person's story of the surrounding events. Dawn felt as if he didn't respect her enough to hear her explanation. Even though the situation and person were different, for her the test was exactly the same.

Dawn needed to learn to become unaffected by other people's opinions of her and validate her own self-worth. Another measure of self-respect is the ability to think and act independently and with self-confidence, without seeking approval from others.

As you become more powerful, other people may react negatively to the transformation in you. Don't let their reactions deter you. One woman told me, "I've never been more spiritually awakened, yet my friends don't want to acknowledge it." I told her, "That's okay. As the old 'you' falls away, they are afraid that they will have to change in order to relate to you. Give them time." This same resistance can also apply to members of your spiritual community, who may be challenged by your growth. Don't let their old vision of you stop you from expanding. Your expansion will shed light, and help others to expand as well.

This period of growth can also mean letting go of the approval of your teachers. Sometimes, your teachers may even let go of you. After spending a year in Africa, I came back to London briefly, before going to Canada. Dadi Janki gave me no instruction. She just said, "I want to see what you will create." Those were her words. At first her words were a dagger in my heart, because I interpreted them as another reason to feel abandoned and turned away.

It took some time before I could understand what Dadi meant and accept the wisdom of her action. For the next few years, we didn't talk much. I would check in with her, from time to time, and tell her what I was doing. She would say very little, nod, and then send me away again. But under the calm gaze of those soft brown eyes, I knew she was watching.

One year, I confronted Dadi in her small room in India. "Why did you let me go?" I protested. "Why did you say, 'I want to see what you will create'?"

She smiled. "I wanted you firmly established on your own two feet. I wanted you to be your own master."

This statement seemed absurd. I had always been so independent. What did she mean, "established on your own two feet?"

Two years later, I was sitting on the same bench by the same river in Canada. And although my victim's voice had already left, a rush of past pain suddenly moved through me. I didn't budge. My feet were firmly planted on the earth. Dadi's words, "firmly established on your own two feet," came back to me. My thoughts turned to God. I didn't cry out or ask for help. I just sat there with this mountain of pain surging through me, and felt total self-acceptance. I was a master, taking responsibility for every aspect of my life.

Then I saw what Dadi had seen. No one, not even your most beloved teacher, can be accountable for your spiritual growth. Soul power is a totally private matter, between you and God.

That realization made me joyous. By pushing me away, Dadi had made me come closer. I was closer to her in self-mastery, than I ever was as a victim.

In Indian mythology, there is an image of Krishna dancing on the head of a cobra. The cobra represents negativity and vice. It has no power of influence over Krishna, which is why he can dance on its head. This power symbol applies to us all. When we are stable in our soul power, our weaknesses no longer frighten or delude us. We dance right through them. This is the dance of illumination.

Then there is light, so much light.

REFLECTIONS ON ILLUMINATION

Reflective Questions

1. In your most recent moments of stillness what new insights have you gained about yourself? And in what way do these insights move you forward?

2. From the list of the five main vices or flaws (anger, greed, attachment, desire, and the ego), which is the one that most closely matches your weak spot, your Achilles Heel?

3. From the list of the main virtues (love, generosity, happiness, peace, non-attachment, contentment, humility, self-respect), which is your greatest strength, your main virtue or specialty?

4. In what aspects of your life do you trust God implicitly? Under what circumstances does your faith falter? How can you develop a more complete faith?

Exercises for Spiritual Practice

1. For the next week, spend ten minutes a day meditating on your special virtue. Experience yourself to be a beautiful being of light, filled with the strength of this quality.

2. During the day use this special virtue in your actions and interactions. Observe how this virtue grows in you. Observe the ways in which you are tested in your use of it. Let this virtue illuminate your life.

3. Practice introversion. Go deep inside yourself and observe what is there. As you watch the thoughts, feelings, and emotions that come up, do not judge, but merely take note of them. It will help if you can create the feeling that you are watching an internal movie, and that each thought, emotion, or memory is merely a scene in a film about your life. You are both the observer and the observed. This practice of self-observation will help you to be less attached and disturbed by the negativities that may surface during your dark nights of the soul.

4. Many people wonder how it is possible to remain calm when there is anger, conflict, and upheaval all around. The method is simple. Practice being an observer of what is happening around you. You are participating as a silent witness. Consider that you are an actor playing a part in the big drama of life, and that "all the world's a stage."

Think of all the other people around you as actors as well. See the beauty of the drama. See the splendor of the essence of things.

5. Go into the depth of the following thought five times a day: "There is goodness in life, God is benevolent, and all will be well." Watch for any resistance that you may have to this thought. Your resistance will teach you what you need to work on.

Meditation on Self-Respect

Be gentle with yourself as you sit in meditation. Do not force your thoughts, rather allow them to focus naturally. Find that place inside where you feel centered, alert, and empowered. In this moment you are deeply aware of who you are, a child of God, a being of light, a soul blessed with God's grace and compassion. Look into the mirror of your heart. Find the courage to see what God sees. In this moment of spiritual splendor, know that your weaknesses and problems have no hold over you. You are beyond the pull of negativity, drawn to God by your simple acceptance of all that He is offering you. Say out loud, "Dear God, I am here before You, with an open and honest heart. I love and respect myself and feel myself to be worthy to receive Your gifts. I believe in the power of Your love. I believe in the illumination of Your company. As a golden vessel I am ready to be filled by You."

STAGE SIX

SURRENDER

I cannot dance O Lord, unless Thou lead me.
If Thou wilt that I leap joyful
Then must Thou Thyself first dance and sing!
Then will I leap for love
From love to knowledge
From knowledge to fruition,
From fruition beyond all human sense
There will I remain
And circle evermore.

– Mechtchild of Magdeburg –

HEALING INTO WHOLENESS

When the soul is affected by sorrow, it then affects the body.
When the body is wounded the soul feels pain. When the soul is
happy, the body is also happy.

THE NATURAL STATE of the body is to be in balance. Sickness is the body's way of telling us that something is wrong. The body doesn't lie. It is the barometer that indicates where there is a lack of harmony and integration between body and soul. Disease, I have discovered, is the 'dis-ease' felt by the body as the soul works through it improperly. As Aristotle said, "A change in the state of the soul produces a change in the state of the body." The journey to wholeness, therefore, depends on how we as souls master the art of living in the body correctly.

The soul is the luminous entity. The body is the temple through which the light of the soul is able to shine out into the world. The soul guides the body, enabling it to function and move around. The body is the vehicle through which the soul expresses itself. When the soul departs, and the body ceases to function, it becomes lifeless.

Though body and soul are clearly distinct from each other, they are in constant dialogue. Picture this. All day long an intricate maze of energetic impulses course back and forth between your spiritual and physical forms. Everything you see, touch and hear through your five senses impacts on the soul. Similarly, thoughts, emotions, attitudes, and beliefs produce a chemical response. For example, a positive thought has the power to generate healing energy and create healthy cells. A negative thought has the power to block energy and damage the body's cells.

This concept is further substantiated by the work of Japanese researcher Masaru Emoto. In his book *Message from Water*, Emoto presented photographic evidence of the effect of thoughts, words, and music on the molecular structure of water. This is relevant to the body since seventy per cent of it consists of water. By freezing drops of water and then examining them under a microscope that had photographic capabilities, Emoto discovered that the crystalline structures of water were different dependent on their environment and vibrational influences. Water from polluted and toxic locations showed signs of distortion, as did water affected by negative thoughts and emotions. In contrast water from fresh mountain springs, and water influenced by loving thoughts and emotions showed pristine formations.

Modern medical science now accepts that positive thoughts, belief, and faith contribute to our ability to heal. The body is a mirror of what the soul believes to be true. Even the way we treat our bodies reflects an attitude of mind. Whether our minds are racing or our emotions are in upheaval, our bodies will reflect those states.

Professor Herbert Benson of the Harvard Mind/Body Medical Institute states in his book *Timeless Healing*, "Our bodies are very good at healing but too often we hinder that process with worries and doubts which bring on what we call 'fight-or-flight response'...Perpetual worry also makes an impression on our nerve cells...Believing you are sick or in danger can bring about the very illness you fear."

This is borne out by a story that someone told me recently about two cancer patients who both were given six months to live. One man went home, made arrangements for his funeral, and within two weeks was dead. The other man went home to his children and thought, "How will these kids manage without me." Twenty years later, he was enjoying life and playing with his grandchildren.

Disease is the result of negative energy becoming locked in at the cellular level. Anger, fear, frustration, depression, guilt, self-hatred are powerful enough forces to make us physically sick. Benson also states that belief can work in a negative way against us. The mind takes in negative images and fulfills self-made prophecies. For instance, crime victims often die from heart attacks brought on by the fear of having been attacked rather than from any actual injuries. On the other hand, according to Benson's research, spiritual practices contribute to good health and healing.

This is what Gary discovered. Gary was a successful businessman who developed multiple sclerosis and became paralyzed. After being told by doctors that he would die in less than two years, he made a last desperate attempt to find a cure. He put his frail body on a plane in San Diego and flew to Australia. And there in the desert outback, he went through a rigorous reprogramming with some aboriginal healers. There are many healers today who are able to read the energy field of the body and use it as a road map to reveal the underlying emotional and spiritual causes of disease.

Using muscle testing or what is known as 'applied kinesiology' among other techniques, Trista, the woman healer, enabled Gary to see the connection between the trauma in his body and the false beliefs he held about himself. She asked him to say the words, "I want to live," and at the same time to resist the force as she pressed down on his arm. His arm fell like dead weight. The thought did not ring true for him and so he had no strength to keep his arm up.

Then Trista asked him to repeat the words, "I want to die." His arm held strong. Gary was dismayed. It was an unbelievable discovery. His conscious mind wanted to live. But the hurt side of him -- the subconscious mind that did not believe he was worthy -- wanted to die. Gary went through a lengthy process of exploring which false beliefs were responsible for destroying his nervous system. Once he could accept where his blocks were, feelings started to return to his once-numb body. Gary was eventually healed and came out of the experience feeling spiritually renewed.

Anyone who is deeply engaged on a spiritual path knows just how profound the act of healing is. We don't heal once or twice and think the job is done. Healing is the constant attention we pay to being aware of the way that spirit works through matter. It is also the correct use of matter through a spiritualized and awakened consciousness.

Often sickness comes as a return of emotional patterns and negative actions carried out through the body, either in this birth or previous lifetimes. This is known as a karmic return. However, if there is a positive attitude toward the settlement of this karma, then suffering isn't experienced. It isn't always the case that sickness in the soul will translate automatically into sickness in the body. Disruptions in our relationships, finances, and work, are other avenues where the settlement of negative karma can occur. Still, illness is inarguably one of life's most persuasive indicators that a change is due.

I learnt this lesson as a result of a painful back injury. I discovered I had misused my body by over-stretching it in my youth through competitive sports, and by not exercising sufficiently later on in life. I was also aware that emotional patterns from this life and before had penetrated to the cellular level of my body. Eventually, I reached a point where if I used my body without love or kind attention, even in small ways, my body would scream at me. Quite literally, it would cry out in pain. I understood then that I would only be able to move properly if I became loving and present with my body as I performed each action. This meant being fully aware of myself as a soul as I washed the plates in the sink, turned the key in the door, pressed the button for the elevator to arrive. When I was not soul conscious I was not in integrity with my whole self. Then it felt as if nails were being driven into my body.

I remember one day walking along the sidewalk to the store. My legs were throbbing, almost ready to collapse. I felt that I was not whole. So I stopped on the dark asphalt, took a deep breath, turned to God and said, "From today I will only walk with kindness. I will walk with You in kindness for the rest of my life."

In this way, my legs became the barometer of my spiritual practice. Ultimately, to walk with strength, I had to walk with truth. Truth was big. It demanded that I, the soul, respect my body and operate through it from the highest, purest level of consciousness. A sacred stillness came upon me whenever I did this, removing all thoughts of force and attachment. God had given me this body in trust. Learning to take care of it was part of my healing.

Physical and spiritual well-being depends on a balance of love and non-attachment, care and self-control. To become whole we must learn to become intimate with our bodies -- truly loving toward them, but not captivated by them. This means being in our bodies, yet also beyond the pull of them at the same time. Evagrios the Solitary, one of the Desert Fathers of the fourth century, sums up this concept well. He wrote, "A monk should always act as if he was going to die tomorrow; yet he should treat his body as if it was going to live for many years" *(The Philokalia, Volume 1)*.

There comes a time when truth like a magnet will pull you to itself. The image of your highest reality is a memory that returns. Once you have set yourself on your spiritual path, your destiny is to become whole. You cannot avoid it. I see this as some kind of spiritual law, a 'fail-safe' mechanism propelling the human spirit toward integration and wholeness. It is as if the soul is compelled to embrace and heal its incomplete parts, all of those weaknesses that had torn it apart, so that it can come back into harmony of being.

Many people describe coming out of severe illnesses with lessons learned and a fresh approach to life. Women with breast cancer, for instance, talk about developing more loving relationships and acquiring a greater sense of self-love. One cancer survivor said in a recent interview, "It was a gift. It taught me to appreciate each day."

Some people are afraid of illness because it brings them close to death. It makes them confront the belief that life in this present form is permanent. In reality we are immortal beings living in bodies that do not last. The more non-attached we become toward our bodies, the less fearful we are of losing them. We then enter into the big open space of eternal reality. In eternity, living and dying are part of the same continuum. There is no separation, no line drawn between life and death.

Four months ago, my friend Lesley died of cancer. She was only forty years old. We had come onto our spiritual path at the same time. I saw Lesley shortly before she left her body. Her face was awash with light, she was totally surrendered to the inevitability of passing on. She did not see her death as a failure or a lack of healing. For her, dying was a sacred event, a deepening connection between herself and God.

I cannot forget the look on Lesley's face. It told me her whole story. She had been to the edge, faced that razor-thin line distinguishing life from death, and discovered the whole continuum. By embracing wholeness, she reached a place inside where, ultimately, there is no fear or death, only deep certainty.

I remember standing in the doorway as Lesley said "Good-bye." I knew it was the last time we would see each other. I wasn't saddened by that thought. Instead, I felt immense gratitude. Lesley had shown me serenity of soul. Her accounts of this lifetime were settled. There was nothing to hold her back, no one to prevent her from moving on.

In dying Lesley was healed. Her body was translucent. She had the face of an angel.

LETTING GO

It is the law that where there is the consciousness of "mine," there is the feeling of belonging, and where there is a feeling of belonging, there is a right. You have made weaknesses your own, and so they do not let go of their right. Under their influence you request the Father to set you free.

LAST THURSDAY Judi, a fitness coach, dropped by during her lunch hour. I told her I was in the middle of writing a chapter on letting go. Judi's mouth curved into a large smile. "I've got a story for you," she said, her grin getting wider.

"Go on," I nodded.

"When my sister Tanya and I were younger, we experienced a lot of sibling rivalry. I was always trying to compete with her, but, being the youngest sister, it was often physically hard for me to keep up with her. One day Tanya came home from a fitness test with the award of excellence. One of the exercises in this test involved Tanya pulling herself up on a metal bar, elbows to her chest, and holding herself there for as long as she could. On hearing of her accomplishment, I mentally programmed myself so that when my turn came to take the test, I would hold on for as long as Tanya.

"Finally, the day arrived. I pulled myself up and dangled from the bar. After a while my arm muscles started to twitch. The gym teacher said, 'Judi, you can let go now.' I thought to myself, 'A little longer, a little longer.' My muscles twitched even more, and began to shake. The gym teacher said, 'Judi, you've got the award of excellence, let go!'"

"So did you?" I asked.

Judi shook her head. "I couldn't. My mind was saying, 'When do I let go?' but my body failed to respond. You see, I had programmed myself to hang on. Even though my muscles were shaking violently and my friends were staring at me, I just kept holding on."

"But that's crazy," I said.

"I know. Finally, my body couldn't take any more and I fell into a heap on the floor. It was such a humiliation."

After Judi left I continued to write. But the image of that bar and her twitching muscles stayed with me for the rest of the afternoon. What had gone on in Judi's mind back then? What kind of emotion had paralyzed her on the bar to the extent that she seemingly lost mental control of her body? Was it her desire to win? Her need to prove herself? And how was it that the pattern of her mental programming had been so strong that she was unable to break it, or even to change the direction of her thoughts?

I stopped typing and pressed the 'save' key. The text vanished. I sat staring at a blank screen. "What?" I exclaimed out loud. "Come back! You can't just disappear like that." Frantically, I worked the keyboard. The text wouldn't come back. I must have pressed the delete button by mistake.

I called Judi at work, "Guess what?"

"What?"

"The letting go essay has gone. The computer just swallowed it. All of it," I said mournfully.

Judi laughed. "That's great."

"Yup," I said. "Letting go is great."

That's what I said. But letting go of those words wasn't easy. It's human nature to want to hold on to the people and things in which we invest our energy. Just as we target and claim them for our own, equally they stake a claim in us. Wherever our energy goes, feelings of ownership inevitably follow. When energy is invested in a situation, idea, or a person, the thought arises, "This is mine. This belongs to me." Ownership is the need to possess and is a form of attachment. Attachment is not real love but a hidden fear that what we hold dear might be taken from us.

I tell you this now. Yet for a full ten minutes after I lost the letting go essay, I battled with myself. Frantically, I started to retype the whole text from memory. But the words fell like heavy tombstones onto the page. Coming from the past, the ideas had no freshness or vitality. It was fear that made me want to hold onto them and recreate them exactly as they had been before.

With the dawning of this realization a beautiful thought formed in my mind, "Only this moment is real. What matters now is how I choose to respond." The answer was simple. I would begin again.

To release anything that we are attached to, whether it is an object, person, or idea, without looking back, requires great courage. Something inside of us has to snap, open up, or just stop resisting. The mind has to change tracks and go in a totally different direction.

In rising above our fear-based patterns of holding on, we come to a place of acceptance and love. In my case, I needed to accept that hours of work had been lost and that by creating the essay anew something better would emerge. Acceptance is that wonderful ability to embrace life as it is, with all of its ups and downs, crises and opportunities.

A friend of mine is in the process of learning this lesson. As the president of a large international corporation based in Canada, he is responsible for a huge creative output. Recently, Luc underwent a major operation, but his recovery has been seriously affected by his inability to accept his illness. He still thinks he can leap out of bed and run the show. His fear of being ill and vulnerable, coupled with his desperate need to control his life and business, is holding him back, preventing him from healing and developing spiritually.

Where there is acceptance, the mind can open up and expand, and a creative energy filled with new possibilities rushes in. Right now, Luc is at the threshold of something big. He has the opportunity to enter into a new phase of life and growth. Only by accepting that life moves on can he let go of the past and find other ways to channel his many gifts and talents.

The mind is a strange creature of habit. It clings to the program we give it. If we think, "I like living in this house. I would never leave it for the world," then even if the roof continues to leak after numerous repairs, we don't consider moving. It's easier to stay put in familiar surroundings than to venture out into unknown territory. Staying put makes us feel safe.

Some of us even become comfortable with thoughts and attitudes that are destructive to our well-being, simply because we are accustomed to their presence. One of my clients is afraid of leaving his management position because he may not have the same salary or security elsewhere. While he is anxious about the levels of stress associated with his current job, he won't let go and take the initiative to move on.

For mystics the mental and emotional patterns to which we are habituated restrict spiritual growth. Jealousy, comparing ourselves with others, feeling insecure in a relationship, even deep-seated, almost imperceptible patterns of low self-worth can bubble for years under an apparent calm facade of growing spiritual maturity. While the obvious forms of these negative traits have been transformed, their more subtle traces are less distinguishable and therefore harder to remove.

Where to begin? Begin by acknowledging to yourself that your patterns of fear and attachment are like golden chains. They have held you captive for many years. Now visualize yourself taking a pair of cutters, snipping the chains, and setting yourself free. Visualizing this act of severance sets in motion your intention to be free. Do this visualization each day for a week or a month. Letting go won't happen all at once. This visualization isn't a magical formula that will immediately clear all the things of the past. But having the intention to be free will open a space for your patterns to be released.

And the time came
when the comfort of staying tight
in a bud became more
painful than the
risk to blossom.
– Anais Nin

Many of us are under the illusion that to enjoy life we have to be in control. But control is just a fear-based response to ensure that life goes according to our plan. Control generates tension and anxiety, leaving little room for synchronicity. Letting go of the need to be in control isn't a passive act, it's a courageous leap of faith. Our lives are not our own. They have a higher purpose.

In a documentary review about her life and work, Canadian author P. K. Page reflected on the creative process. She said, "You stop doing and creativity takes over." Later she added, "You get into a trance-like state and this rests something in you." For the author, surrendering to this creative flow of energy involved letting go of control. Many artists find they are at their most creative when they go with the flow.

P. K. Page's description of the creative process is also true of life. Living is our most creative act. We are creative when we live with life's natural rhythm. Renouncing our desire to control creates a welcoming, peaceful space into which unforeseen possibilities can enter. But if letting go is the key to our opening up to life's unlimited bounty, it does not imply a lack of commitment to life or an inability to make decisions. Rather, it is the ability, once a decision is made, to relinquish wanting to be in control of the outcome. Once we let go, all that we need will come to us.

W. H. Murray from the 1951 Scottish Himalayan Expedition expressed the beauty of synchronicity that can happen the moment a person is committed and trusts in a decision taken. "Then Providence moves too," he wrote. "All sorts of things occur to help one that never would have otherwise occurred. A whole stream of events issues from the decision, raising in one's favor all manner of unforeseen incidents and meeting, and material assistance, which no man could have dreamt would come his way."

On the mystic path learning to let go is fundamental to the process of surrender. God is moving and guiding us toward our destiny and purpose. By placing ourselves in the palms of God's hands, we no longer resist life's challenging circumstances. There is nothing more creatively rewarding than sitting in the back seat, with God at the wheel, and watching our journey unfold.

A few weeks ago, I had a spiritual conversation with another writer. I told her that "Stage Six" of the spiritual journey was about surrendering to God. "Why would anyone want to do that?" she asked, appalled. For her, the idea of handing over her life to a higher power was clearly disturbing.

When I shared this conversation with my friend Joy, she said, "Why, Nikki, surrender doesn't happen all at once. We let go in some areas because we feel comfortable doing so. We hang on in others because we are still trying to develop ourselves."

"You mean we are still afraid," I said. Joy was silent for a moment.

"Let me tell you something. Last week, I woke up every morning with indescribable joy. I felt that everything was all right between me and the world. Being a freelancer, I would normally worry about paying the bills. But somehow, I got into that place of really trusting God. I just knew He was going to take care of me.

"And did that feeling last?" I asked.

Joy laughed. "No. But at least I had a glimpse of what it is like."

It's true. We hand over to God in stages. We surrender the little things we don't care about so much. We think, "I'll let go of control of these." But when it comes to the really important things, the job we want, our future security, the difficulties we're having in a relationship -- we think, "I'll hang on to these myself." This is our unconscious attempt to stay in control.

Handing over to God is not a preventative from facing life's challenges. The lessons that we are meant to learn will still come. Confucius once said, "A gem cannot be polished without friction, nor a person perfected without trials." God's guidance doesn't take away our challenges but gives us the strength to work through them.

A few years ago I met a woman executive in London. As an unmarried mother in her youth she had given up her daughter for adoption. And even though she was now reconciled with her daughter, the pain of her past loss kept returning to her. One day she sat in meditation and asked God why she was still experiencing deep pain. The answer came, "Because you are holding on to the child whom you considered to be lost. That child has now been found." With this realization came the power to accept her past and put it behind her. She let go of the lost child and enfolded in her heart the daughter with whom she was now reunited.

Once difficult situations are accepted the painful feelings around them can be set free. Acceptance leads to release. Where there is resistance, painful feelings will persist. With acceptance comes an unflinching trust in a higher order and a belief that each scene in our lives has a reason and purpose.

I wake up in a sweat. The room is silent. "Hello!" Early morning light turns the walls slimy gray. Involuntarily, my right hand shoots down and touches my right leg. It hangs motionless and numb. I am struck by the sheer weight of lifeless matter. Since my fall on the stairs, there are some days when I cannot move. I am afraid whether I will ever move again. In my mind I call out, "God if You are my Friend, move my legs. Please."

I feel vulnerable now, no longer master of myself or of my own destiny. I want the touch of a human hand, a gentle voice telling me everything is all right. I crave sunlight, laughter, the memories of a body that is supple and strong.

"What's going on?" I demand. But God is silent. She has seen this game before. "Don't hide Yourself. Not now." I throw accusations at God as if it were She who had turned away, and not I. "Tell me what what's wrong with me!"

God is silent and still. She knows that the imperfections of many births cannot be healed so quickly. I must look inward for answers. She pulls away ever so slightly, leaving a space for me to make unwelcome discoveries...

"Yogis aren't afraid," I tell myself. But I am deeply afraid. Afraid of being alone, of not being useful, of slipping away from this body without a trace.

Finally God speaks. "Let go!" She says.

"Alright," I agree. I'll relinquish the urge to get out of bed and embrace the sun on my face. I will be dull and lifeless. I accept the fact that today You like my body lying motionless on the bed. Unable to move unless You move me. Unable to breathe unless You breathe life into me.

At that moment, my mind goes back to a class in 1986 when my teacher, Dadi Janki, asked a group of us, "Which would you prefer to be: a server, an instrument, or a puppet?" She directed the question to me first. "An instrument," I said quickly, as the image of a knife flashed onto the screen of my mind. I saw the knife cutting a red apple into four equal parts. The knife was a perfect instrument, razor sharp, clear, clean. God could use it to get any job done.

Dadi listened to all the students' answers. Then she said, "A puppet cannot move without the puppeteer." Her dark eyes flashed. "Even if the puppet wants to move an arm, it cannot unless God first pulls the string."

As Dadi was speaking I saw a pathetic Pinocchio scrunched up in the corner of the toy maker's shop, dull and lifeless. But when the toy maker lifted him up and pulled at the strings, Pinocchio came alive. He flapped his arms, tapped his shoes and sings. The toy maker's love breathed life into him.

Dadi continued, "Don't you realize that the string of your life is in God's hand?" My heart flooded with emotion. I desperately wanted my string to be in God's hand. Dadi saw the look on my face and nodded slowly, "So, first become a server, then an instrument. Then learn how to be a good puppet."

That day I made my vow to become a good puppet. But I never thought it would lead me to this place, to this sweaty bed and paralyzed legs. Suddenly, I want to be a knife. At least knives work. They cut, make things, are useful. But they are also sharp. Just like the ego. "So where do 'I' go if You hold the string?" I ask God. "Do 'I' just disappear? That's what You want, isn't it?"

God smiles at the futility of my resistance, at this Pinocchio body sprawled on the bed, arms and legs splayed out all over the place. I know God is smiling, because very easily I roll up into a little ball and drift back to sleep.

Later that night, I am suddenly awakened by a soft pink glow above my bed. The pink hovers near my face in the form of sparkling light. Then it spreads a blanket of warmth over my entire body. I feel as if I am sinking into a bath of rose-scented water. A voice seems to be telling me, "Relax." My consciousness seems to be hovering somewhere between dream state and conscious awareness.

I am not afraid of the light, nor resistant to it. I want to melt right into it. I want to merge in love with this Being who is infusing love into every part of my body and mind, massaging me into a state of tranquility and surrender. And because I am not fully 'awake' in the conscious sense of the word, I find myself awakening to a miraculous unraveling of my energies.

Suddenly, from deep within the structure of my body, not the flesh and bone body but the subtle body that is made of light, there is a jerk, like the straightening of a bent fork. A massive tidal wave of vulnerable, undefended energy that previously had been blocked by my desire to hold on is now sweeping down from the top of my head to the soles of my feet, creating an after-swell of pink currents that tingle through every pore of my physical and spiritual being.

God is my Friend sweeping out my pain with tender and attentive strokes. Now She is my Surgeon performing the most delicate of operations -- in the middle of the night -- when I am least resistant, least able to question Her methods or marvel at Her intentions.

I am not in control. Not of any of this. Looking down, I see that my body is now calm and still. In my mind I whisper, "You are mine. I am Yours. I surrender."

THE BELOVED

Remain absorbed in the love of God. Do not just take a dip in the Ocean and then come out again.

MY FIRST EXPERIENCE of the Beloved happened ten days after I started meditating in London. His sudden, powerful appearance left me shaken, but also overjoyed. Then, over time, as God made Himself known to me, revealing the softer side of His love, I was able to relax. I allowed the Beloved to draw me to Himself, whenever He chose. No longer did I question His thoughts or intentions. "Not a single lover would seek union if the Beloved were not seeking it," Rumi says. Indeed, we could not connect with God, if God did not make the first move.

I call to You...No, it is You who call me to Yourself.
How could I say, "It is You!" if You had not said to me, "It is I"?
– Al-Hallaj

But as quickly as the Beloved entered my life, He disappeared. I wasn't troubled or even surprised when He left. In His place came Mother, Father, Teacher, Friend and Guide. God has many different roles. Soon I was busy exploring all the relationships one can have with the Divine. It would be many years before I would see the Beloved again.

Strangely, we met again while I was working as a management consultant in the Middle East, in a place where God seems to be knitted into the very fabric of society. The first question most people tended to ask me was, "What is your name?" and the second question was, "Are you married?" Even though I knew this stemmed from cultural curiosity more than anything else, the questioning became so intrusive one year that I actually began to lie: "My husband's in Canada. Yes, he's coming for a visit soon."

At first I felt uncomfortable about lying. But a startling encounter with some Bedouins in the southern desert of Jordan strengthened my resolve. Some colleagues and I had just visited a development project near Petra. We were driving out of the desert along the main highway when we saw the familiar black-and-white-striped tents at the side of the road. We stopped the car, and sent the driver ahead to ask permission for us to visit. A man in a flowing gray robe and white *keffieh*, Arab headscarf, beckoned us to approach.

As we came toward the tent, a short plump woman grabbed me by the arm and pulled me into the women's quarters. My female colleagues came with us. The woman pointed to long flat cushions on the ground and invited us to sit. Soon the fire was being stoked, dishes were washed, and I was presented with a steaming cup of Arabic *chay*, tea.

After tea, an elderly Bedouin woman came and sat next to me. She held my hand in her warm lap, looked intently into my eyes, and began to speak in a slow, guttural Arabic. My colleagues started to smile but seemed too embarrassed to translate. "Go on," I told Maha, "tell me what she said."

Maha cast her eyes downwards, then said blankly, "She's just proposed to you. On behalf of her son."

I gulped. "Where is he?"

"In the men's tent," Maha said, pointing behind my back. I kept my gaze steady on the old woman's face and, with as much dignity and politeness as I could muster, shook my head. Undeterred, the old Bedouin carried on. "She's offering you goats and camels, as well as the good fortune of living in a cement house for six months out of the year," Maha said, covering her mouth to suppress a smirk.

I pressed the old lady's hand. "Don't I even get to meet the proposed groom?" I asked. Maha didn't translate. The old woman was still looking into my eyes. I smiled, and shook my head, "Tell her I am already married." In my mind, I begged the Beloved to return, so that what I said would be true.

From that day forward, I wore a ring on my marriage finger, like a wedding band. The ring became a form of protection against straying eyes, but it also represented for me an important shift in consciousness. I was surrendering to God at a whole different level of being.

As my Beloved and Companion, God was more dutiful and attentive than I ever could have imagined. I handed over each important and small detail of my life: my work schedule, finding a parking space, even how to navigate heavy bags through long airport walkways. God never let me down. Under the canopy of His protection, I felt safe, secure, and loved above all else.

At the same time, a new and exciting element entered our relationship. I felt the stirrings of a tremendous, mind-blowing, expansive love that was completely different from what I had experienced in the early days of my spiritual journey. Although I knew God wanted me, more importantly I wanted God. Now, I was the passionate one.

Mystical literature is full of descriptions of the Beloved. In all religions and cultures, more poetry and literature has been produced about this relationship with God than possibly any other. The *Song of Songs* from the Old Testament is perhaps one of the most beautiful series of lyrical love songs ever written. Historically, the *Song of Songs* has been interpreted as an allegory describing the deepest love between God and the people of Israel. At another level it can be seen as the soul's relationship with its Beloved, "I am my beloved's and he is mine."

Relationship with God, the Beloved -- also known in some traditions as the Bridegroom -- lies at the heart of the mystical experience. This relationship is not simply about ritualistic prayer, ascetic practices, or following a strict code of conduct. It is more about a mystic's ability to open him or herself to the deeply personal aspect of the Divine. This is also when the Divine steps out of the realm of conventional dogma and invites the individual seeker into an intimate and directly transformative experience. What happens between God and each soul is precious and unique. It defies comparison to any other type of relationship. And yet, even though God is not human and does not operate in human ways, the soul's experience of this relationship assumes familiar human characteristics, such as feelings of possessiveness and joy, inseparability and passion:

> *O my Joy and my Desire and my Refuge,*
> *My Friend and my Sustainer and my Goal,*
> *Thou art my Intimate, and longing for Thee sustains me,*
> *Where it not for Thee, O my Life and my Friend,*
> *How I should have been distraught over the spaces of*
> *   the earth.*
> *How many favors have been bestowed, and how*
> *   much has Thou given me.*
> *Of gifts and grace and assistance,*
> *Thy love is now my desire and my bliss....*
> *– Rabi'a*

As the first woman Sufi mystic, Rabi'a's poetry reveals both the ecstatic devotion and burning passion a mystic has for God, the intense longing for union with the Beloved that rises above all other human desires. Most Sufi poetry uses rich metaphor and imagery to convey the intensity of this experience. The soul is compared to a bird searching for its nest or a reed flute desperate to return to the reed bed from which it was cut. God, on the other hand, is portrayed as an all-consuming fire, an eternal flame in which the soul surrenders to an all-conquering love. This 'fire of love' is important to the Sufis, for it also represents the power of purification, the 'burning' process through which ego is sacrificed in order for the soul to reach perfection. Rumi compares this purification to chickpeas boiling in a pot. Only by surrendering to the boiling, he says, may we "come upon the embrace of our Beloved."

In India, the devotional movement, *bhakti*, began around the sixth century. It became widespread in the Middle Ages through the popularization of sacred poetry by wandering singer-saints. In this way, *bhakti* offered a counterbalance to the strict Brahmanical tradition that had come to embody ritualism, caste distinction, and the domination of religious learning by the elite. By placing love and devotion at the heart of the spiritual experience, *bhakti* brought the concept of a personal and accessible God to the uneducated masses. The twelfth-century poet Mahdeviyakka took to wandering the streets in search of mystical union with the God Shiva. She wrote:

I love the Beautiful One
with no bond nor fear
no clan no land
no landmarks
for his beauty
So my lord, white as jasmine, is my husband.

Of all the Hindu singer-saints, Meera is perhaps the most revered due to the strength of her renunciation of the temporary things of this life and the eloquence of her poetry. Meera was a sixteenth-century Rajput princess who left the security of her husband's palace and became a wandering devotee of Krishna, whom she considered to be an incarnation of God. Meera's *bhajans*, songs, capture the intense love and faithfulness of a devotee, waiting, life after life, day after day, night after night, for her Lord.

Life after life
I stand by the road
and look for a home
with my lord

At times, Meera's emotional outpouring seems unjustly ignored. In spite of her vigilance, Meera only manages to catch rare glimpses of Krishna. Often he doesn't come at all, and this elusiveness is a source of great torment for her:

Look how he wounds me
    again.
He vowed to come, and the yard
    is empty

When the Beloved does appear, however, it is when Meera least expects or desires His presence. This letting go, this surrendering to the Beloved, is the key to experiencing Him. The mystic's heart has to be unencumbered in order for the Beloved to sit there.

Outside of the historical context in which it emerged as a spiritual movement, devotional love is considered an important aspect of a mystic's inner development. However, it is also perceived by many as a stage that must be worked through and then moved on from. In my own case, having an emotional connection with God, the Beloved, was necessary in my learning how to surrender. For me, this emotional bonding brought a greater balance between my heart and head. It made my spiritual understanding richer because now I could access it at the level of feeling. Once I was intimately connected with God and felt secure with the Beloved, my heart was ready to engage with Him at a more mature level. This meant moving beyond the experience of emotional stirrings into a relationship of companionship and partnership. At this stage, there is no more mystical questing. One doesn't have to pine or search for the Beloved; the Beloved has been found.

St Teresa of Avila understood this process well. With characteristic insight, she drew attention to the dangers of over-emotionalism and false raptures. She described these experiences as being quite distinct from mature love, distinct also from ecstatic love. Whereas an emotional engagement is captured externally through physical sensations, the rarefied experience of ecstatic love is felt deeply within, at the purest level of soul. This love literally takes a person outside of his or her physical perceptions into an experience of "joy beyond the senses." In this state, one's emotions are not engaged at all. Having been purified in meditation by the cooling power of God's love, they are stilled into peaceful waves or vibrations of pure energy. The heart is connected, but now at peace. All of the work we do with God is meant to prepare us for this experience. Mature love eventually leads us to this ecstatic state, which in yogic traditions is referred to as 'bliss'.

St Teresa was a master of mature love. The down-to-earth approach she took in creating intimacy between herself and God was refreshing. In all of her writings and letters, Teresa demonstrated how she built a relationship with Her God, claiming Him as her own. As previously mentioned Teresa attributed to God as well as to Christ different personal and meaningful names, such as His Majesty, True Friend, my Spouse, my True Lord, my Good, my Mercy. The names are not important in themselves, only for what they represent to the one who coins them: the reality of a personal, palpable relationship with God.

For Teresa, as for many other mystics, the ultimate goal of her relationship with the Beloved, her Spouse, was to experience the union of Oneness. Teresa described in her book, *The Interior Castle*, how spiritual betrothal is like the joining of two candles, "To such an extent that the flame coming from them is but one, or that the wick, the flame, and the wax are all one." Or, she compares it to when streams of light, although separate when entering a room, "become one."

Whether Teresa actually meant that she became One with God, or that the love was so great it was as though she had become One, we shall never know. From my own experience and understanding this deep and loving union occurs metaphysically, not physically. The soul does not actually merge into God and disappear. Rather by merging "in the love of God," the experience is "as though both had become One." God is God, soul is soul. The purpose of union is not for the soul to lose its identity in God's but to be strengthened and made whole. Power, light, love from the Supreme makes each soul complete and unique in itself just as God is complete and unique in Him/Herself.

I remember how when the Beloved first came to me, I was afraid to let go and plunge into the Ocean. I thought I would get lost in His being, or would disappear into an expanse of light. In my diary, I wrote, "Your Ocean goes on forever, my Lord, and once I start sailing, I am afraid I won't come to its end. Your depth overwhelms me, since I, myself, have become that shallow. No, I won't dive in just yet. I'll just sit at Your shore and listen to the sound of Your mighty Being."

Many people who take up meditation face this same fear. What they are really afraid of is losing control, of dropping their ego-defense mechanisms. Yet to achieve an unbroken and constant connection with God, the ego must go. It is the false self, not the real self that dissolves into the ocean of God's light. The real self, the soul, remains intact. In loving union the soul is not lost, but found.

For other people there are still lessons to be learned about how to accept God's love at a more mature level. They assume that mystics are naturally blessed with this gift of intimacy with God. Actually, mystics work for it. One student who had issues around intimacy and partnership, told me, "I don't know if I can be in love with God. I like God as my Friend. But having Him as my Beloved implies a deeper level of commitment and surrender. I'm not ready for it yet."

Many times we fear intimacy because of the attention it demands, and also because of the attention it draws to ourselves. Some meditators have trouble in their relationship with the Divine because they project their own human failings and weakness onto God. Painful memories of past relationships with parents and partners at the human level can also block the soul's ability to come close to the Divine. This is why many modern mystics first have to resolve deeply held patterns of grief and mistrust before they are able to accept God's love.

If this applies to you, consider that as you become cleansed during your dark nights you will discover a new kind of strength. This increase of spiritual power will enable you to feel worthy to receive. The stronger you become, the more God can offer you.

Whereas before you were the one seeking union, now you make no effort at all and God's eyes fall on you. Whereas before you might have half accepted God's love, now you are certain of your ability to claim it. Your certainty is like a rock. God is your backbone, your support.

At any moment, the Beloved can call on you.

GOD'S VISION

The sign of love is to surrender yourself completely.

MORE THAN SIXTEEN CENTURIES AGO, while living in the Egyptian desert, Evagrios the Solitary wrote, "Do not pray for the fulfillment of your wishes, for they may not accord with the will of God. But pray as you have been taught, saying: Thy will be done in me." In his text *On Prayer (The Philokalia, Volume 1)*, Evagrios went on to describe how he would often ask God for what he considered was beneficial. But upon obtaining what he sought he was sorry he had not left it to God after all, "because the thing turned out not to be as I had thought."

Evagrios discovered the painful lesson that the fulfillment of his wishes did not always bring the expected result. As he wrote further, "What is good, except God? Then let us leave to Him everything that concerns us, and all will be well." God knows best. Many of us have had the experience of asking God for things and receiving the unexpected. When God does not accord our wishes, He has something better in mind.

> *I asked God for help that I might do greater things;*
> *I was given infirmity that I might do better things.*
> *I asked for riches that I might be happy;*
> *I was given poverty that I might be wise.*
> *I asked for all things that I might enjoy life;*
> *I was given life that I might enjoy all things.*
> *I was given nothing that I asked for;*
> *But everything that I hoped for.*
> – *Anonymous*

In the vastness of God's mind lies a reservoir of pure undiluted thought. There is love in its depths, but also quiet dispassion. God doesn't think unnecessarily. His every thought is filled with powerful intent. His is not an extravagant mind, but a mind that is purposeful and far-reaching. This has been my experience. God is without desire. He has no thoughts for Himself. Since God is free from self-absorption, He is free to guide each soul in a benevolent way. Understanding God's mind and personality is the key to surrender.

Picture an open umbrella with long thin spokes radiating from the centerpiece. God's rays of light and love are just like that. If you open your third eye, you can see a huge canopy of light fanning out from a still center-point. And sitting under that canopy, you can experience complete love and protection. Place your trust in the Divine, knowing with absolute certainty that your life is safe in His hands.

As Creator, God is an Artist who paints on a large canvas, the Almighty-Builder who works to a broad plan. Whereas God has an unlimited perspective, we human souls are myopic. We tend to see ourselves at the center of God's world and everyone else on the sidelines. But God's mind spans the whole. His vision is flawless. God is concerned with the benefit of all.

The Golden rule "Do unto others as you would wish them to do unto you" is found in most religious teachings. It is a divine principle for experiencing happiness in life. God's vision is for us to perform acts of kindness and not to give sorrow to others. Our willingness to follow God's vision depends on our belief in His wisdom, together with the belief in our ability to follow it.

Surrender is the conscious act of committing to God's vision, "Not to do things my way but God's way. Not to put other things first but God first." It is a question of priority. Most of the time our wishes come first and God's wishes second. This concept of putting God first is difficult for those of us who live in a culture that values independence. We are conditioned from birth to believe that through self-reliance and hard work we can achieve what we want. Our fear about handing over and surrendering our lives to God is that we will lose our sense of self, or simply not have our needs met.

People tend to assume that living according to God's will means they will have to give up their homes, families, jobs, and even their dreams. This is not so. God does not ask us to abandon the world, just the negative ways that we live in the world. God does not take away our freedom of choice, but gives the assurance that by aligning our will to His, our deepest needs will be met. As the French writer Charles de Foucauld said, "To love God is to will what He wills." In accepting God's vision, we enter into a different dimension of consciousness, whereby our minds meet and our wills unite. Ramakrishna, the Hindu sage, described it another way. He said, "The wind of God's grace is incessantly blowing. Lazy sailors on the sea of life do not take advantage of it. But the active and the strong always keep the sails of their minds unfurled to catch the favorable wind and thus reach their destination very soon."

In the East, I've met yogis who taught me that surrender is a natural state of being in relationship with God. Last year in India, I asked one of my teachers, Brother Atam, to describe how he lives with the consciousness of surrender. As he spoke, the light of spiritual happiness shone from his face. "God is my Father. He looks after me. I am a small boy. My finger is in His hand and He is guiding me. God always has good wishes for me. I experience myself to be under His canopy of protection. God is the great Bestower of Blessings. I feel that I am receiving many treasures from the Father. God gives me so much. And so I become a faithful and obedient child."

When I am in Brother Atam's presence, I am aware of how my Western mind tends to complicate things, whereas the Eastern mind prefers to simplify things. From Brother Atam's perspective, surrender is not so difficult. He says, "I do it out of love. I do it because I know the benefits. I receive love and peace, happiness and contentment." If Brother Atam has what some would call a child-like faith in God, he is still very much a master, a yogi in full control of his thoughts and emotions. Incredibly, he maintains the consciousness of being a master and yet also a child.

For many mystics this master-child dynamic poses a spiritual quandary. How is it possible to reconcile these apparent opposite states of consciousness? The master is independent and wise, the child innocent and trusting. The master's strength comes from inner discipline and self-control; the child's strength from handing over control to God. The master works with a clear vision, mission and purpose; the child lives fully in the present. The master knows his or her destiny; the child knows that destiny lies with God. Bringing both these states of consciousness into balance deepens the level of surrender.

Having mastery over the mind gives a mystic self-awareness and clarity, confidence and strength. We like the feelings of empowerment that self-mastery brings. But self-mastery must be balanced with innocence and surrender, otherwise it becomes a negative power that can turn against us. The imploding energy of "I am a master" can lead to an intensification of subtle forms of arrogance and pride. Without even realizing it, there can be such thoughts as, "I am in control," "Look how I've got my life together," "I deserve the credit for doing this." On the other hand, adopting the child consciousness allows us to feel carefree and light, energetic and full of wonder. But this natural exuberance and joy needs to be balanced with wisdom and discipline, otherwise it can lead to carelessness and a lack of responsibility. Without responsibility and self-control the imploding negative energy of the child leads to selfishness and a desire to have needs immediately fulfilled.

Not only do the negative sides of these states of consciousness have to be purified for a mystic to advance, both master and child need to be harmonized within. In a balanced state of consciousness, we can surrender to God and yet pursue freedom of choice. This is a paradox. And as scientist Darryl Reanney suggests in *Music of the Mind*, "Things which seem opposite in ignorance are reconciled in knowing."

Just over five years ago, I had to reconcile the paradox of surrendering to God and honoring my own freedom of choice. I had arrived at that thin line of tension that separates and yet unites opposites -- which is the meaning of paradox. I could straddle one side of the equation, but not the other. I could embrace self-mastery, but had forgotten how to be a child. Being unable to reconcile these two states threw me into turmoil. I was plunged into my second dark night. St John of Cross referred to it as the "dark night of the spirit" in which the soul faces the less obvious and more hidden forms of negativity through internal struggles that are not always visible to others. On the surface, my dark night of the spirit was an infinitely less dramatic event than my ego-crunch experience. There were no obvious external situations or provocations from other people that triggered this sense of desperation that I now felt. The agony was entirely driven from within.

I had gone into the mountains of British Columbia to meditate and experience solitude. It was July. The weather was warm, purple peaks stood at my back, and dragonflies turned golden-red by the sun darted in front of my log cabin. I was sitting alone in a field of green when all of a sudden I was gripped by a suffocating fear. It was like wearing a coat that was too tight, and wanting to throw it off, but at the same time needing to keep it on. The tightness I was experiencing was my desire to still be in control of my life. I had been struggling with this conflict for several years.

Ever since I became determined to step away from ego-consciousness, God's breath was becoming more of an operating force in my life. The more I let God in, the less I could tolerate any sign of my own ego-based thinking. I knew that the fulfillment of professional and creative work, even the subtle attachment I still had to seeing the results of my actions, were in conflict with my spiritual life and could not bring me lasting happiness. I could not move forward spiritually by continuing to will things to go my way. And even if my way brought temporary success, that would not be enough. Happiness would elude me as long as I continued to put my vision for my life ahead of God's vision for me.

This time alone was my second greatest spiritual test. I became entranced with silence but also frightened by it. Silence has such a depth, it stretches you beyond yourself. It's like going deep under water, where all is calm and still, dark and unknown. There, I touched the underbelly of the beast. And I didn't like what I saw. I saw a woman weighed down by the burdens of many births, by accumulated imprints of attachment and ego.

> *The Name*
> *is loud*
> *on the lips:*
> *the heart*
> *doesn't seem*
> *to hear:*
> *Help me fling off*
> *these clinging*
> *wants*
> *and turn to You,*
> *says Meera.*

Then one day, this ghost of wanting things to go my way left me. It happened on the narrow pathway, down by the river. I was walking slowly, taking strength from the metaphor of the river's curve as she wound her way from the mountains to the city. She kept going no matter what -- in spite of the weather, in spite of the terrain. She was purposeful and strong, but also surrendered to the destiny of her course. With each drop of her body, the river kept on flowing.

And as I walked, I talked aloud, not to myself but to God. We were conversing privately in public. Around me autumn leaves were falling from dust-colored trees, squirrels and birds were retiring from their playful games, and gardens usually so full of color were now drab and bare. As a soul with my own sense of the seasons, I was ready to hibernate.

All of a sudden, my physical senses were pulled away from the river. And as my perceptions altered, I spontaneously closed my hands together and held them to my chest, as if in prayer, concentrating on this act of quiet offering. This moment was holy. I wanted to honor it, here and now, on the black asphalt next to the Elbow River.

"Dear God," I said, "Release me from my wants." I paused, then said quickly, "No, release me even from that thought. I want not to want anymore."

As soon as I said those words, my head felt light. I may have been walking on the river path but I felt as if I had entered a timeless dimension, in which I was suddenly no longer attached to myself, or to my journey through life. God was beckoning. It was as if He wanted me to leave this world and come and sit with Him in His world. "Come, my child, come," God said.

All of a sudden, an understanding flashed before me of what the mystics meant by the loss of self, or self-forgetting. Of course, they didn't mean a loss of soul-identity. They wanted to lose their ego-centeredness -- that part that considers the self to be the all-important pivot around which all things revolve. They knew that this loss of selfish self-absorption would open up a new flow of energy within them. By transferring their focus to God, as the center-point of spiritual activity, they could come to see things through His eyes, learn to love others His way, surrender their actions with happiness to His guidance and care. This transference of focus was so powerful it could alter the whole of one's field of vision irrevocably. As a result of such paradigm shift the unattainable could now be attained.

St Catherine of Genoa summed up this shift beautifully when she wrote, "Since Love took charge of everything, I have not taken care of anything, and I have never been able to work with my intellect, memory and will, any more than if I had never had them. Indeed every day I feel myself more occupied in Him, and with greater fire" *(Life and Works)*. In surrendering to God, Catherine discovered that she utilized more of God's energy and less of her own.

My prayerful hands told me that I had to surrender more deeply. "It's not about me anymore," I said to God. "It's about You." Those words, which I would repeat many times, over many months, were part of my shift out of ego-centered consciousness into what I call the 'non-ego state.' This meant that my needs, my wants, my fears, my desires were no longer relevant. There was nothing of mine I could hold onto. It was all God's. I was surrendering myself entirely to God.

If the magnet were not loving, how could it attract the iron with such longing? And if love were not there the straw would not seek the amber.

– Nizami

As the more subtle layers of ego and attachment are shed, mystics receive the joys of illumination and the abiding peace that comes from residing with God. Some people have a burning desire to be used by God. They want to have their talents and abilities utilized in God's work. In this stage of growth, we even have to let go of the longing to be used. How God wants to use and when is His concern. We just have to show up.

I remembered the example of Mama, who was like a mother for my teacher Dadi Janki. Mama was a wonderful example of a person who was both master and child. She was both disciplined and obedient. Even though her own mental powers and personal virtues were well advanced, she didn't employ them based on what she thought should be done. She handed over her mind to God so that all her thoughts and decisions would be directed by Him.

Once Mama asked a group of yogis, "What does it mean to put your hand in God's hand?" She spoke about how it took courage and strength. A person has to reach a certain spiritual stage and level of practice before he or she is ready to surrender. Then Mama said, "The more we surrender everything to God and follow His directions, the more He becomes responsible and inspires us to act."

In the vastness of His unlimited mind, God works to make each of us strong. Silently, consistently, God, the Ocean of Love draws each soul near and inspires our hearts to receive His vision.

A WORK OF GRANDEUR

Just as a rose spreads its fragrance into the atmosphere, are you the one who spreads the fragrance of your spirituality in all directions?

ON JANUARY 1ST, 1997, I celebrated New Year's Day with friends on the island of Aegina, Greece. That morning we drove into one of the tiny villages to visit an old fisherman and his wife. In his retirement, George had begun carving hearts out of stone. In the courtyard outside their small, whitewashed cottage, leaning against walls, trees, chicken coops were thick slabs of stone hearts, all shapes and sizes.

I stood in the courtyard and stared in amazement. Out of the middle of nowhere, I had stumbled across an Olympian heart-factory. As the sun's strong rays bounced off the white pristine walls, stinging my eyes, I lifted my right hand to shield my vision so that I could view George's hearts more clearly. There were big ones, fat ones, crooked ones, and little baby ones. The sculptor had captured all the emotions of the heart, happiness and sadness, intensity and joy, rebellion and hope. Yet despite their beauty, seeing these raw emotions depicted through the medium of stone filled me with a sense of incongruity. I turned to George, "Why hearts?"

He replied, "I don't make the hearts, they just find their way out of the stone." As soon as he spoke, I got it. Here, on this small Greek island was a Michelangelo of hearts.

His words reminded me of a story about the great Renaissance artist. Apparently, one day Michelangelo's attention was drawn to a block of marble that the owner said had no value. "It's of value to me," said Michelangelo. "There's an angel imprisoned in it and I must set it free."

For his biographical novel of Michelangelo, *The Agony and the Ecstasy*, Irving Stone drew on the artist's biographies, private letters and poetry, as well as journals of other contemporary artists, to capture the sculptor's relationship with the medium and tools of his work. Michelangelo worked with marble, which is derived from the Greek word meaning "shining stone." The higher up the mountain the marble's source, the purer it was. Michelangelo considered white marble to be "white purity," the "purest substance created by God." He believed that the sculptor and marble formed a partnership and spoke to each other as if they were one.

The sculptor could never force any design onto the marble that was not indigenous to its nature. Michelangelo said that "in each piece of marble there were rich and base images in so far as our genius can draw them out." No two sculptures could be carved identically, for marble contained many forms. Each stone had its own character and would shatter if not handled with love and care. Only with sympathy and love in the sculptor's hands would the stone become more "luminous and sparkling."

With chiseled touch
the stone unhewn and cold
becomes a living mold.
The more the marble wastes
the more the statue grows
– Michelangelo

If Michelangelo is considered a genius, then how great an Artist must God be? God understands the true nature of our being as well as the design and character of our stone. In the eyes of the Divine we are works of grandeur waiting to be released from prison slabs. As Supreme Sculptor God chisels away at our negativities and imperfections, working day and night with patience and compassion to free us from the blemishes of our past. Only then can we emerge, shining in the beauty of our luminous and splendid forms.

Just as no two sculptures ever end up looking identical, similarly, God does not fashion identical human works of art. While God's techniques of sculpting are the same, when applied to each of us, the end result is unique. We are each beautiful in our own way.

God doesn't see us as little or weak. God sees us as mighty divine beings, humble and pure, free from the constraints of negativity. As Supreme craftsman God holds within His mind a vision of our most perfect and glorious selves. What turns us into works of art is the acceptance of our grandeur. We must accept God's vision of us and take that leap of faith. Dadi Janki once said, "We have to realize how great we are. Everything else comes out of that."

For a long time I have believed in the possibility of taking what I call spiritual 'quantum leaps.' These leaps were either orchestrated by God in moments that I did not choose or were willed by myself personally during meditation. On those occasions, I was in one state of consciousness and then visualized myself magically transported, through a leap of consciousness, into another. Each time, I arrived in that new dimension completely transformed. On other occasions God pulled me into this transformative process. It was as if He released me from my mediocrity and gave me wings to fly. In one moment I was a work in progress, waiting to be released from my slab, and in the next I was an angel in flight, full of energy and light. In this other reality I was no longer becoming that resplendent image of beauty. I was it.

Shifts of consciousness depend on our own efforts as well as God's grace. The effort we make is invisible to most people most of the time, and sometimes invisible to ourselves, but always acknowledged by God. When God sees our effort, as a gift to us, He grants us insights and flashes of illumination. We not only glimpse our most perfect selves, but live in that moment as if we are already in that perfection. These gifts are encouragements to draw us further down the path so that we can become the image of what we have experienced.

I like the idea that within seconds, if God pulls me or if I stretch my consciousness far enough, I can become completely different from what I was before. This experience is like standing on one side of the river in my current state and seeing my perfect form on the other side. God acts as the bridge. God can pull my vision to the other side in a second. But I still have to make the journey across the bridge to ultimately be united with my resplendent form. The more I meditate on this image, the closer I come to making it a reality.

Once when I took one of these spiritual leaps, I became so free from everyday thoughts that even if I had wanted to create them, I couldn't have done so. I tried to bring myself back into ordinary consciousness, but it was impossible. It seemed as if I had broken through some kind of spiritual glass ceiling and entered another level of existence that was more real than any other I had previously known. In that altered state of consciousness, I was impenetrable. Nothing could pull me down or destabilize me. There was such an accumulation of spiritual power inside of me that I was able to direct the pure energy of my mind to whatever places and people I chose for long periods of time. My mind was so clear, so focused, I saw myself reflected in the mirror of God's mind. I saw the divinity of the human soul,

God-like in nature, and knew this was the truth of my existence.

For several years now I have stood at the gateway to this elevated realm of consciousness. Though I know what lies ahead, at the same time I feel like Alice afraid to leap through the looking glass into this magical world and stay there.

Ultimately, I know that to surrender to our highest reality, we must relinquish mediocrity. Often I've asked myself: What stops us from becoming great? If we are born to reflect the grandeur of God, why then do we resist with such intensity? Again, it is mediocrity's pull. We prefer to stay at a mediocre level of spiritual attainment rather than to reach over to the other side and embrace the greatness that is our destiny.

Laziness is one of the main detractors to spiritual growth. It is a symptom of loss of hope and loss of faith in one's efforts. According to Julian of Norwich it is one of the most insidious of negativities. Behind laziness is the fear of moving onto the next stage of growth, and a lack of willingness to receive all God's splendor. To accept that we are powerful beings -- powerful beyond measure -- is the most courageous leap we can take.

In some ways, it is easier to play small than to be big. The further along the path a mystic goes, the more focused he or she has to become. To reach the final destination requires courage, determination, clarity, and acceptance. When the final destination is accepted there is no room for mediocre behavior. In day-to-day life we have to measure up to that image of grandeur. It is for this reason that the last few phases we pass through while completing the stage of surrender are the most crucial.

The same is also true when running a marathon. Judi, my friend who is a fitness trainer, told me that the last few kilometers of a marathon before the final meters at the end are the most challenging. A good trainer will always train his or her runners for the last segment of the run. That's when the mind will start to be overcome by negative messages. Mind and body will separate. Judi told me, "Your body is screaming at you to stop, while your mind is saying, 'you have to keep going. I prepared you for this." To finish the marathon, Judi continued, the mind has to muster all of its willpower to overcome the body's negative messages. Most runners who drop out experience a sense of failure and of having given in to their worst fear of not completing the race.

Alan Hobson, the Canadian mountaineer who climbed Mt Everest in 1997, also told me that the last meters to the summit are the most difficult. They have to be carefully managed because they can make or break a climb. Called the 'death zone,' this area will only support life for a very short time due to a lack of oxygen. Forty per cent of mountaineers who die on Everest die during the initial phase of their descent, having expended too much energy on those last few meters to the summit. Some expeditions are never completed. They halt just before reaching the summit, either because conditions are not right or the mountaineers know they have run out of the necessary inner resources to make it back down.

For some mystics, by the time they reach stage six, the destination can seem too far, and the rigors of the journey beyond their perceived capacities. They love God but are uncertain how far spiritually they can be stretched. In many cases, they have more resources than they suspect. But the feeling of not being adaptable enough to cope with where God is leading them, stints their growth. For others, the resistance to surrendering is conditioned upon knowing that once they do surrender, their lives will not be the same. They will no longer be able to carry on in ordinary ways. Their bodies, minds, hearts will all belong to God and will be operating according to God's will and not their own. Spiritual greatness implies that every thought and every act be worthy in God's eyes.

In the final stages of surrender there are times when we are longing for the next leap forward, but it feels as if we have come to a standstill and nothing is happening at all. We think, "I'm not progressing," and this thought causes distress. We forget that spiritual process takes into account the need for a breathing space, time to accommodate change and allow the pangs of growth to settle. Just as a child doesn't grow all at once, but in intermittent spurts, spiritual growth doesn't occur all at once. We reach certain plateaus and are given time for reflection and rest before continuing the journey. Do not rush yourself through to your next phase of growth. This waiting period is more valuable than you think.

There is a beautiful story in Nikos Kazantzakis's *Zorba the Greek* about the need for trust in the natural rhythm of growth. The narrator of the story tells how he came upon a cocoon in the bark of a tree and watched a butterfly trying to make a hole in its case in preparation to emerge. Impatient at its slowness, he blew onto the cocoon to warm it. The butterfly started to crawl out, but he was horrified to see that its wings were folded back and crumpled. A few seconds later the butterfly died in the palm of his hand. The lesson he learned is that one should never force a butterfly to appear prematurely, but leave it to unfold naturally in the sun.

We are like these butterflies that must emerge from our cocoons at the appointed moment. Any attempt to come out too soon causes a setback. It is better to wait for the warmth of the sun and allow our feelings of worthiness to mature so that we can spread our wings and fly.

So how can you know that you are moving toward a more complete level of surrender? One of the signs is the feeling that your negativity is not just being removed, but being replaced by something greater. Each quantum leap taken into divine consciousness, even for just a few minutes, allows you to bring back some of the magic of that state into your everyday life. And, bit by bit, as you graft this experience of greatness onto yourself, you will find that your confidence increases.

I believe it is possible to take this quantum leap into greatness, and then to continue to live in that consciousness. I know people who have made it to the other side. Their light shines like a beacon for all of us on the mystic path.

When I think of a model of spiritual grandeur I think of Dadi Prakashmani, who has been an inspiration to me. What struck me most the last time I met her in India was the detached perspective she had toward her own self. Whatever people say about her, whether it is praise or criticism, she just nods. It is as if in the nodding, she accepts whatever is being said but doesn't take it personally. Instead, she channels the flow of energy that comes her way upward, toward God. She hands everything over to Him. She is free from the opinions of others, free from thoughts about herself. This is the ego-less state.

In fact, Dadi Prakashmani is so non-attached herself, so uninfluenced by how she might appear to others, that she is able to have a tremendous spiritual impact on those who meet her. She doesn't just accept her own grandeur, she lives it.

The following spiritual practices will help you to become a work of grandeur:

1. *Fire of Yoga meditation.*

Set aside times during your meditations where your sole intent is to free yourself from your hidden forms of negativity. Sit before God with the purpose of being made free. Become aware that God's energy is so strong that it can penetrate the darkest of defects. The combination of God's light and power is like a laser beam blasting through any accumulated debris in the soul.

The Sufis called this action "burning." As Rumi said, "I burnt, and burnt and burnt." In yogic terms this specific meditation is known as the "Fire of Yoga." The fire is the current of pure energy that flows from the

Divine to the soul, flooding it with purity and light. Sometimes there can be a feeling of being heated up from the inside, consumed by a fire of love so intense it penetrates the darkness, purifying the soul, burning away the different layers of negativity accumulated over many births. This is a cathartic experience that leaves the soul shaken, but also stronger and cleansed.

At other times, the heating up is more quiet, as if the soul is being illuminated by a Divine light that is filling it with warmth and power. Then comes a peace so sweet, so clear, you can melt right into it, feeling as if all of your burdens have been lifted.

2. The art of refreshing yourself.

It is useful at various points along your spiritual journey to think of how you can renew your energy, enthusiasm, and commitment to the path. Think of the last time you saw an amazing sunrise, how it looked as if a great artist had mixed red, gold, and pink paint and brushed these colors across the sky. Remember how awed you felt, thrilled at the newness of this fresh discovery.

In the same way, go back to the spiritual insights that you most love. Think about those truths that previously set you tingling with happiness and joy. Begin to work with these truths as if for the first time. Think of yourself as a novice, back at the beginning of your journey, discovering the joy of it all over again. Remember how you felt when you were discovering that you are a peaceful soul. Think about the ineffable beauty you experienced upon receiving God's grace for the first time.

Of course, you are not starting your journey again. You are merely going deeper and more freshly into what you already know.

As a friend once wrote to me, "After years and years, I'm finally beginning to understand what it means to be an eternal soul. We are so much more than we have ever dreamed of. I have been experiencing a state of being that I don't have words for, except that it feels like grace moving through my life, not just for myself but flowing outward to others." Consider for yourself this joy of re-discovery.

3. Keep the vision of your grandeur.

Keep allowing the vision of your own grandeur to emerge. Connect to how you feel when see yourself as God sees you. Imagine the beauty mirrored in God's eyes and see that you are a reflection of that. You are a glorious, luminous being. Create that image in your mind, and stay with the light.

4. *Become aware of your blocks.*

Think about what prevents you from accepting yourself as a work of grandeur. Is it fear, laziness, feelings of unworthiness, or arrogance?

Reflect deeply on the four main phases that the soul goes through in dismantling the ego. At the start of its journey the soul is operating from an ego-based consciousness, pandering to tendencies of self-absorption and selfishness.

To move beyond this stage, the soul will go through some kind of ego crisis in which the obvious patterns of ego must be shed. The process of growth continues as the soul learns to move beyond judgment and criticism, either of the self or others, before arriving at a place of greater love, acceptance, and self-respect. By this stage, the soul is no longer adversely affected by events and circumstances inside or outside of itself. This inner quietude is the non-ego state where the soul is no longer operating from egocentricity but is not yet entirely free from the subtle traces of ego. Love is the opposite of ego. In the non-ego state the soul no longer disturbs itself but has mercy. It becomes a silent and compassionate witness of itself and others. This is the place the soul must reach before it can fully accept and embrace its image of grandeur.

The ego-less state is the final spiritual frontier. Becoming free from ego requires full concentration and dedication to the will of God. Until a soul reaches its final complete stage (stage nine of the mystic path) when it is emptied of all negativity and filled with the light of virtue, imperceptible traces of ego will still remain.

Now ask yourself: Where am I in the process of dismantling my ego?

5. *Practice taking spiritual leaps.*

Consider that the more you enter into higher levels of consciousness, the closer you will come to God. Having an unbroken, constant connection with God is the peak experience. When operating from these most elevated states of consciousness, a mystic becomes naturally attuned to life, clear, awake and enlightened.

By increasing the practice of taking spiritual leaps you will touch, experience, and bring to life the grandeur that is yours.

REFLECTIONS ON SURRENDER

Reflective Questions

1. Was there a time in your life when you were able to release something that you desperately wanted to hold onto? Did you release it out of choice or necessity? How did you feel when you let it go?

2. Look inside. What attitudes, beliefs, and mental or emotional patterns are still blocking you, preventing you from taking a spiritual leap forward?

3. What are the old fears, attachments, and expectations that you need to let go of and transform so that you can become spiritually free?

4. In what way do you still try to control your life? Make a list of the situations that you still resist. Which ones require change and which ones more acceptance from your side?

Exercises for Spiritual Practice

1. Try spending an hour in soul consciousness becoming aware of yourself as a soul, as you walk, talk, drive the car, and wash the dishes. Feel the beauty and harmony of your soul-body connection as you c arry out your daily activities in this meditative state. Even as you read these words, become soul conscious. Notice how you sink into gentleness, even in the way you hold this page and receive these words through your eyes. In soul consciousness, the mind doesn't intrude on matter. It caresses it, without any thought of holding on.

2. In meditation take time to review your relationship with God. Practice filling yourself with the love of the Mother, the protection of the Father, the guidance of the Teacher, the support of the Friend, the companionship of the Beloved.

3. If you are still holding onto any painful situation from the past, try writing it down in a letter to God. Then light a small fire in your fireplace, or in your garden, and perform a simple ceremony in which you let go of the past. Hand it over to God by throwing your letter onto the fire. Feel as if God is supporting you to let go of your energy that has been stuck in the past. Now you can live in the present.

4. Consider how you might begin to surrender your life to God. Try visualizing each aspect of your life -- your mind, body, talents,

relationships, career, etc -- as tiny seeds sitting in the palm of your hand. See yourself handing over each seed in turn to God, allowing the Divine to fill it with light. Say aloud or silently, "Dear God, I hand over this seed to your love and care. I release all thoughts and expectations about how, and in which way, this seed will grow."

5. Practice creating the firm thought, "God is freeing me from all chains of negativity. As I return to wholeness, I trust that all the scenes of my life are for my benefit and are taking me forward."

Meditation on Gentleness:

This is a meditation you can practice while walking.

Become aware of yourself as a soul and that your energy is sparkling from the still point behind your forehead. Allow your spiritual energy to spread from the central point of the soul throughout your body, so that little by little you begin to feel light and effortless in your movements. Focus on creating thoughts of peace. Become aware of your breath as you breathe in peace and breathe out any negative tension. Become aware of each step as you tread lightly but firmly on the earth. By walking with kindness you won't hurt the earth or your body. Let each thought, each movement, create a feeling of lightness and happiness inside of you.

Call on God to be with you as your Companion. As you walk, feel that you are a child and that your hand is tucked safely in God's hand. The gentle hand of God is moving you, guiding you along the path. As your arms swing gently by your side and your legs move you forward, steadily, peacefully you surrender to your destiny.

STAGE SEVEN

WALKING THE TALK

However many holy words you read,
however many you speak,
What good will they do you
if you do not act upon them?

– The Dhammapada –

THE POWER OF VIRTUE

Any virtue you have will definitely create an impression because
virtues cannot be hidden.

AFTER PAIN, THERE IS JOY.

After three harsh winter months, the frozen river cracks open. I can
hear the ice popping under the warm heat of the sun. In some places, the
river is still encased in solid white blocks. But further along where the
cracks are, the river bubbles up and races downstream. It's late February in
Canada, not yet springtime, and I am bursting with an indescribable joy.

The battles I had in the past, whether they were with fear, attachment,
or low self-esteem, seem to have subsided and a quiet certainty has stolen
over me. It is as if I have become innocent to all that went before and a veil
of forgetting has dropped over my eyes. I have no heartaches to attend to,
no strong pull to do anything or be anywhere special. I have reached the
place where I am meant to be, and will travel where I am meant to go.
There is no greater moment than this one...

Down by the river I am distinctly aware of the beauty of my own
being. What a gift it is to feel so light-spirited. As a soul, I am. I just am. I
have no need to do. My sole purpose is to be.

Sitting on a nearby bench a ripple of contentment moves through me.
Just as nature has its seasons, so too there are seasons on the spiritual path.
A person can go through times of enormous difficulty and pain and then
break through into a springtime of creativity, a marvelous sensation of rushing energy. When pain is released all of the dark energy that accompanied
it is also released, into a river of light.

In this moment I have no worries, only a strong sense of the unassail-
able, as if no person or circumstance can invade my space or take away my
new-found contentment. With the benefit of this internal stability, I seem
to be poised at the threshold of a different phase of spiritual development.

Or at least, for this moment, I have insight into what could be.

Then I remember something that Angela of Foligna had once written in *Conversion and Penitence*, about coming through the trials and tribulations of her dark nights and into a "peaceful abiding in God." Angela's last major battle lasted more than two years, after which she wrote, "A divine change took place in my soul, which neither saint nor angel could describe or explain." Angela did not come to this place on her own, rather God had led her to it. "...And I possess God in such fullness that I am not longer in the state in which I used to be; but I walk in such perfect peace of heart and mind that I am content in all things."

"Perfect peace. Contentment in all things." This is the natural state of a human. To exist is to be, without desire, or force, without even the necessity to prove oneself. In being a natural radiance creeps onto one's face and lights up the eyes, and accompanies a person's presence. This radiance results from a flowering of virtue. Our inner beauty rises to the surface and becomes visible to all. Virtue is the noble essence of the self. It makes the invisible visible, the ugly beautiful, and the imagined real.

By stage seven of the spiritual journey a mystic will have done enough inner work to be stabilized in the strength of virtue. Indeed, with virtue as the main operating force, a spiritually mature person will be able to observe and accommodate negativity in others and will remain unaffected by negative traces in him or herself. Weaknesses may still exist, but they no longer irritate or cause unpleasantness to the mystic. Such a state of equanimity is the doorway to an almost unimaginable depth of peace -- one that St Francis of Assisi poignantly noted "passes all understanding."

> *Fire of love,*
> *breath of all holiness*
> *You are so delicious to our hearts.*
> *You infuse our hearts deeply with*
> *the good spell of virtue.*
> *– St Hildegard of Bingen*

The Greek philosopher, Socrates, was the first to speak in the West about spiritual memory or nemesis. In Plato's *Republic*, Socrates talked about the nature of virtue and whether or not it could be taught. Socrates argued that it could not be taught for virtue already existed within the soul, given to it through some kind of divine dispensation. And since virtue was there, accessible through memory, it could be drawn upon at will and utilized.

Virtue is a strange word, and for some people a little old fashioned. It comes from the Latin *virtus*, meaning strength and refers to the inherent qualities and powers of the soul. At another level, virtue is associated with moral excellence and abstinence from vice. According to this definition, I perceive virtue to be a source of empowerment, and use it in this context.

Ever since I was a young girl I was fascinated by stories of people who had gone through the most grueling of situations and come out the other side. How did they ever survive? From where did they get their amazing strength? I trace this fascination back to when at the age of twelve I read the story of a woman who contracted polio. For five years she lay in an iron lung, only able to communicate by blinking one eye. What struck me was her resoluteness, her unflinching will to live and improve her life.

Now, many years later, I understand the power of virtue. At the precipice of any difficulty or danger we humans inevitably fall back on our hidden resources and strengths. Without our virtues to support us through the tough times, many of us would give up hope, lay down, and die. But thanks to virtue, the human spirit triumphs over unimaginable challenges. The more I contemplate my own virtues the more aware I am of their power to transform darkness and pain. This power comes from the fact that virtue lies at the root of everything.

I was living in London at the time when Terrry Waite, John McCarthy, Brian Keenan, and Terry Anderson were being held hostage in Beirut. Their stories on the news touched me deeply. Perhaps I was affected because I had met Terry Waite the year before he was captured while working on a United Nations-related project and I felt some affinity with John McCarthy because he was a journalist. Yet, there was another reason why my thoughts turned to them during their dark years of confinement. I had the feeling that even if these men had plunged into the deepest pit of despair, at the bottom of that pit would be the light of virtue. They would endure through virtue, be upheld through virtue, and would survive through virtue.

In my meditations I saw their bedrock of virtue giving them the will to carry on. Which particular virtue had supported them? Was it wisdom or courage? Hope or humor? Was it forgiveness for their captors, love for a dear one, or deep friendship with each other? Or was it simply a basic love of life itself, which in its crudest definition is called survival.

This was the experience of Odette Churchill, a British spy captured and interned at Ravensbruck during World War Two. What kept Odette going during two years of almost total solitary confinement in a dark, airless cell was a small leaf she had picked up in the courtyard on her way to interrogation. Back in her cell, Odette spent hours fingering the leaf's patterns and veins, flying on the vehicle of her mind to capture and savor the essence and origin of life. The leaf led her into a contemplation of the rarest kind, where beyond the horror and pain of confinement she connected with all that was good and true.

> *When your constant virtue does not go astray,*
> *you'll return to the condition which has no limit.*
> *– Lao-tzu*

Virtues lie in each and every one of us, awakened only to the extent that we contemplate them. Sometimes our virtues are so natural that we do not even realize their presence. And when others admire a particular quality that they see in us, we may even think they are being over-generous in singling it out. A common response is to shrug off the compliment, "Really? You think I'm courageous? Maybe, I don't know." Of course, we don't see our courage as something extraordinary the way others do. To us, it's just like an arm or a leg, a basic part of us.

The writer Jacques Lusseyran talked about this in his autobiography, *And There was Light.* Whereas others pointed to his courage in dealing with blindness Lusseyran, who had been blind from the age of eight, felt it was nothing unusual. He considered that children do not view courage as adults do, but see courage as the most natural thing in the world, at each moment through life. "A child does not think about the future," he wrote, "and so is protected from a thousand follies and nearly every fear. He relies on the course of events, and that reliance brings him happiness with every step."

Virtues are naturally displayed in children. What makes virtues so apparent in them is that they live very much in the present. Children are powerful mirrors. They haven't yet learnt the self-protective mechanisms of adulthood -- those harsh reflexes that ultimately make a person become defensive or afraid. And because children live out of their virtues a great deal of the time, they remind us what it is like to *be.*

In the courtyard of the Abassi Hotel in Esfahan a tinkling of water fountains fills the early evening air. Plane trees stand stark against the dark blue sky, gradually fading into soft azure as the sun goes down. The dome of the mosque hangs above the madresah like a detailed miniature painting. From the adjacent minaret an invisible, melodic voice calls the faithful to prayer. The fragrance of the stocks and flocks, arranged before me in haphazard rows of whites and purples and pinks, reminds me of music.

At the end of the courtyard is a teahouse where guests are talking and drinking chay. The chatter and clinking of cups does not disturb my peace, but somehow adds to it as I sink further into the poetic silence and mystery of this ancient city.

In Parsi the word for Garden is 'pairi-daize,' -- Paradise. I am here.

In the pairi-daize, there is a gentleness about my being that I cannot explain. It is as if I have become a flower or a fountain in God's Garden, fragrant with the emanations of peace and the uncontained vibrations of love.

Sitting upright in the garden chair I begin to meditate. I start by spreading love and peace to all creatures and plants of the earth. To the guests enjoying the garden, I also send love and peace, invisible droplets that mingle with the waters, becoming an orchestra for their pleasure. I send out all manner of pure and happy vibrations, to the people of Iran, and to all peoples and countries, and places that I haven't even seen. The rays of love and peace grow stronger until a rainbow of light surrounds the world.

Then into my mind steps Miriam. She is the twelve-year-old girl I met two days previously in Shiraz. We bumped into each other while standing at the Tomb of Hafiz, one of Iran's most revered poets. I send love and peace to Miriam, as well. She couldn't speak to me in English, nor I to her in Parsi. But somehow she understood that I wanted her to read to me one of Hafiz's poems from the little book she was carrying in the palm of her hand.

Miriam read like a nightingale, her dark eyes flashing underneath those stern spectacles. And when she was done, we just looked at each other and smiled, not communicating in words, communicating only through vibrations, though the language of virtue.

Then I knew. The poem she had selected was Hafiz's finest. It was on love.

THE AUTHENTIC SELF

If you have the experience of any virtue or power for even one second,
your happiness increases so much.

LOOKING BACK AT MY YEARS at university, studying literature, I realize that I walked away with one special lesson. It came from reading Voltaire's *Candide*. This was the story of a young man who searched the world for the meaning of life and finally discovered, on returning to the place where he had started, that it is about each person cultivating his or her own garden.

At the time I considered Voltaire's message to be a great philosophical secret. I took enormous delight in knowing of its existence, little realizing that Voltaire may have had something more practical in mind.

In the summer of 1979, I returned from holiday in Canada to the island of Jersey where I was born. Across the road from my mother's house lived a French farmer's wife. Every day she was in her garden, planting, weeding, and watering. My mother said, "Why don't you go visit Madame. She would be so happy to speak to you in French." I was nineteen and didn't want to be bothered with an old lady. Finally, overcome by guilt, I crossed the road, and hopped over the wall into her garden.

The old lady stood before me in a torn dress. She had a dirty apron tied to her waist and bulging slippers hanging off her feet. She waddled up to me and smiled. Then she took my hand in her gnarled, earth-cracked fingers and led me with shining eyes through the gates of her paradise.

"These are broccoli," she said, pointing to a mass of green. "These are cabbages. Over here are strawberries, over there radishes." Her eyes were moist. Silently, she surveyed all of her colorful children, those dear ones born through her hands from the earth.

In the middle of the tour, somewhere near the gladiolas, she stopped and looked tenderly toward the sky. "I only have to look up to God," she said. Then she pointed to the ground, "I only have to look here." Then she paused, resting her arms contentedly on her belly, "And I have everything."

Yes, she had everything, that old woman. She had the skies, the earth, salt-sea air, and the warmth of harvest. She had worn-out, blistered hands and only one dress. But in that moment I loved that old peasant woman. By cultivating her own garden she had reaped the finest crop of all: contentment.

It took the old woman only half an hour to teach me in real life what Voltaire had taught me on paper, a lesson I have carried throughout my life's journey. Often I think of her simple love for God and how her garden represented the divine blessings she had received. She was at peace with herself and with her surroundings. She sought admiration from no one. The old woman's garden was her love, her life, and she enjoyed it to the full. There was a natural congruence between who she was and what she did. Her authenticity shone like the sun and I wanted to be like her.

When I think of authenticity I think of a garden full of fragrant flowers, each one rising out of the rich soil of inner virtue. Each flower is unique, distinguished by the shape of its leaves, color of its petals, the aroma it emits. A rose may be round and red, a jasmine petite and white. A rose doesn't try to be a jasmine, a jasmine doesn't pretend to be a rose. Each flower remains true to its own essence. What you see, touch, and smell is what the flower genuinely is.

A person filled with virtue is like this. A virtuous person will not compare him or herself to another, but will sit comfortably in the presence of who he or she is. This comfort and ease with the self translates into natural transparency. In other words, whoever a person is on the inside is automatically reflected on the outside. There is no filtering between the inner experience and the outward expression of it.

You know when you are in the presence of someone authentic. The fragrance of his or her virtue puts you at ease, enables you to appreciate your own essence. In a world filled with inauthenticity, many of us long to be in the company of people whose lives, and not merely their message, inspire us to greater things. One of the hazards on the spiritual path is coming across teachers, writers, or workshop leaders who have a message to give but who do not embody that message. The hazard is that they lead us to believe that spirituality is a surface phenomenon rather than a life-long learning. This is why it is important to separate the message from the messenger and, at other times, to discriminate between those who just talk and those who live what they say.

Mother Teresa of Calcutta was an example for many. Her mission, message, and practice were the same. Her outer world was congruent with her inner world. What she said she did, what she did she was. Her message was simple: love the poorest of the poor. And, every day, while working in the slums, that's exactly what she did.

"Be kind, be merciful. Let no one ever come to you without coming away better and happier," Mother Teresa advised. "Be the living expression of God's kindness. Kindness on your face, kindness in your eyes, kindness in your smile, kindness in your warm greeting. To children, to the poor, to all who suffer and are lonely, give always a happy smile -- give them not only your care but also your heart."

What was also intriguing about Mother Teresa is that she combined a bold and active life of service with a rich inner life of prayer. There is a story about a bishop who met Mother Teresa at a conference. The conference finished at midnight. The next day, the bishop was surprised to learn that Mother Teresa, in spite of her advanced years, had risen early in the morning to pray. "She never missed her prayers," the bishop said.

A good tree does not bear rotten fruit; a rotten tree does not bear good fruit. Are figs gathered from thorns, or grapes from thistles? Every tree is known by its fruit.
The good man produces good things from his store of goods and treasures; and the evil man evil things.
For the mouth speaks from a full heart.
– Jesus

'Walking the talk' is the term used in spiritual circles to describe genuine spirituality. People who walk the talk are considered to be authentic in their demonstration of spiritual truths. Indeed, these truths seem to be etched into their very being, their wealth of virtues visible to all. People who walk the talk do not flaunt their radiant spirituality, but are quietly innocent of it. They just get on with their own spiritual practice, becoming examples that others can emulate and follow.

In my life I have been fortunate to meet a few such spiritually integrated people. What I have observed about them is that there is no difference in their thoughts and words, nor in their words and actions. Their inner and outer lives are totally in harmony, they are well balanced.

Mystical traditions recognize that there are two routes to spiritual fulfillment, the active and the reflective. Some people are more naturally drawn to silence. They prefer hours of meditation over the call to action whereas others are more naturally inclined to be actively serving the community instead of spending valuable time alone in silence. To be drawn into one more than the other reveals a lack of integration and a state of imbalance.

For your own progress you will need to look at where you are inclined to spend your time. Spiritual process is full of surprises. You may find, as I did, that there are periods in your life when the outer route to spiritual fulfillment is infinitely more appealing, and also periods when the inner route will totally captivate you. It is normal and necessary to go through such swings before finding the common ground between a life of meditation and a life of action out there in the world.

Spiritual authenticity is achieved not through the separate mastery of the inner and outer domains, but by making them one and the same. Thus actions become a meditation and meditation a means of service in the world. Being content with yourself, and having others content with you, is an indication of spiritual progress.

In the Soul Power seminar that I run I talk about the importance of spiritual integration. I tell participants, "It isn't enough to read spiritual books or to play with concepts intellectually. Spiritual truths have to become visible in your lives. Without virtue there is no grounding of your spirituality, no realism about what you do. If you just read and meditate but do not become loving and kind, caring and compassionate, then spirituality is just a mask or a means of escape. If friends and colleagues couldn't see the proof of spirituality in your behavior they would feel deceived by you. They would look at you and think, 'You are only pretending to be spiritual.' They would pick up on your inauthenticity. But when spiritually is grounded it has a considerable impact."

Last year a friend of mine was invited to speak at the Institute of Noetic Science (IONS) conference in Palm Springs. During one of the workshops Barbara sat peacefully at the back of the room, while another facilitator was talking. After the workshop a woman came up to her and said, "None of the speakers attend other people's workshops, but you do. I love the way you sit and hold the space for the other speakers."

My friend was amazed that someone had noticed. She was using her virtues of love and peace as a support to the other speakers without them even knowing. This was a selfless, invisible act, straight from her heart. The work she did inwardly impacted outwardly. Love and peace were not just qualities she thought about. They were a part of her being that seeped out from her and became a tangible part of the workshops she attended.

In Hindi the word *dharma*, means religion, righteousness, or way of life. *Dharma* is closely connected to the word *dharna*, which means inculcation or assimilation of virtue. In the spelling of these two words, there is just the difference between an 'm' and an 'n.' In this way, the extent to which we assimilate virtue -- have *dharna* -- is the foundation for our *dharma*. In others words, the virtues we embody create our way of life.

Spiritual life is built from the inside out, not from the outside in. How does this work? Think back to a time when you tried to change a situation from the outside, before addressing your thoughts and feelings about it from the inside. Maybe you tried to patch up a conflict with a friend verbally, but found that your words just made things worse. Or maybe you ran around with your resume and networking plans, only to be told that your impressive list of skills were incompatible with the job requirements.

An easier method is to work with virtue. I have found that whenever I put virtue first, and action second, my life flows. Since the seed of virtue is silence, the power of silence does most of the work. So before going out and doing anything concretely, I focus first on virtue. Before beginning a project with a new client, I meditate on self-respect and personal power. Before tackling a situation of potential conflict, I meditate on peace and harmony. Before teaching meditation to a new group of students I connect to love and humility. By meditating on virtue, I think less and achieve more. A task that used to take me five hours several years ago, now takes me two. I don't try to change situations or people, instead I rely on the power of virtue.

This attention to virtue is essential to the process of spiritual integration. If being knowledgeable is at one end of the spiritual spectrum, and walking the talk at the other end, then the assimilation and demonstration of virtues in daily life is the bridge between the two.

What can you do to enhance your level of spiritual integration?

I'd like you to consider the Soul Power Model that I use in my seminars. The model is comprised of four equal components. These components are like the legs of a stool. If one of the legs is missing, the stool becomes lopsided and cannot serve its purpose. In the same way, if one of the components of the model is weak, you will feel spiritually lopsided. By bringing these four components into balance you will achieve deeper levels of spiritual integration.

1. *Begin by visualizing a square in the middle of a piece of paper.*
Now divide the square into four equal parts. In the top right hand box write

'knowing.' In the lower right hand box put 'connecting.' In the lower left hand box write 'deepening/integrating.' In the top left hand box write 'serving/demonstrating.'

Knowing relates to your increasing ability to understand yourself at a spiritual level. Connecting is the strengthening of your spirituality by linking to a higher order, namely your higher values and your relationship with God. Deepening is the constant nurturing and integration of your inner qualities so that who you are inside is reflected naturally outside through your behavior. Serving is the proof of your spirituality in your work and in your relationships. It is your gift to the world.

2. *Now go within and visualize this model on the screen of your mind.*

See how it relates to your spiritual development at the present time. See which box of the model has the most meaning for you or is the most illuminated. That will indicate where your strength is. Which box of the model appears to be the most dim or blurred? That will indicate an area where you are weak and need work. Among most audiences I find the deepening component of the model to be the weakest. In other words, since most people tend to jump from awareness straight into action, spiritual integration is the area requiring the most spiritual work.

3. *Further your own process of spiritual integration.*

Begin by choosing a virtue, such as contentment, and go through the following steps:

First, become aware that contentment is one of your most essential qualities of being. Tap into your already existing memory of it. Inside of you lies the memory of what it feels like to be deeply content.

As a second step, connect to God. Contentment is a divine gift. Feel God's energy filling and strengthening this virtue in you.

Thirdly, to deepen this quality of contentment, meditate on it. Hold contentment close to your being. From the still point within, your seat of soul, visualize a ray of light filled with the energy of contentment moving through every part of you. Feel as if it is assimilated into each and every thought, each and every cell of your body.

To further deepen your contentment, bring it into your actions. When you get into your car and drive to work, drive with contentment. When you enter the door of your office, step forward with contentment. As you make a coffee, turn on the computer, prepare the budget, do it with contentment. All day long let your thoughts hum with contentment.

Fourthly, the more you begin to demonstrate contentment in all that you do, it will serve your relationships. Instead of being affected by what others say and do, you will carry a gentle smile into all of your interactions. Unexpectedly, friends and family members will comment, "You are so contented."

Your contentment has not only become an integral part of you, but also a source of inspiration for others. Once you have become the visible proof of contentment, pick another virtue.

Benjamin Franklin, one of America's founding fathers, understood the value of working with virtue. He believed that good leadership rested on the foundation of moral and spiritual character. In his desire to be virtuous and to live a life "without committing any fault at any time," Franklin began to cull from his readings a catalogue of moral values. From this research he extracted a list of thirteen virtues. Among them were tranquility and humility, sincerity and cleanliness. These virtues became the basis of a chart that he used daily to check his attitudes and behaviors, his inner achievements and failings.

It's worth reading Franklin's autobiography just for the benefits of this list and the insights he gained from using it. Living according to his chart was more difficult than Franklin had imagined. There was always some occasion where he didn't meet his goal. This was mainly due, he wrote, to the force of "habit and inattention." Still, by using his chart, Franklin discovered a rhythm to his moral and spiritual progress.

Just as Benjamin Franklin did, you can benefit from creating your own personal chart. Check yourself: What virtues are still lacking in me? What habit or inattention is reducing my stock of virtue? What virtues require practice on a daily, weekly, or monthly basis? Check and change.

If you don't change yourself, you will become disheartened. But the more you acquire the power of virtue, the closer you will be to your authentic self.

ONE FAMILY

*Have love for the eternal soul. By considering others to be your broth-
ers and sisters your vision of love and relationship will become firm.*

NEXT TO GOD human beings are our greatest teachers. In no other
arena of our lives are we challenged so severely, or called upon to act so
humanely, as in our relationships. Other people are like mirrors, reflecting
our strengths and weaknesses. Through all of our dealings with them we
receive opportunities to learn, windows of grace through which to grow in
tolerance, patience, understanding, and wisdom.

The ability to foster happy and harmonious relations is a sign of spiritual maturity. The proof of this maturity is seen in our love of God and in
the love that we are willing to share, not only with friends and family members but also with people of different backgrounds and races, with whom
we would not normally associate. It is easy to love the lovable. It is less easy
to love those to whom we are indifferent or with whom we find fault.

Seeing the faults in others is a huge spiritual detractor. Criticism and
judgment are an unseen violence. We all know when someone doesn't like
us. Their negative vibrations cut the air like a knife and we feel the pain. By
the same token, to have critical or judgmental thoughts in our minds for
another is a double-edged sword, a sword that punctures our spirituality in
two ways. First of all, as instigators of the wound we feel the reverberations
of our own negativity, draining away inner peace and contentment, suck-
ing our energy levels as low as the floor. Secondly, real damage is done just
by thinking about other people negatively. They, in turn, start to view us
with hostile eyes.

A writer friend of mine recently had an unsettling experience with her
co-author. The other woman, who was from an indigenous culture, accused
Sarah of being a racist and an opportunist. My friend was devastated by the
accusations and felt the repercussions of the woman's pent-up negativity.

For weeks afterward Sarah, herself, harbored many angry thoughts and feelings toward the other woman.

When the co-author unexpectedly became seriously ill and was taken to hospital, Sarah said, "All of my bad thoughts about her disappeared." Sarah realized that her negativity could affect the woman's capacity to get well. So she decided to stop being negative. "We never know for sure what our careless thoughts can do to someone," Sarah told me. "I couldn't be a party any more to putting out that level of negativity into the world. Instead I decided to see that woman as my teacher. As soon as I sent her thoughts of gratitude for all that she had taught me, my joy came back."

Animosity does not eradicate animosity.
Only by loving kindness is animosity dissolved.
This law is ancient and eternal.
– Buddha

What most people want from their relationships is to be loved and understood. They want to be treated with dignity and respect. Yet in this modern, self-obsessive world, many relationships seem to have gone off track. While reciprocity of love is much desired, most of us prefer to be on the receiving rather than the giving end.

When people do not treat us as we expect, the tendency is to withdraw our love. Yet these are the precise moments when we need to keep on giving. I cannot forget the words of the celebrated poet and author, Maya Angelou, who appeared on the Oprah Winfrey Show several years ago and explained the responsibility implied in any relationship. Her words were simple, "The silence stops with me, the bitterness stops with me. From me there will only be love. From my throat there will only be kindness and sweetness..."

Yet to do what Maya Angelou suggests requires a certain vigilance about our behavior. It implies an ability to keep spontaneous moods and reactions in check. If we speak or act out of arrogance or anger we can hurt the hearts of many people. Anger is a form of violence that inflicts pain and sorrow on the self and others. The effects of anger can last for months, often many years. Spiteful words or the banging of fists is remembered long after the kindness. And once anger is taken into another person's heart, it turns the relationship sour. A person can spend a lifetime showing kindness and goodness to another, yet it can all be erased in a moment of anger.

So, check yourself. When were you last angry? What was the impact of that anger on the people around you? How did it affect your own state of being? Answering these questions will show you where you need to change.

And if you are ever tempted to strike out and hurt another person, remember that you are only hurting yourself.

When discontentment is harbored within, the tendency is to project that feeling onto others. "They are to blame. I am angry because they said this. I am depressed because they did that." Much of the disillusionment found in relationships is the result of projection. In an attempt to make others responsible we blame them for our fears, resentments, and emotional turmoil. But as Maya Angelou cautioned, "the bitterness stops with me…"

Last year my friend Ros was involved in a painful situation with a colleague whom she believed mistrusted her. "I had always felt that I was a trustworthy person. So it deeply hurt me to be mistrusted," Ros said. "But I also appreciated the theory that if you see something you dislike in someone else that dislike is a reflection of what you see in yourself. I do not consider that I mistrust people, so why was my colleague treating me this way? I was confused."

"Did you figure it out?" I asked.

"Well, it took some time. But when the answer finally came, it was profound. What I saw was my own mistrust of me. In that moment I recognized how little was my faith in myself."

"And you projected that feeling, thinking that your colleague didn't trust you," I said.

"Yes, but this time I really got it. I saw clearly how we project our vision of ourselves onto others. I'll give you another example. Let's say you see someone and think, 'I hate the way she wastes money.' Look inside and see what you hate about yourself. You may not waste money, but you waste time. In fact, you hate the way you waste anything. It's so simple. Whenever you react to others, whether to the good or to the bad in them, what you are really reacting to is that something inside yourself."

"It's like seeing the world, not as it is, but as you are," I said.

"Yes. And when you finally get it, that realization gives you so much freedom."

We were silent together for a moment. Then Ros said, "I stop the denial as soon as I accept the whole of me, the light and the dark. Now, I see the darkness inside myself that I was just trying to pass off onto someone else as his or her mistake or fault. I recognize that I am perfectly capable of doing precisely the same thing that I disliked seeing others do. But I also know that once I accept my own darkness, I can move into the light, and in a real way have compassion for others. Why? Because, finally, I have compassion for myself. No one can make me feel anything. My feelings are my own choice, my own responsibility. How I see others really depends on how I see myself."

What Ros said was true. I had reached a point in my own life where I was vigilant about my own projections. If a single negative thought came to me about others, I stopped it in its tracks. I asked myself, "Where is this discontentment coming from?" Then I changed it immediately. I went inside and replenished myself with the necessary virtues.

The more I practiced inner contentment, along with self-control, the less I thought negatively about anyone. Just last month I went for days without having a careless thought about another. And even if someone said something or behaved negatively toward me, it was as if I didn't see it. Even if I had wanted to think badly about that person, I couldn't, there was so much fullness of contentment within me. My vision of myself had changed. And since I myself was luminous now I could see others as luminous beings.

Seeing others as souls is a gentle, respectful way to communicate. Dispensing with age, gender, religion, and race, it honors the being within. I find that little children are immensely sensitive to this soul-conscious vision. I try it out on them in supermarkets as they are wheeled around on carts by busy mothers raiding the food shelves. When I look at children as souls, they gaze back in amazement. Their eyes don't leave mine, not for a second, until either they are whisked off to grab a box of sugar puffs, or I am obliged to step forward and pay for my purchases at the till.

How is soul-conscious vision developed?

First, become aware of yourself as a soul. Then, when you communicate with another human being, do not focus on that person's body, look for the soul. Do not see your mother as your mother, see her as a soul. See your boss as a soul. See the girl at the checkout counter as a soul. See the man who stole your money as a soul. See the street person with the cardboard sign asking for food as a soul.

This practice is powerful. Simply by keeping your vision on the eternal soul, you will see others as they really are -- tiny beings of light obscured by their physical forms. This is how God sees them. Behind the veil of a person's face, behind the window of the eyes, lies the beauty of soul. Once you see that dazzling beauty, you wonder, "How did I ever perceive any man, woman, or child, as anything other than divine?"

As a family of human souls, we are children of God, soul brothers and sisters. No matter how different or apart we may be, an invisible thread of spirit-love connects us. All the world's religions speak about the importance of unconditional love, a love so expansive and pure it transcends limitations. This love is a gift of the spirit, conceived and nurtured through soul-conscious vision.

Spirit love is big. It is generous and bold. Spirit love overlooks surface deficiencies, searching out the light, while ignoring the shadows. Once other people are seen for their qualities, they begin to shine in our eyes, and their deficiencies pale in significance. In the presence of love others feel accepted, liberated from the wheel of criticism and judgment. In relationship to us, people can be up or down, happy or sad, according to their own rhythm and mood. Spirit love sees beyond such fluctuations and allows people the space to discover their own goodness.

Last New Year's Eve my friend Joy attended an evening of Sufi Dancing. There was a man at the dance who made jokes at other people's expense. All night she was careful to avoid his company. But at the last dance she found herself matched up with him. Participants were asked to hold their partners' hands, and look into their eyes to "honor the god or goddess within."

"At first I recoiled," Joy told me, "but then when I looked into his eyes, I saw the soul. I saw that his arrogance had been a defense mechanism. All his life he had been so courageous in dealing with many hardships. When I realized this, I looked at him with love. This big arrogant man stood silent before me. Tears welled up in his eyes. Really, we know so little about people."

Seeing the good in others makes perfect spiritual sense. Beauty, when appreciated, augments not only the one who is seen but elevates even more the beholder. As Plotinus once said, "The soul that beholds the beautiful becomes beautiful."

Seeing the good in other people is like holding up a kindly mirror, reflecting a vision of beauty to which they may aspire. Research has shown that children develop better if parents and teachers are encouraging rather than critical, if they see children passing exams instead of failing them. Similarly, souls develop faster spiritually when they are reminded of their strengths rather than their weaknesses.

It is only imperfection that complains of what is imperfect.
The more perfect we are, the more gentle and quiet we
become toward the defects of others.
– *Fenelon*

A mature mystic will see in others only their positive qualities and as a result will experience a wave of good feelings and good intentions for all. No matter how difficult, or negative, or bereft of conscience someone may be, each soul has at least one redeeming quality. A spiritually trained person will be able to spot that quality, bring it to the fore, and make the other person aware of it.

Not all of us have this natural inclination to look for the good, especially when there is so much darkness around. Often our happiness is lost just by seeing people's weaknesses and, conversely, on occasions, when we compare our virtues to the ones they possess. Comparison is that age-old dark emotion born out of jealousy. Like criticism, it diminishes the light and robs us of precious energy. The moment we compare ourselves to another, we feel, "I am of no use." Then our own virtues diminish and we begin to feel dry inside.

But when the process is reversed, the opposite is true. By seeing virtues in others, our own increase. This is a natural law. Soul-conscious vision stabilizes us in the power of our own strengths and qualities. Over the years, I have seen what the power of virtue can do. As a silent force for good, it can reach out and touch people, healing them, in ways that words and actions cannot always do.

People are sensitive to our good feelings for them. They know when our motives are pure, even though they may not always want to admit it. Several months ago, a meditation student was hesitant to talk to me. At times she treated me with veiled intolerance and dislike. Yet I sensed that her mistrust was not about me but had something to do with her past. I knew she needed to talk and that, deep down, she wanted to connect.

Previously, I would have tried to fix the relationship by talking to her directly. But on this occasion I remained silent. At the time, I was experiencing a groundswell of good wishes, and whenever I thought of her, waves of good feelings washed over me. I decided to let the power of good wishes bring about change.

One evening, at a crucial point when I sensed that she needed to communicate, I consciously focused on the virtues of love and contentment. In meditation I sent her good thoughts, filled with the power of those virtues.

The next morning at nine o'clock, she called me. She apologized, saying, "I'm sorry I haven't treated you with the respect you deserve." I listened. "It was my own lack of trust," she continued. "Because I couldn't trust myself, I couldn't trust you."

I was touched. This realization was her victory, not mine.

There have been times on my spiritual path when I found it singularly daunting to carry this soul-conscious vision into all aspects of my life. Like many people, I was afraid of what others thought of me. In the face of criticism and judgment, I shut down to protect myself from unkind words or behaviors. And in shutting down fear blocked my ability to love.

Much later on the path I have come to understand that people's patterns and behaviors, their anger, moodiness, or simple lack of kindness, may not have anything to do with me personally. Rather their patterns are part of their own inner terrain, response-mechanisms to how they were once treated. This is why I now can witness other people's transgressions with more compassion. Though my ability to see everyone with soul-conscious vision has been sorely tested, my capacity for giving love is getting stronger day by day.

Now in all of my relationships, I just want to be kind. I don't want a single thought of mine to disturb the atmosphere. So I think to myself, "Just as I have learned to tread lightly upon the earth, let me not disturb another's space. Let me tread lightly in their company. Let my thoughts and words be comforting and beautiful, bringing joy to those around me. Let the contentment in my heart radiate out and be a healing presence."

REFLECTIONS ON
WALKING THE TALK

Reflective Questions

1. What makes you content? What takes away your contentment?
2. Under what circumstances do you feel discontented with others? In what ways do you affect the contentment of others?
3. What subtle fault or vice still pulls at you? What habit or lack of attention reduces your stock of spiritual power? Which virtues still need to be strengthened in you?
4. If you could list the eight most important spiritual qualities for your life's journey, what would they be?

Exercises for Spiritual Practice

1. Just as Benjamin Franklin did, create a system or chart for self-checking, using the eight spiritual qualities you consider essential for your journey. Select a time during the day when you can check to what extent you are modeling these virtues in your life. You can give yourself percentages or just a simple tick.
2. Stand back from yourself and observe. Try to see yourself as others might see you. Observe your own level of spiritual transparency. Notice the places where you are restricted. Notice the degree to which your honesty and integrity shine.
3. Think about the way you see others. Instead of picking up on their faults try to locate one of their hidden virtues. Just by acknowledging these qualities in others, you will help their virtues (as well as your own) to blossom. At the same time, begin seeing others as the sons and daughters of God. See each person as a soul, a divine being in a human form.
4. Create a groundswell of good wishes for yourself and others. A good wish is a pure thought, a pure intent, a considerate and genuine hope for someone else's success and well-being. Create the following thought for someone you care about, "I see you as my soul brother or sister. I see your God-given beauty. From the depths of my heart I wish you well. I rejoice in your well-being." After creating this thought, fill

it with pure intent, then release this arrow of pure thought in the direction of the chosen person. Know that he or she will benefit immeasurably from receiving it.

Meditation in the Garden of Virtue

I have conducted the following spiritual experiment as part of my workshops. It might take days, or weeks, or months but people generally experience a significant shift in their relationships as a result of doing this.

Visualize yourself standing in front of a walled garden. This is your spiritual sanctuary, your garden of inner virtue. Your garden has no gate, you can revisit it at any time. You make your way through a beautiful archway covered with purple bougainvillea. You stop on the threshold before stepping into an enchanted land.

In this garden are all the flowers that you recognize and love. Silently, you acknowledge your garden, reaching out your hand to touch the flowers. Taking in their fragrance connects you to your inner beauty. You touch yellow happiness, pink kindness, blue serenity, jade wisdom, white innocence, and all the other myriad colored children that live in this tranquil land.

In the middle of your garden is a large circle of soft green grass. You spread out a blanket and sit down comfortably. You are quiet and at peace. A ripple of contentment flows through you, enveloping you with the graciousness of your now expanded being. You take in a deep breath and appreciate the groundswell of silence rising out from your inner being

Now that you are comfortable and safe in your sanctuary, you can begin the experiment.

Call to mind the name of a person with whom you are experiencing a difficulty or conflict. Notice your feelings as you remember the reason for your conflict. Acknowledge that you have been harboring some negative thoughts and feelings for this person. With the advantage of your inner sight, calmly begin to observe this person. Try to look beyond any characteristic that may have upset you in the past. Search for one good quality in this person. Think of this quality as a flower. Give the flower a name or a color. Allow this flower to emerge and blossom before your eyes.

Now look up and out across your garden. The person you were thinking about has just walked in. Are you surprised? Of course not. You were expecting them. Now calmly observe this person as he or she begins to walk around, quietly admiring the abundance of exotic flowers, plants, and trees.

From a safe distance consider that you are ready to see this person as 'a brother or sister soul.' Notice if any resistance accompanies this thought. Acknowledge your feelings, then remind yourself of the strength and beauty of your virtue. This is a garden seeded with goodness.

Now select one thought of good wishes and pure intent for this person who is visiting your garden. Visualize this thought as a ray of light, filled with the warmth of good feeling. Your intent is to wish this person well, thus creating the space for forgiveness and for the past to be released. Visualize this ray of light reaching out and touching this person. Create the thought that this ray of light is removing all negative feelings between the two of you, opening the possibility for change.

For a while you hold the silence. Then spontaneously you find yourself picking a flower, walking over, and giving it to this person. You smile, then turn graciously, and walk toward the archway leading out of the garden.

Creating good wishes for someone's happiness, well-being, or success is an incredibly powerful practice. At the beginning of our journey most of us have to learn how to generate good thoughts for others, especially for those whom we dislike. But over time this practice intensifies. The more you focus on your inner beauty in meditation, the more a natural benevolence will rise up from the core of your being. Like a hot spring from the earth, it releases a soft mist of virtue that will permeate everything you do.

STAGE EIGHT

BLISS

But if anyone asks for a further description of ecstasy, let him cease to do that, for how can a thing be described which has no description but itself, and no witness to it but itself, and its reality is known from itself to him only who has it?...He who does not know its existence, and both he who knows it and he who does not know it are altogether unable to deal with the matter...For it is felt by experience only.

– Ziyab Al Arabi –

THE DRAMA OF LIFE

Once you finish the question "Why?" you stabilize yourself in the destiny of the drama. When you understand the drama you become stable and unshakeable.

THE ANCIENT CIVILIZATIONS of Greece and Rome, like others before them, resorted to the mechanism of theater as a means of exploring the meaning of life. Understanding the world, and the role of humans within in it, was inextricably linked to religious practice. In those days, the theater was almost always built next to the temple. Thus, acts of celebration and performance grew right out of the ancient rites of worship.

Ancient performances presented life as a drama consisting of scenes where actors playing out their various intricate parts. The drama vacillated between happiness and sorrow, comedy and tragedy, subtlety and intrigue. These states were portrayed by the actors using 'comic' and 'tragic' masks.

I remember sitting once on the original stone seats of an ancient theater in Athens. I was watching a Euripides play in Greek, not understanding a word but finding myself the observer of an amazing chain of events. Actors were rushing on and off the stage. Some actors played the villain while others played the hero part. Some played the role of confidant while others the learned and wise. What struck me was how some characters were unaware of the unfolding scenarios that would ultimately affect them.

Since I was a member of the audience I was a witness to all the scenes and could perceive the intricate web of the drama, linking the characters to their and each other's parts. I remember thinking at the time that I too was an actor in its drama called 'life.' The drama was within me and around me. The scenes that I created and walked through were the backdrop to my performance. My attitude toward life could alter my interaction with other actors, affect their lives, and the outcome of my own drama. Similarly other scenes played offstage could equally affect me.

Later, on the spiritual path, I realized it was an art not to be pulled into the drama, but to be an observer of it. An observer can stand back and witness the interconnectedness of patterns that shape the personal and collective destiny. With this insight an observer is better equipped to play his or her part.

The drama of life consists of elements of both destiny and freedom of choice. So often viewed as opposites, fate and free will are reconciled through understanding. In a shift of perception they appear as one and the same. In the West the preferential outlook is freedom of choice; in the East life is seen to be governed by fate. As an observer of the drama it is possible to harmonize both outlooks. If you look behind the mask of external events you will come to know that your destiny is indeed your choice. What you choose to do with your live is also destined.

Fate is unmoved by one's pitiful hopes; what changes,
bowing to fate, is what one hopes for.
– Murasaki Shikibu

This is a world of significance. Sometimes we don't perceive the connection between the events, people and signs that surround us, the everyday miracles that occur. Sometimes we do. This realization came to me while I was sitting in the gardens behind the health clinic in Guatemala. I had put my head in my hands and was staring at the ground, thinking how peaceful I felt sitting on the bench in the sun. As my eyes surveyed the ground, it seemed to erupt in a flurry of spasmodic movements. Some kind of insect was burrowing its way deep into the earth. To do what, I wondered? Build a home? Look for food?

Suddenly, I became aware that there were hundreds, maybe thousands of animals, birds, and insects populating these gardens. Every day they went about their business, digging, foraging, and going here and there. But who really noticed? Who even cared?

It was a strange leap of thought. A minute ago, I had been thinking about my health and now I was contemplating the life of an insect. The mind is good at this. One minute it can be totally focused inward, the next it can expand to include an awareness of the world outside of itself.

Soon my thoughts turned to the conversation I'd had the day before with Else, the German nurse born in Guatemala who was helping me with my Spanish translations. Else had told me how as a young girl during World War Two, she was unwillingly repatriated to Germany. She had seen

Hitler several times from a distance, and had bumped into his top aide Himmler at a restaurant near her boarding school. When the war ended, Else returned to Guatemala, married, and ran a farm with her husband in the east of the country, near the border with Honduras.

How strange life is, I thought. Else had lived through the war and played a part in history before I was even born. Now our paths had crossed for a few days in Guatemala. Soon we would go our separate ways again. I thought about the other six billion people on the planet, about whom I knew nothing, each one with his or her own amazing stories. Under the hot sun, all of these thoughts connected in my mind: the disappearing insect, Else's strange meeting with Himmler, and all of the billions of people who, like the animals and insects in this garden, went about their daily business without the rest of us seeming to notice them.

How often did I see the whole picture, I asked myself? Or was I mainly caught up in my own affairs? When I stood back and observed, I could see the interconnectedness of all things, like tiny threads woven together forming the tapestry of 'life.'

The drama can be viewed in different ways depending on our attitudes, life experiences, and character formation. Either we become too personal in our approach, bogged down by the little things, or we flee from the personal and see the drama as too big, too unwieldy, for us to make any sense of it. Similarly, we may become overly optimistic and lose our sense of realism. Or we can become so negative toward ourselves and others, and entangled in webs of fear and mistrust, that we lose our ability to make effective decisions. Being an observer enables us to dispassionately view the drama as it is and come to a place of acceptance.

Once the drama is accepted then each scene in the drama can be accepted. The drama is an amazing unfolding of many scenes that keep changing. Once a scene is finished it is over, and that scene has now become the past. At any time a scene can end and a new one begin. The scenes of the drama are fleeting, just like the fast flickering of an old movie reel. The moment you accept this concept, your perspective changes and you begin to develop a new outlook on life. For instance, you may be going through a scene of financial disaster, but this scene does not last forever. Tomorrow you can wake up to a new scene. You can see your situation through fresh eyes and accordingly make decisions that could alter your destiny. You decide to train in new skills, move to a different country, or you meet a person in a café who offers you a new job opportunity. What is important is to realize that no one scene envelops an entire lifetime. Each scene is a doorway to another.

With acceptance comes an understanding of all the dimensions of the drama. Acceptance allows for a gentle appreciation of our own roles, seeing them as beautiful and unique. It takes a giant step to accept ourselves and the parts that we play. Sometimes we envy others and want to play their parts instead of our own. Our role is not to covet, judge, or try to change the role of another because each actor has chosen his or her own part within the drama. Learning to appreciate that each person has his or her own life and destiny does not mean that we should condone aggressive, abusive, or violent behavior. Acceptance is not a passive response, merely a compassionate one.

Look around. See how all six billion human beings within the drama of life are accurately playing out their parts. What they say or do is part of the script and is accepted by the drama. Whatever happens, happens for a reason. Even the most difficult and painful situations reveal a hidden gift. There are documented cases of people who have come through great hardship and torture and yet managed to make a difference both to themselves and others. In his book *Man's Search for Meaning*, Viktor Frankl wrote that even in concentration camp, "Man can preserve a vestige of spiritual freedom, of independence of mind, even in such terrible conditions of psychic and physical distress." He went on to describe the acts of heroism by men who comforted others by giving away their last piece of bread. This was the proof, he wrote, that every dignity could be taken away from a human being except, "to choose one's attitude in any given circumstances, to choose one's own way."

What Frankl's story reveals is that the external events are less important than our responses to them. This is affirmed by the experience of another holocaust survivor, Dr Edith Eva Egar *(USANA Magazine, July/August 1998)*, who was imprisoned in Auschwitz. Even though she suffered horrors that defy most of our imaginations, Dr Egar survived by cultivating an indomitable spirit that endures to this day. It was the power of positivity and the wisdom of her mother that saw her through her darkest moments. On the train to Auschwitz, before she died, her mother had told her, "No one can take away from you what you put in your mind."

As observers of the drama we come to accept all of life, the pain and sorrow, the happiness and joy, and this acceptance gives us the courage to make the best of each opportunity. Life and death are seen as part of the same eternal cycle. Death is not a bad thing, it's just another experience that happens to the soul. The soul moves on. Life moves on. The drama keeps changing.

In 1972 Faye, a businesswoman from Calgary, experienced an event that changed her life. Her seventeen-year-old sister Sandra was killed in a car crash. "It was like someone had snatched my body," Faye recalled. "For a long time, there was just this emptiness inside."

What eventually helped Faye through her grieving process was something that her mother had taught her, "Everything is for the best." This seed of a thought grew in her. Faye said, "I went through a great deal of anger, especially at God. But slowly, I began to accept that what happens in the external world is not the only reality. Because my outer world had just been blown apart, I had to go inward for answers. Then I knew her death was meant to be."

Thirteen years later, both of Faye's parents were killed in an airplane crash.

"How did you cope?" I asked.

"First of all because I had already experienced the death of my sister years earlier I felt I had survived. When you go through something like this you come out very strong. When my parents died I understood that it was meant to be. I guess 'fate' was the word that came to mind. My mother had taught me many things such as unconditional love. My father taught me not to be afraid. He said I could do anything I wanted to. When they died the lessons I had learned from them became more important then ever."

"How did you gain from this experience?" I asked.

"My siblings and I were forced to grow. I had to take over the family business and this made me strong. It wasn't easy but my mother's words helped me, 'Everything is for the best.' Even now I say those words to myself every day. It's easy to believe them when things are going right. But when you are faced with trauma, you just have to keep reminding yourself."

At the beginning of my spiritual journey, I thought I understood this concept of drama. Applying it proved to be more difficult. Like many people, I easily embraced the good times and was happy when my life went the way I wanted. But when the tough times came, I resisted them with all my might. My resistance took away my happiness. And for a long time afterward I had regrets. I wished that those terrible events had never happened.

Looking back I see the futility of my resistance. How much easier it would have been, how much more dignified, had I wholeheartedly accepted the drama rather than wishing for it to be different.

"Life is good. It is really good." Now, many years later, these words emerge naturally from my heart. They are a part of me. With a heart full of acceptance, I can afford to be joyous. To accept the drama of life in this way doesn't lead to complacency, as some people fear, but to love. You just open your arms wide and allow the drama to unfold.

I can trace this seed of acceptance back to the deep spiritual efforts I made four summers ago. Each day I went walking and practiced a combination of non-attachment and loving acceptance toward myself and the drama. Out of this experience a natural feeling of happiness and bliss emerged in my attitude toward all things.

That September I went to Seattle. I was driving downtown when a gray Mitsubishi crossed three lanes of traffic and crashed into the passenger side of my car. An electric shock reverberated down my neck and back. As my car came to a standstill, I remember looking down at my legs and saying, "Oh." It was a simple, "Oh, I guess I've just been hit." My next thought was, "It's okay. It's good."

As Brian, the other driver, and I worked out insurance details, no thoughts of concern entered my mind. I was physically in pain, but internally at ease. I didn't have the thought, "Why did this happen?" I just accepted the accident, even though at the time I was in the final stages of recovery from a previous back injury.

This was a drama and I was an actor playing my part. A natural feeling bubbled up inside of me: some kind of good would come out of this. Strangely enough after some prolonged treatment for whiplash my previous back ailments improved. My spiritual practices had gone deep. I was living them at another level of reality.

When Mama, the teacher of my teacher Dadi Janki, was asked, "What is truth?" she replied, "That which is accepted by the drama." What Mama meant is that whatever happens in the drama is accepted by the drama. And because the drama is beneficial, it is therefore true.

How the drama is, how it was, how it will be --we learn to take all of it in our stride. And when all is accepted, nothing is wrong. Then there is bliss. Bliss is the indescribable joy that comes from being able to embrace what comes toward us with love, wisdom, and compassion.

Many of us have had glimpses of this bliss, times when we suddenly, miraculously find ourselves in synchronicity with the drama. These are the magical moments of meaningful coincidences when life seems to flow easily, we are in the right place, at the right time, making the right decisions. It's like surfing in the ocean and catching the crest of a big wave, not too early or too late, but just before it breaks, and then riding that wave all the way to the shore. The power of that perfect wave takes us far. A writer friend once told me, "I often thought about the things that came into my life as waves that I could choose to ride or resist, as well as waves of opportunity that I could catch if I was vigilant and aware."

Five summers ago I made a decision that put me in total synchronicity with the drama. I was about to leave Vancouver airport for Cranbrooke, in the interior of British Columbia, when a freak lightning storm hit the city. The flight was delayed and instead of boarding the plane, I sat in the departure lounge and watched the lightning rip open the skies. But the longer I sat, the more I had a strange intuition that something important was waiting for me at home. So I left the other passengers stranded in their seats and caught a cab.

As soon I walked in the door, the telephone rang. It was my brother Guy calling from Toronto. He wanted me to officiate at my niece, Isabel's, christening in October. Guy and his wife Laura were planning a spiritual, non-denominational service. "I'm touched, Guy, really honored," I said.

Since my parents' divorce, our whole family had been split apart. The christening would be the first time in twenty years that my parents, my two brothers and their partners, my niece and myself would all be in the same room. In a flash I saw the potential for healing. Guy's invitation was a magical, heart-opening moment.

As soon as I put the phone down two crises erupted, one after the other, involving friends who were in urgent need of help that required my undivided attention until late that evening. "I guess I was meant to be in Vancouver, not in the interior," I thought to myself.

The next morning my plane took off into clear blue skies. I arrived in Cranbrooke, got in my car that I had left there, and set off down the highway. As I passed fresh emerald lakes and green forests smelling of pine, I felt the hand of God pulling me forward. God whispered, "It's time to step onto the center stage of your life."

"What do you mean?" I asked.

"Step forward. Become big. Become bold."

The events of the previous day flashed before me: the lightning storm, the intuition to go home, the invitation from my brother, the crisis and emergency phone calls. "It's all perfect," I said to myself. "Yesterday, I was where I was meant to be. Today, on this highway, I'm where I'm meant to be. It's perfect."

My heart expanded and took in the blue open sky, the purple peaks, the sun-baked road. The largeness of nature was a symbol for the largeness of my life. I was big in that moment because I was present with all things and all people. I was in love with the many scenes and strands of my life. My love was big enough to accept it all, equally.

I cannot forget the bliss of that moment when the drama opened up to me. It was as if I had prized open a secret treasure chest and found the jewels. Each second of the drama was a sparkling gem linked inextricably to the next second. Past, present, and future were all one. I knew the past, could see into the future, but was sitting in the present. I had this amazing feeling that I had been here before. I had traveled before down this highway, and was traveling here once again.

As this eternal reel of the drama played itself out before me, I had access to all of it. This was not just some momentary glimpse. I had stepped into the realm of the eternal now. Before me lay a vast expanse of unlimited goodness. It was all good. As Julian of Norwich once said, "All is well. All is forever well."

In the advanced stages of spiritual development, mystics have these kinds of experiences all the time. Bliss comes from being in step with the drama, which is a natural state of self-mastery. Questions such as, "Why is this happening? What will be the result?" simply do not arise. There are no unnecessary thoughts at all. In this advanced state mystics achieve an internal state of peace and stability, regardless of the situations that come and go.

To accept the drama in all of its dimensions is the doorway to enlightenment. It means that we can sit in a place of peace, with the drama revolving around us, and not lose our happiness. The ecstatic or blissful state comes from the realization that we are not just players in the drama, but masters of it. We create the drama through our thoughts and vibrations. What lies before us is the creation of our individual and collective consciousness.

When we are in bliss, we can see it all, and know it all. Ecstasy is in the knowing.

LIVING IN THE
PRESENCE OF GOD

*Because the Father has so much love for you He tells you to go to sleep
remembering Him. When you awaken, you awaken with the Father,
when you eat you eat with Him, and when you walk you walk with
Him. When you become sad at times, the Father becomes your Friend
and tries to cheer you up. God also becomes your Friend when you
shed tears of joy and love, and comes to wipe away your tears. He
places your tears in the jewel case of His heart, like pearls. So with
whom do you spend your whole day?*

IT IS AFTER FOUR O'CLOCK in the morning. The *adhan* is
calling the faithful to prayer. There are at least four mosques near my hotel
in Amman, Jordan. "*Allahu Akbar*, God is Great," rings out four separate
times, each cry following seconds after the one before. I count the mosques
in turn: one, two, three, four. The last call fades into silence. Now there is
only the gentle humming of the radiator in my room.

I love the early morning hours. At this time the mind is fresh. Perhaps
this is why the faithful rise early to remember God. In meditation my
thoughts turn to a child's poem I once read. The child wrote, "Blood is the
same color in all human beings." I like this thought and play with it in my
mind.

As patches of light seep into the morning sky, I reflect that the same
orb of light turning the sandstone houses pink in Amman also rises over the
sleepy hills of Jerusalem. The same artist paints the sea of Aqaba red,
whether on the Egyptian, Israeli, Jordanian, or Saudi side. We are children
of the sun, living on the same earth, under the same sky. It is the same God
for us all.

In Islam there are ninety-nine qualities that describe the greatness of God. God is the Almighty, the Merciful, and the Compassionate. He is the Noble, the Giver of Virtues, and the Powerful One. In meditation I too focus on God's qualities.

There is no end to the depth of God. Hours can be spent contemplating the beauty of the Divine yet only a few, I think, ever truly experience God in all of His dimensions.

As well as being an Ocean of many qualities, God is the Origin of Wisdom, the Living Consciousness and Creator of Life. God is the Seed from whom the whole human tree receives its nourishment. In most religions the tree represents life and knowledge. In my practice I contemplate the tree as a symbol for the connection of all souls to God and their interconnectedness with each other. Each branch of the tree represents the various religions and beliefs, tracing their origin through the trunk back to the Seed. Each soul is like a leaf on the tree with its own unique place on that branch and its own way of relating and being in relationship with God. Without God, the Seed, we souls of the world would have no place from which to renew our consciousness or receive spiritual strength.

These are my thoughts as I meditate. In the silent hours of the early morning I hear the soundless voice of God calling me to start my day in His Presence. I am aware that life is a divine gift and that each human being in the world is a child of the Divine and therefore my brother and sister. Silently the vibration of God's love fills my mind. I am not alone. It is as if I can feel the entire family of human souls responding to God's early morning call. He is drawing them back to the Seed and Source of Life.

Some fifteen minutes later the *adhan* rings out a second time. The sound comes from the loudspeakers hidden somewhere inside the green-lit minarets of the mosques. The Jordanian skyline is dotted with these permanent reminders of God's presence.

"Just turn to God and remember Him with love," I think to myself. "God is always with you."

The more I progress in my meditations the more I am pulled to be constantly in the presence of God. To remain in God's company throughout the day, even while performing daily activities, is an advanced meditative practice. Mystics who have reached this advanced state describe it as remembering God with every breath and every thought. The Hindu mystic Meera said, "A moment without God is no moment."

The pure soul feels a constant fire of love,
which desires above all things to be one with God,
and the more the soul obeys the attraction of God the more it feels it,
and the more it feels it the more it feels to be one with God.
— *Ruysbroeck*

Loving God is an all-day affair. The love doesn't stop just because you have to clean the house or cook the evening meal. The secret is to bring God into every task, into every action, to make each part of your life divine. This love does not stem from the thought that God is there anyway. Rather it results from the conscious attempt to make the Divine present in all that you do. Remembering God at all times is achieved both by sitting in contemplative prayer or meditation, and through the remembrance of the Divine while performing actions. In yogic terms this is known as karma yoga -- yoga in action.

It is easy to concentrate on two tasks at the same time. You can have a conversation with a friend or family member while doing the ironing, or drive the car and listen to the radio. The mind splits in two directions and is aware of both activities. Since you can talk to a friend or listen to the radio, equally you can focus on God and do other activities at the same time. If you remember God while preparing a meal, cooking becomes a delightful task and pure vibrations fill the food. Similarly, if your mind is focused on God while speaking to a friend on the phone, that person will feel spiritually uplifted.

When a person is in constant remembrance of God, the actions that he or she performs become God's responsibility. Remembering God makes life simple and stress free.

In the seventeenth century a lay Carmelite named Brother Lawrence wrote of his experiences of living in the presence of God. He mostly worked in the kitchen and performed other ordinary tasks such as mending shoes and picking fruit in the orchard. The simplicity of his lifestyle allowed him the opportunity to cultivate his practice. At the same time, he explained how the awareness of God in all actions made life simple and pure, "We must act very simply with God, and speak to Him frankly, while asking His help in things that occur" *(from The Practice of the Presence of God)*.

Rather than taking him away from other people, this God-focused life brought Brother Lawrence closer to them. Behind his letters, conversations, and maxims, lies a great humanitarian spirit, one that was able to comprehend the most troubled heart. Brother Lawrence's spirituality was open and loving, without force or frustration. He anchored his practice in the virtues of humility, simplicity, and faith.

Last May Rima asked me, "How can I remember God more? I want to be with God all day long." Like many people in the Middle East her passion for God is high.

I told her, "When you remember a friend or loved one, you feel as if that person is with you. In your mind you enjoy his or her company. In the same way, as you consciously keep God in your awareness, you bring God's presence in front of you."

"Yes, but I want more of Him," Rima insisted. "I don't just want a bit of God, I want all of God."

I laughed. "A relationship is built one step at a time, Rima. The more you remember God with concentration and with love, the more you will attract God to you."

Keeping God at the forefront of our minds is the meaning of constant and conscious awareness. This is not the same as thinking, "I remember God all day," when in fact He is in the background of all our other thinking. The sign that we are with God is that we are filled with His power. By maintaining such a focus in our remembrance, we are actually filled with God's light and can then feel His presence clearly.

To reach this advanced level of spiritual practice is like going for gold in the Olympics or striving for a Ph.D. Whether we are willing to make the effort is entirely dependent on what we want for ourselves. For some it may seem an impossible challenge. Yet others may appreciate that as in any other pursuit, motivation and dedication are required.

As a former tennis coach, I know the value of discipline and practice, the importance of staying focused on a singular effort. Years ago I was invited by British Olympic Gold Medallist David Hemery to attend one of his seminars on the power of effective questioning. The seminar aimed to improve performance at work and in the sporting arena. One of the exercises was to try out a range of sporting activities, such as golf and hurdling. We were invited to work in pairs and use effective questioning to coach each other. I hadn't ever done hurdling in my life. My first attempt was disastrous.

"How did you feel?" asked my coaching partner.

"Like a lump of lead. My paces were uneven and lacked rhythm. My legs were all over the place."

"What were you focused on?"

"I was looking down at my feet and counting my paces between each hurdle. I was trying to keep them even."

"So what could you do to improve your performance?" he probed. I thought for a while as I looked out over the course. There was a wall at the far end. Then I smiled, "I know. I have to keep my eyes on the destination. See that wall, I'm just going to race till I get there."

On my next hurdling attempt, I focused on the wall and sailed over without touching a single bar.

"How did you feel?" asked my coach.

"Like a swan," I smiled.

Just as an athlete must keep his or her eye on the goal or final destination, similarly, a gold medallist meditator needs to increase the hours spent in God's remembrance. God comes first over and above all souls, as well as any other possession or human activity. As Brother Lawrence said, "Having found different methods of going to God and different practices to attain the spiritual life in several books, I decided that they would serve more to hinder than facilitate me in what I was seeking -- which was nothing other than a means to be wholly God's. This made me decide to give all to gain all; so after having given all to God...I began to live as if there were no one in the world but Him and me" (from *The Practice of the Presence of God*).

Such a constancy of remembrance ultimately leads to experiences of bliss. Just as athletes have their highs, bliss is one of the ultimate attainments for a mystic. I have met many blissful yogis at the spiritual university in Mt Abu, India, where I go each year to study. Many of them are able to maintain eight or more hours a day in concentrated remembrance of God. This remembrance occurs not only when they sit to meditate but also as they perform their activities and daily duties.

I have seen the light shining from their eyes and a glow radiating from their faces. This glow is not an uncommon phenomenon on the mystic path. It was said about Rabi'a, the famous woman Sufi saint, that light rose above her head whenever she was deeply in prayer. It was also said of Buddha that when he entered Deer Park at Benares after his enlightenment, and met his former companions, they were stunned by the bliss radiating from his person and the light of ecstasy in his eyes. Angela of Foligna also could not hide from her companions the ecstasy which years of contemplation had benefited her "because at times my face was all resplendent and rosy, and my eyes shone like candles."

As for the mystic yogis of Mt Abu, when I looked at them closely, I could also see an aura of bright light surrounding their physical forms, giving them the appearance of being luminous beings. And when I came close to them, I could feel the heat of divine energy flowing from their beings and energizing mine so that I too began to shine without any effort on my part. The ecstatic look on their faces came from the bliss of deeply experiencing God and having no need to speak about it except through their vibrations and presence. Theirs is such a natural, constant, and loving union that I am inspired to achieve the same.

Dadi Gulzar is another of my senior teachers. She doesn't speak much, but her eyes are like deep pools that speak volumes. I have the feeling, when I am in front of her, that she is with me, but not with me, that she is of this world, but not of this world. At the same time, I feel that she is fully in the presence of God. There is a divine energy, a refined and loving vibration that is wrapped around her like a warm blanket, which makes me feel that I too am wrapped in the warmth of God's embrace. Dadi Gulzar has made God her constant Companion. The two are inseparable, totally combined. If I were to invite Dadi Gulzar to tea, I couldn't imagine her showing up without God.

Last year I interviewed Dadi Gulzar, asking her the question, "What is bliss?" This was her reply:

"When one is in a blissful stage, at that moment it feels as if one is filled with everything, with all powers and virtues from God. And nothing is lacking. Being filled with everything, there is the joy of complete fullness. Only when one is completely full, does one experience deep internal happiness."

Dadi Gulzar continued by linking this ecstatic feeling to her relationship with God. She said, "Whenever a situation arises, then it is as if my Father is my Companion. I do not feel that I am alone. In an unseen way, He gives me power. Or He gives me a direction, 'Child, do this.' I am given a touching and am guided as to what to do. I've had hundreds of experiences where before God gives me His direction, a task might seem impossible. And an hour later, things change in such a way that I don't understand what happened. It feels as if I did not do the task, but rather that God gave me the courage and help to do it. And with God's help that task, which was like a mountain, becomes easy. This companionship with God in action is also a form of bliss."

I also interviewed Brother Surya and asked him how a state of bliss could be reached. This was his reply:

"Ecstasy comes from maintaining higher consciousness and a constant link with God. When one has loving and ecstatic thoughts that are directed toward God, then no ordinary thoughts arise. The best ecstatic thought arises when the mind is stable and focused on one particular thought. This is full concentration. In this state, I receive so much from God. I am completely content. I am so full of everything that I need nothing."

"But how did you reach this concentrated union with God?" I asked. Brother Surya replied, "I made a chart to improve my yoga practice. To achieve total union with God, I had to reach eight hours of remembrance a day. Even now I spend a lot of time in solitude, at least four hours a day. If I miss my solitude, I feel I have really missed something because I will have missed the company of God."

From all of my research, I have come to understand that living constantly in the presence of God is not an intellectual activity but a tangible experience. Several years ago I wrote this in my diary, "When the love of God runs thicker than blood through my veins, expanding my lungs, filling my breath, transforming my eyes, ears, hands, and feet, when every thought is naturally created out of that sweet union, then I will know that I have His constant company and that He is mine. And the bliss that rises up from this state is similar to a rose bud that has come into full bloom simply by virtue of having turned its face toward the sun."

Even now I can see the large darkened kitchen at the university in India where a solitary light bulb hangs from the ceiling. Outside, even the stars give off more light.

It is early morning. A small group of no more than fifteen men and women crouch down on small wicker stools before large straw baskets filled with potatoes, carrots, tomatoes, and peas. We begin our work in silence, preparing the vegetables that will be eaten later that day.

I sit in front of the basket containing carrots, pick up a short blunt peeler, and begin to remove the outside skins. The peeler doesn't work well, and bits of skin get stuck in the wedge of the blade. After every two or three shavings, I wipe the wedge free with my fingers.

It is cold out. This is evident from the steam that bellows out from my mouth and mingles with the crisp dark air.

I call You to myself. You are my Friend and I need Your help in peeling these carrots. There is a whole basketful in front of me. At least an hour's work.

"Don't rush," You say. "Peel slowly and in rhythm with your inner breath. Let the rhythm do the work, not your speed."

Mountains of orange sticks pass through my hands and lose their skins. Soon a mound of peel lies at my feet. I do not look up, do not compare my basket to anyone else's, do not mind the bits that get stuck on the blades of the peeler.

I am aware that You are with me, pouring light over my head, down my back and arms, into my scrunched-up fingers. You are teaching me to love this work, each carrot, even the flaky bits of skin that are lying on the floor.

My hands work powerfully. They have discovered new strength. Time moves slowly. I am lost in Your love, energized by Your constant Presence.

The basket is empty, yet I am reluctant to leave. I am unable to tear myself away from the bliss of peeling carrots in Your Company.

TRUTH

Know that the Greatest and Highest Authority of all is with you. God knows everything. Therefore He is known as the Blissful One.

WHAT IS THE ULTIMATE EXPERIENCE OF GOD?

Many of the ancient mystics have spoken of God as Truth. Although a number of them experienced this Truth, many were at a loss to describe it.

Mystics considered the experience of Truth to be beyond human rationale. They said that language (that "sad incompetence of human speech" as Wordsworth once put it) was insufficient to convey what could only be understood by those who had experienced it. As Catherine of Genoa wrote *(Life and Works)*, "But how can I describe in words the immeasurable and the indescribable? I am at a loss to speak of its greatness and excellence; it is impossible to express it in words, or for anyone to understand it who had not experienced it." Kabir, the fifteenth-century Hindu sage, also said, "Even if I could express in words what I see, who would believe my words anyway!"

If Truth is indescribable how did these ancient mystics arrive at their understanding of it? A close examination of mystical literature reveals that theirs was an intuitive understanding born out of years of contemplation, spiritual practice and occasional visionary experiences. These experiences were not created of their own accord, but were divinely granted to them. What they 'saw' was shown, what they 'heard' was sent, what they 'felt' was given. As Teresa of Avila wrote in her autobiography, *Life*, "Thus I understood what it is for a soul to be walking in truth in the presence of Truth Itself. And what I understood comes to this: the Lord showed me that He is Truth Itself."

These experiences of God were so powerful for these mystics that all other insights paled in comparison. When Jacopone da Todi, a thirteenth-century Italian mystic, achieved his vision of the Absolute he realized that what he had earlier supposed to be Truth was merely a veil obscuring that which he so eagerly sought.

Thus it appeared that as these mystics progressed spiritually their perceptions of God changed. Catherine of Genoa wrote *(Life and Works)*, "I see without eyes, I understand without mind, I feel without feeling, and I taste without taste. I have no shape or size, so that without seeing I see such divine activity and energy, that beside it, all those words like perfection, fullness, and purity that I once used now seem to me all falsehood and fables when compared with that Truth and Directness."

No one knows exactly how visionary experiences occur. They are gifts from God. Many believe that visions are the definitive route to Truth, and become disappointed when they are not granted access. And yet having a vision of God is not the only indication of God's grace, nor the only means of knowing and experiencing Him in the ultimate sense. Visions are transitory phenomena. And because they are infrequent and do not last, they are not necessarily the most reliable source of God's affection.

With her characteristic clarity, Teresa of Avila shed light on this mystical dilemma. "The highest perfection does not consist in feelings of spiritual bliss," she wrote, "nor in the great ecstasies or visions, nor yet in the spirit of prophesy, but in bringing your will into conformity with the will of God." In other words, ecstatic states and visions are not useful unless they are transformative. A mystic wants to be colored by Truth not simply dazzled by it.

Looking back on my 'out of the body' experience in Paris, I see that God pulled me into the warmth of His Light and granted me, for want of better word, a vision of His grandeur. As powerful as it was, this one-off visionary experience did not lead me to incorporating truth in my life. I was changed by the experience but not transformed by it. Instead, it was the consistency of my daily practice, the accumulation of minutes and hours spent deepening my relationship with God that brought me closer to Truth.

When I recently asked Dadi Janki what she considered to be the basis for knowing Absolute Truth, she said it depended on two important factors that took time to develop. The first is the depth of our recognition of God. The second is our own degree of purity and truth. She said, "A soul who is in search of Truth will recognize God as the Supreme Soul. The one who understands this Truth will follow Truth and thus remove all traces of falsehood from within."

"How do we remove falsehood?" I asked.

Dadi replied that we have to keep our hearts clean and our minds free from negative thoughts and the influence of others. "Through God's love our hearts become pure, and then we are able to experience Truth," she said. "When there is Truth, there is no falsehood. Falsehood is when we are attracted, influenced, or subservient to others. Those who recognize God make Him their sole strength and support. They have no need to look to anyone or listen to anyone other than God. This is Truth."

It seems that there are two main aspects in this exploration of Truth. First of all, to know God as God really is, a mystic has to become very clean inside, free from the pull of any negativity that could interfere in the experience of Truth. God is totally pure. To view the Divine we need a pure heart and pure mind free from the coloring of our own weaknesses, prejudices, and past experiences. There is an Absolute Truth, of which God is the embodiment, and then there is the subjective and personal experience of Truth that is achieved to the extent to which we have brought Truth into our lives.

The second aspect is that once a person has known and experienced Truth there is a transformative effect. That person will then be filled with the characteristics of truth. His or her words and actions will be truthful, without a trace of anything false. Nor will such a person perform any harmful acts toward others. Others will seek out that person's company just to benefit from his or her honesty, simplicity, and truthfulness.

Dadi Janki pays careful attention to her thoughts, words, and actions. This attention is an indication of her unfailing love of Truth. Dadi has taught me that Truth can only be attained by someone who is willing to live a life of truth. What inspires me about being in her presence is that I know Truth is attainable.

As lovers of Truth, our passion and goal is to know God fully. And yet I am convinced from all that I have read and studied that only a few know God as God really is. St Teresa of Avila confirms this. She wrote in her autobiography that once in a meditation Truth said to her, "Ah, daughter, how few are they who love Me in truth! If people loved Me, I should not hide my secrets from them."

To reach this advanced state of knowing Truth is a peak mystical experience. I have found this state singularly illusive except on those occasions when I peeked through the keyhole and experienced God in a way that is difficult to put into words. All I know is that I was pulled into another dimension by the absorbing presence of God and into an experience of Truth that was not of my own making. God's Majesty was not overwhelming, as I would have expected, but blissfully Real. Instead of finding myself lost in love, or swimming in a jumble of emotions, I just was. I was beyond time and space, suspended before the All-knowing. As Truth, God was. Eternally Pure and Holy. Indeed nothing of 'me' seemed to cloud the experience. God was simply there before me, in all of His fullness.

The presence of God
Is like grains of sugar
In a pile of sand;
An elephant
Can't pick them
But an ant
Knows the way!

O Kabir, listen:
Truth is very subtle
Be humble to seek it.
– Kabir

Although I believe it is possible for each of us to have glimpses of the Absolute during profound meditations, it takes years of meditation and prayer to come to know God as God truly is. This is because Truth can only be approached with humility and purity. Ultimately it is the result of our spiritual efforts and the degree to which we as souls have become cleansed from our negativities that enables us to see God clearly. Over time, our experiences match up with Truth. Then the Majesty and Beauty of God become less of a theory and more of a Reality.

There is a saying that light and darkness cannot exist together. The experience of Truth is the experience of Light. Light removes darkness and fear. And this connection to Truth makes our lives shine like beacons in the dark.

REFLECTIONS ON BLISS

Reflective Questions

1. To what extent has God become your main source of strength and support?
2. Go back to some events in the past where you experienced the power of synchronicity. What convergence of ideas, people, and events allowed this to happen?
3. How often do you catch the little signals in life guiding you toward your destiny? What recent signals have you been conscious of that have indicated that new pathways could open up for you?

Exercises for Spiritual Practice

1. Carl Jung once said, "We are players in a divine world drama." Consider how you are playing your part. Give thanks to each person for the role he or she is playing. If the other actors didn't play their parts, you wouldn't be able to play yours. We are all part of a bigger story.
2. Consider the well-known serenity prayer, "God grant me the serenity to accept the things I cannot change, the courage to change the things I can, and the wisdom to know the difference." Begin by observing the scenes that come to you in the drama of life. Visualize opening your arms wide and embracing these scenes in an act of acceptance. Now create a space for God to guide your response.
3. Try for a day to remain attentive to remembering God while you work. What helps is to consciously invoke God's presence before beginning any task, no matter how small or how important. This practice brings sacredness into whatever you do. Try to increase the time you consciously spend in the presence of God.

Meditation on Bliss

Begin your meditation with the thought, "I want to know God as God really is." Let this thought quietly deepen in your mind. It's as if you are traveling down a wide road that becomes more and more narrow as your mind focuses powerfully on this singular thought. Again you think, "I want to know You, God, know You as You really are." Experience the silence and beauty of this pure thought. You slip through a passage of time, a crack in the wall, and the staggering intensity of this thought raises you up.

You are like a bird flying beyond all limitations. You burst open into an immense field of light. God, the Blissful One, is waiting for you...

Sitting next to God I have the feeling, "This is where I belong. I have waited my whole life for this. I am meant to be here, face to face with Truth." God fills me with rays of Love, and Peace, and Power. I feel the current and become charged with this perfect union.

In the open spaces of my mind I see the seed of Your love and know that it is inextricably connected to my own essence.

One thought anchors my mind, "I love and I am loved." My mind stretches deep down inside the nature of thought itself, as though it is a melody and I am being played with my own essence. This concentration on Your love magnifies and intensifies all that I know and am. I am a small angel harp and You are pulling my strings.

You rise like the Sun illuminating an endless sky. Your light goes on and on. I am beyond thought, sunk into silence by the vastness of Your presence, by the radiance of your Light flooding my being.

You are the Seed of my life, the author of our blissful union. In Your essence lies the secret of creation, the key to unlocking the universe.

With You I am connected to the whole. My love expands. I am blissful.

STAGE NINE

PERFECTION OF SPIRIT

*When the soul reaches the perfection of the Spirit,
being completely purified from passion, and is joined and
commingled with the Holy Spirit...
then it becomes all light, all exultation,
all heartfelt love, all goodness and loving kindness.*

– Mecarius –

THE HUMBLE SERVER

May you be a humble instrument who considers yourself to be a server, having surrendered your every thought and action to the Father.

I HAD COME TO PARIS to watch the leaves dance. As I sat on Anne-Marie's roof terrace garden in the warmth of the afternoon sun a gentle May breeze blew in from the Seine, gathered up the white-spotted leaves of the wall creeper and sent them fluttering and twirling on their stems.

I thought, "This wind is like the breath of God. The leaves would not move had His breath not touched them. The leaves have no movement of their own, nor do they think, 'I am the one moving.' They are simply pulled to the dance and surrender with humility. I want to be like them."

No sooner had this thought entered my mind than I was transported into another dimension. Just as the French writer Proust had dunked a "petite Madeleine" into his tea, and flashed onto a memory of childhood, I too was granted access to some distant memory, only mine was not of the past but of the future. In this serene Parisienne garden I caught a glimpse of the 'me' I would eventually become, once, like the leaves, I'd allowed the breath of God to move me.

Practically all mystical traditions consider humility to be the greatest of spiritual qualities. St Teresa of Avila advised those who studied with her that there were three important precepts in life: "First to love one another; secondly, detachment from all created things; thirdly, true humility. Though I mention this virtue last," she wrote, "it is the chief one and includes all the others."

People are wary of humility for they do not understand its true meaning. Whenever I bring up the subject in workshops, people comment, "Yes, but if you are humble other people walk all over you." To them humility is a sign of weakness not strength, and not very high on their list of favorite attainments. To address this misconception, I try to define humility within the broader context of dissolving the ego.

I tell participants, "Humility is not the absence of self, nor is it an empty self-forgetting. When you are humble you do not become a doormat but a bridge. As a bridge you lean over and help others to reach their destination. Humility is the opposite of the ego. It is a complete self-respect, a genuine desire to put others forward. A highly spiritual person doesn't brag about his or her achievements, or seek to demonstrate spiritual powers, or feel the need to be applauded. In the face of disregard, a highly spiritual person just continues with what he or she has to do, exuding dignity and respect to others. This is humility."

The other redeeming aspect about humility, I tell participants, is the natural inclination to give credit where credit is due. In spiritual circles, just as in life, the human ego is frail. The ego wants to believe that human intelligence is the motor for every known achievement, that humanity alone can do what God does. But spiritual greatness cannot be claimed in isolation, nor can it be made in a test tube. Spiritual knowledge is God-given, and without the guiding hand of God a mystic cannot reach full spiritual accomplishment on the basis of his or her merit alone. God's power does the work. This is why I tell people, "Humility comes from the deep recognition: all that I am, all that I have, comes to me from God."

Yet the more a mystic advances, the more humility appears illusive. A fine line exists between considering oneself to be humble, even demonstrating it externally, while inwardly taking the credit for such exemplary behavior. Just one misplaced thought, "Aren't I humble, look what I've achieved," and humility is immediately displaced by the subtleties of the ego.

This is was what happened to Arjuna, the famous warrior in Hindu mythology. He believed that his skill and strength alone had defeated his enemies, the Kauravas, in battle. Seeing this, Lord Krishna (the Hindu incarnation of God) decided to teach Arjuna a lesson. He sent the warrior into the mountains to consult an eagle. The eagle, which had witnessed the whole battle from the air, revealed to Arjuna the secret of his success. The eagle told him it was not Arjuna's power, but Lord Krishna's power working through him, that had won the war. In this kind of spiritual battle, victory only came with God's support.

God is full of knowledge and spiritual power yet is totally without ego. God sustains each soul in a myriad ways, but doesn't take the credit, send a mega bill, or demand recognition from anyone. Drawing on humility from God, a truly humble person will not accept praise for any accomplishment, but will continue to point to the true Source of his or her strength and inspiration. As the Christian mystic Ruysbroeck said, "For to pay homage to God by every outward and inward act, this is the first and dearest work of humility."

This is illustrated by the following abridged story from Anthony de Mello's *The Heart of the Enlightened.* Legend has it there once lived a godly man who was so holy he had no notion of his own goodness. One day an angel came to him and told him that any wish of his would be granted by God.

"Would you like to have the gift of healing?" the angel asked.

"No," said the man, "It is best that God did the healing Himself."

"Would you like to help those who have gone astray?"

"No," said the man, "It's not my job to touch human hearts. That work belongs to angels."

"Maybe you would like to become a model of virtue for others to emulate."

"No," said the holy man, "Because then I would become the center of attention."

The angel then told him that if he did not ask for a wish one would be granted anyway. "Alright," said the holy man, "My wish is that good be done through me without my even being aware of it."

So from that moment on the old man's shadow was filled with the power of healing. And wherever his shadow fell, as long as his back was turned to it, the sick were healed, flowers and trees sprang into bloom, and people in all manner of sorrowful circumstances were granted relief.

And since people were focused on his shadow and not on him, the holy man knew nothing of the good that was being done through him. In desiring that he not be credited for his goodness, believing that all good acts come from God, the holy man was free from ego. And in this sense he was a true server of God.

Swami Vivekanada, the twentieth-century Hindu sage, described this same state in one of his inspirational talks. He said, "Our best work is done, our greatest influence is exerted, when we are without the thought of self. All great geniuses know this. Let us open ourselves to the one Divine Actor and let Him act, and do nothing ourselves. Be perfectly resigned, perfectly unconcerned; then alone can you do any true work."

Throughout history mystics and saints have considered selflessness to be a mark of spirituality maturity. It implies the surrender to hand over all of our acts to God so that the Divine can work through us. One of the best ways to cultivate humility is by giving to others. Most spiritual traditions include within their practices the notion of "service" -- the importance of giving back to the community. If this giving were not an integral part of spiritual development, spirituality would quickly become dry and self-serving. To be of service to others covers a wide spectrum of activities -- from small acts of kindness and generosity to any work done, when connected to the Divine, that brings benefit to people and society as a whole. The Jewish teacher Baal Shem Tov defined service this way, "The essence of sacred service dwells in the mind. When a person's thoughts are connected to Divine wisdom and nobility, even the simplest actions become holy."

This is such a beautiful concept. Imagine making your thoughts and actions so beautiful, so holy, that their very vibrations are a means of uplifting others. The highest sacred service is to inspire others to honor the divine within. For when another soul is connected inwardly and has the facility to connect with God there is an expansion of faith and an increased ability to stand strong. Serving is not about making others dependent on us. Rather it is encouraging them and providing them (when appropriate) with the necessary tools to progress on their own.

Such acts of service are only made noble when carried out invisibly. Each day countless individuals perform selfless acts of charity, such as caring for bed-ridden relatives, or rescuing children from a building in flames. They go about their business quietly, bravely, seeking no reward or acclaim. A similar attitude is required at the spiritual level. A humble server is always ready to serve but acknowledges there is beauty and safety in unseen acts. As the Sufi poet Rumi wrote, "Work in the invisible at least at much as you do in the visible."

You can begin to work invisibly by developing the clear awareness: "God is with me. God is getting this work done through me. I am just God's helper." Think about this deeply. Meditate on what it means to be a spiritual helper and agent for God. Consider that when you go to the office, or out into the community, this is God's work and God is getting it done.

Many people ask, "How does God do everything?" Perhaps they have an image of God in a human form, with hands and feet, physically doing all the work. But God doesn't have a body, or hands and feet. God doesn't paint walls, dig gardens, or drive the kids to school. We divine souls in human forms are the ones performing physical actions in this world. When we are attuned to God, and keenly feel His love and power, our actions become easy and inspired. Thus, sacred service is not what we do but the power by which it is done. Higher energy attracts. And a soul connected to God exudes spirituality and automatically attracts positive situations and results. It is this spiritual energy that comes from God and does the work.

St John of the Cross described this advanced state as a "perfect and self-forgetting harmony of will with God." Whereas before a person was "moved toward a life of Spirit," St John wrote, "Now he is immersed in it; inspired and directed in all of his actions by the indwelling love of God."

Other occasions arise when unpredictably God Himself would seem to choose us for His higher purpose. Perhaps you have had the experience of being at the right place, at the right time, able to offer assistance to someone in need. That person says, "God must have sent you." You smile, thinking it could easily have been a coincidence. Was it destiny or chance that that put you in that place? Or did God really send you? Did it have to be you? Or could God have equally chosen someone else?

There are no simple answers to these questions. Some modern writers such as Carolyn Myss talk about the fact that we can't help but be used by God, that God infuses everything that happens in human life, whether we are aware of it or not. This may be the case. It is not for anyone to judge or to say. Perhaps only God can say when He is making use of someone to brighten up a person's day, such as when a truck driver in Oklahoma stops in a road cafe and listens to a waitress's problems, or when the Dalai Lama gives a lecture to millions and his words transform a person's life.

God can make anyone an instrument at any time. But instruments are not all equal, alert, or available to be used by Him any time of the day or night. It takes humility to grasp the nature of God's work and selflessness to play an invisible part in His plan.

At this stage of spiritual development mature mystics will distinguish between when they are being used by God directly and when they are operating on the basis of their power. A common failing of the ego is to confuse the two. Many times people are just tapping into their own creative resources, while claiming to be a 'channel' for God. A true helper doesn't talk about being used by God but quietly gives thanks when it happens.

For those of us not yet at this stage we can begin by being totally honest. First of all, honest attention is required to consciously bring the Divine into all of our actions. Then, when we are no longer operating solely on the basis of our own thinking, there is a good chance for God to make use of us. God can step in at any time but what matters, ultimately, is the humility in which we receive His grace.

An old English proverb states that, "The bough that bears the most fruit is the bough that bows the lowest." The degree to which we make ourselves completely available to God is a sign of advanced spirituality. It's not simply a question of willingness, for instance of saying, "Here I am, God. Use me." It's more about having made ourselves worthy of God's consideration.

The ultimate stage of spirituality is distinguished not by our abilities or talents but by our purity of intention.

PEAK OF PERFECTION

Remain stable in the complete form of all attainments.
The sparkle and intoxication of that stage of perfection should be
visible on your face.

MYSTICS AND SPIRITUAL LEADERS down the ages have known how to conserve and transform energy and use it for a higher purpose. They do this by breaking through a spiritual glass ceiling, and tapping into a huge stock of purified energy that is then released and made available to them. St Teresa of Avila, for example, described in her later years having access to a boundless energy that was previously unknown to her. It allowed her to perform, she said, a mountain of spiritual work that she ordinarily was incapable of doing. During the last twenty years of her life the saint traveled across Spain, frequently in poor health, and under the most appalling road conditions of the sixteenth century. She set up convents, taught and administered, wrote her most insightful books, and penned a voluminous correspondence to key figures in the Church.

Many of the elders on my spiritual path are similarly endowed. They have indefatigable energy sources and use none of it for themselves. Though they get on with the ordinary acts of eating, talking, and driving to appointments like the rest of us, their entire focus is on the well-being of others. With just a kind word or a smile and through an extraordinary vibrational presence they elevate people's spirits. Though their timetables are strenuous, each thought and word is put to good use. I look at them and wonder, "How are they able to accomplish so much and yet continue to radiate such vibrant energy?"

One contributing factor is their total disinterest in praise for anything they have done. They just want to serve. Dadi Janki once said, "Just like a river doesn't drink its own water and a tree doesn't eat its own fruit, so too we keep on doing our work." The underlying principle is that giving is a joy and a demonstration of love for humanity. The more a person gives, the more that person is energized. When giving has no vested interest, energy is accumulated, not drained.

The second contributing factor is absolute closeness to God. Having reached a state of constant union with the Divine, a mystic gains a spiritual strength and energy that are a complement to God's. In *The Interior Castle* St Teresa explained that the process is of becoming, "holy with the holy" and through this "high union of spirit with Spirit shares His strength." Due to the complementary nature of their energies God and the mystic now work as a team.

In many mystical traditions achieving Oneness with God is the ultimate goal. However, the nature of this final destination varies according to each tradition and across traditions. I like the definition offered by St John of the Cross who said that "marriage" or union of the soul with the Divine brings about complete transformation. In *Flame of Love*, St John wrote, "In this state God and the soul are united as the window is with the light or the coal with the fire...this communication of God diffuses itself substantially in the whole soul, or rather the soul is transformed in God." During this process, St John went on, "the soul drinks of God in its very substance and its spiritual powers." In other words through an in-taking of God's energy and attributes, the soul is transformed.

Thus the third factor contributing to a mystic's indefatigable energy lies in the very nature of this transformation. In this altered state, soul and God are united, but remain distinct. Though we are one with God, the Christian mystic Ruysbroeck noted in *Sparkling Stone*, "We must eternally remain other than God, and distinct from Him..." In *The Adornment of the Spiritual Marriage*, he went on to describe this union as the highest stage of spiritual life, "the dual and God-like existence of fruition in God and work for God." The result of constant union, therefore, is a God-like existence. Every facet of character, every aspect of the self is brought into alignment with God's energy and purpose. A soul filled by God is colored with God's essence.

This is perfection of spirit, the stage of being complete. The dictionary defines perfection as being "without blemish, fault, or error," and as "possessing every moral excellence." By this stage, a mystic will have become empty of vice and abundant in goodness, truth and virtue. In this state worldly desires no longer pull the soul, nor is there any experience of suffering or pain. In fact all karmas of the past have been settled. The energy that was being used to deal with those karmas is now available for higher use.

Perfection of spirit signifies a return to the original purity of the soul, a liberation from negativity and ego-consciousness. This liberation is not the same as the Hindu *moksha*, or final emancipation of the soul. Nor is it the blissful goal of extinction, becoming free from the cycle of happiness and sorrow, birth and death, by attaining *nirvana*. Far from being a liberation from the world, perfection of spirit is the state of an enlightened presence available and ready to serve the world.

In these times of unprecedented global change, the attempts any of us make to reach such a light-filled state are of increased relevance and importance. Spirituality would seem singularly myopic if our goal were solely to reach enlightenment and then to forget the world and everyone else in it. For spirituality to be dynamic, as opposed to static, it must have social meaning. It must serve to uplift those around us and the world as a whole.

A mystic who has been made complete by God will act as an "instrument" to reflect God's qualities. God is remembered as the Merciful One who knows our weaknesses, yet doesn't judge our mistakes. God is constantly loving and giving. There is no generosity as great as God's. His love is tireless and without prejudice. As the Compassionate Lord, God is benevolent to all souls, even to those who disregard His presence. In His world all souls are without blemish. And those mystics who attain the peak of perfection -- having been transformed by God and completely filled with His spiritual power -- will mirror those same divine qualities at the human level. Such mystics will be blessed with an abundance of love, respect, and compassion for all souls.

Compassion is an all-encompassing virtue comprising kindness, tenderness, sympathy and love. We all know the outward signs of compassion, such as when a hospice worker helps a person to find comfort and peace in the last moments of this life. Or when a stranger rescues someone from a car accident in the dead of winter and wraps the victim in his or her coat.

But perhaps we are less familiar with the spiritual demonstrations of compassion. This is when a mystic's compassionate thoughts and feelings at the vibrational level are specifically directed towards the benefit of the world. Vibrations are the invisible energies that emanate from the soul and impact at the subtle level. They are felt but not seen. Dadi Janki explained it this way: "Through an attitude of benevolence and compassion and an intense remembrance of God we can spread pure vibrations. On receiving power from God we become powerful, and through those vibrations we are able to change the atmosphere. An unhappy atmosphere can be changed through God's love. On the basis of God's peace and power souls can receive courage and hope."

Once, about twelve years ago, I saw those forces of spiritual love and compassion at work. I was sitting at the kitchen table with Dadi Janki, quietly eating my toast. Out of the corner of my eye I saw Dadi put a spoonful of yogurt into her mouth. It was such an ordinary act. But coming from the stillness of her being, it was visionary.

Dadi's left elbow rested on the table, her head was cushioned gently in the pillow of her hand. Her right arm moved slowly, significantly, through space as if supported and directed by God's unseen hand. Love radiated from God's hand to Dadi's hand, to the spoon, to the bowl, to the yogurt. And then to her mouth. Every part of her sparkled with the light of love -- even the things she touched. The yogurt was no longer cultured milk. It was liquid love.

Love entered Dadi's body. It circulated through her whole system, permeating the pores of her skin. Then it poured out again -- this electric vibration of love -- to the spoon and table, to me sitting on the chair opposite her. In my mind I called out, "Dadi!" I was amazed, but could not speak. She didn't once look up. Her thoughts were fully engaged with the One she loved. God, her Companion, was feeding Her, just as she was feeding herself.

At that moment a wonderful energy entered the room. Everything, including myself, seemed to be energized and transformed.

And as Dadi nurtured herself in silence, that loving silence was nurturing the world.

A LIGHT FOR THE WORLD

A lighthouse stays in one place and spreads its light in all directions. To bring about light into darkness, to bring peace where there is a lack of peace and to bring a sparkle of happiness into a dry atmosphere is known as being a world benefactor. To become such a lighthouse and world benefactor, spread your light across the whole world.

IMAGINE THROWING A PEBBLE into the Pacific Ocean, knowing that the ripples from that pebble will reach the shores of Japan. In the same way, imagine sending out one powerful thought into the world, knowing that the vibrations emanating from that thought can touch any person or place. Thoughts can travel. They move at great speed and with considerable impact.

The task of serving the world belongs to us all. The highest service we can undertake is to direct our thoughts and vibrations benevolently for the greater good. To serve others through vibrations requires a purity of consciousness. Thoughts need to be clean, altruistic in nature, and without any trace of animosity.

Through deep concentration it is possible to spread vibrations of peace, healing, and empowerment to those who are suffering, or in ill health, and for them to receive benefit. Scientific experiments, for instance, have shown that people who are sick are helped in their recovery through intercessional prayer, even when they don't know it is being done on their behalf. Highly concentrated meditation also produces an abundance of spiritual energy. When that energy is directed specifically or sent out to the world in general it can soothe troubled hearts, bring peace to situations of crisis, and moreover affect a positive change in the atmosphere.

For a mystic to direct the full sum of his or her vibrational being toward the benefit of the world requires special dedication. Over many years a conscious effort will already have been made to accumulate within the self the necessary stock of pure energy. And while a mystic is blessed with a light of his or her own, only someone at the advanced stage has the power and transparency to reflect purely the Light from God.

Whereas mystics of the past were hoping to receive visions, modern mystics aim to share visions of light. What is a vision but an experience granted through a dimension of light? Enlightenment is the state of being in the light, of the light, able to generate light for the world. The most effective helpers in this task are those enlightened beings who have reached perfection of spirit. This does not mean that the rest of us cannot participate in spreading the light. However, light reflects more quickly and cleanly off souls who are whole and complete due to the purity of their being.

A soul who has attained perfection of spirit is like a crystal-clear diamond. If you were to hold that diamond up to the light it would sparkle before your eyes. Myriad rays of color would emanate from it. Diamonds are perfect reflectors of energy and light. A soul who is like a diamond is a perfect agent to reflect and mirror God's light. Divine energy intensifies and spreads further when it is reflected off something clear and pure. This is why God utilizes enlightened souls through whom to beam His light into the physical world.

To reflect God in all that is, both here and now,
my heart must be a mirror that reflects it.
– Angelius Silesius

Learning to spread the light is an important aspect of spiritual development. Those of us who have not yet reached perfection of spirit will radiate less light than those who are complete. Yet our thoughts and vibrations can still bring benefit. We just need to know how to channel them properly. Paradoxically, energy accumulates to the extent that it is used. The more a person spreads light, that light increases significantly within. This is why none of us can wait until the end of our journey to begin this work. We have to start now.

When the terrorist- hijacked planes dived into the World Trade Center Towers and unleashed tragedy and terror not only in New York but across the world, millions of people turned to silence, prayer, and meditation. They gathered on the streets, lit candles, wrote condolences, anything to feel solidarity and to spread a wave of love. Churches, temples, mosques, and retreat centers were flooded with people seeking to raise their consciousness beyond the senseless killing to a higher, more noble plane.

In times of chaos people instinctively turn to the unseen and intangible for their support. It is a silent acknowledgement of what has always been known, namely, that spiritual power can unite, and heal, and transcend the powers of darkness. People in spiritual circles talk about being a light for the world. The world is looking for the light. Uplifting the world through vibrations is not the task of one person alone. An entire army of willing and selfless servers needs to be in place. Just as one light can ignite another, and more people join in the task of spreading light, the light increases and envelops the world.

This concept can best be understood through a comparison to Tesla's resonant and magnifier coils in radio transmission. The inventor discovered that when a coil was tuned to the signal of a particular frequency the incoming electrical energy was magnified through the resonant action. He could transmit and receive powerful radio signals when his coils were tuned to resonate at the same frequency. Similarly, if a sufficient number of people are tuned into the same frequency, namely the highest vibration of God's light and love, that energy would be felt on earth.

I have spent many hours observing yogis who are regularly engaged in spreading the light. From what I have seen two special powers enhance this work: the power of purity, and the power of silence. Purity is the actual light of the soul. The more concentration there is on our inner light in meditation, the more it intensifies. Purity also results from focusing the mind on pure thoughts and pure feelings for the self and others. Silence is cultivated in the mind when we think less and speak less. By spending a considerable amount of time in silence, that silence becomes a genuine force for change.

The ability to spread light, therefore, is based on these two powers of the mind. The mind has such great power. It can enhance or harm our environment, strengthen other souls or weaken them. We can do tremendous damage with our thoughts, equally we can do a lot of good.

Using the mind to serve the world through pure vibrations is an advanced spiritual state. In my practice it is known as "service through the mind." To do this invisible work the mind needs to be incredibly strong. If you allow one slightly negative thought to penetrate your mind, it reduces your mind's effectiveness. One weak thought is like a tiny hole in your thinking system. Just as a leak in a pipe wastes water, a hole in your thinking drains precious energy. The more powerful you become spiritually, the less you can afford to waste your thoughts through carelessness.

Advanced mystics have mastered their minds. Their ability to remain in a constant and stable state of spreading the light reflects the highest degree of soul power. But for those of us still progressing on our spiritual journey, this is a level of consciousness we can tap into and perfect over time.

Where to begin? Here are some important guidelines to consider:

1. *Pay attention to whatever thoughts and attitudes you have.*
Your vibrations definitely spread into the atmosphere and affect other people. Over time, and with practice, it is possible to cultivate a benevolent attitude toward all that you do. Have the awareness that you are a being of light and that light not only affects your thinking, it affects your way of talking, walking, your whole behavior. Once your consciousness changes, everything changes.

2. *Think about doing less and achieving more.*
By using your power of the mind effectively, you will conserve energy, and your actions will have a positive impact and result. For example, I take a moment in silence before going to meetings or giving lectures. I create the thought, "This task is good. It will bring benefit to everyone." Then I hand over whatever task I am performing to God, knowing that God is responsible for the outcome. Service through the mind is greatly hampered by thoughts such as, "This task is mine. I'm the only one who can do it. It's because of me that this task is successful."

3. *The mind can never be used for personal gain.*
As people progress spiritually they can be tempted to use spiritual powers for their own advancement, professionally or spiritually. This is a misuse of energy. In addition, along with spiritual advancement comes the ability to understand more clearly the hearts and minds of others. I am not referring to psychic abilities, but to natural soul-perceptions. Yet spiritual insights such as these cannot be used to manipulate people emotionally or have them become dependent on us. If we come to know another person's situation or feelings it is so that, through our link to God, we may send the healing power of light. Our aim is for each person to find their strength and support through God, not through us.

4. *Make time to serve through the mind.*
Keep your mind free from petty matters by reducing the clutter in your

lives. If your mind is distracted by problems and worries, you will not have the necessary force to use your spiritual energy for the benefit of others. Pure thoughts work best with the power of silence behind them.

5. *To have dislike or enmity for any other person creates a negative shadow.* It blocks the mind and reduces your effectiveness in being able to send out light-filled thoughts. Similarly, if in moments of crisis you are negatively affected by another's pain, or by an atmosphere of conflict, your ability to spread light will be weakened. In these situations, empathy and compassion are necessary. But to offer the maximum help stay focused on the light.

6. *The most effective spiritual service is accomplished invisibly.* God can call on you for any task, at any time. Even if you don't feel prepared or worthy, God can make the impossible happen. Just have the awareness that you are a "lighthouse," taking light and power from God, and that you are spreading those vibrations into the atmosphere, to the elements of nature, and to all souls of the world.

I am excited by the idea of spreading light. In my meditations, I send light and spiritual power to the earth, to air, fire, water, the ether, to the birds and plants, to all living creatures and human beings that live on the earth. All need to be fed and nurtured with light of God's love and power. This is a joyful, heart-warming practice. Each time I spread light, I come closer to the Divine, knowing that in some small way I am participating in God's plan. When I am engaged in using my mind to spread light, there is a silent reciprocity and respect between myself and my God.

Over the years, I have come to understand that silent, invisible work carries a special power. Talking about it diminishes its effect. So I have tried to balance carefully what I write in this book for the purposes of clarifying spiritual principles, and what is left unsaid.

On a few occasions I have asked my spiritual elders to explain more deeply about the mechanism involved in spreading the light. They don't answer me fully. It's not that they are being secretive or that they think I'm too immature to understand. They simply recognize the value of my own discovery.

I trust their judgment. I trust my own.

I trust your discovery.

REFLECTIONS ON
PERFECTION OF SPIRIT

Reflective Questions

1. Think back to a highlight moment when you felt that God used you to bring benefit to a person, a community, your workplace. What were the circumstances? Who was involved? And what was your state of consciousness?
2. What do you need to do at this stage in your development to be available to God as His helper as an agent of change?
3. To what extent are you still affected by other people's comments, criticisms, and opinions of you? Do you still require affirmation or praise for the things that you do and the person that you are? Notice the way this dependency takes away your soul power.
4. What stock of spiritual power have you accumulated that can now be used for a higher purpose?

Exercises for Spiritual Practice

1. Reflect on the following words taken from a speech on compassion by the Dalai Lama, "Compassion compels us to reach out to all living beings, including our so-called enemies, those people who upset or hurt us. Irrespective of what they do to you, if you remember that all beings, like you, are only trying to be happy, you will find it much easier to develop compassion toward them." Notice when you are unable to have compassion for the people you dislike, for this is not the true meaning of compassion,
2. Practice becoming a light. Look within to the light of the soul. Concentrate on this light. As your inner light increases, it becomes clearer and brighter and expands. It's as if the outer structure of your body falls away and dissolves into light. You are now a form of pure white light, radiating light.
3. If you know of someone who is in difficulty, illness, or pain, you can send light to that person. If you hear of a crisis somewhere in the world, such as a shortage of food, an earthquake, or plane crash, all those who are suffering can be sent light. Visualize yourself

surrounded with light, and in your mind's eye bring those people in front of you. Surround them with a healing, soothing, restoring light. See them protected and strengthened by the power of this light.

Meditation on Being a Light for the World

Create the consciousness that you, the soul, are operating from your highest place of soul power. Visualize that you are in a dimension of light, in the presence of the Divine. There is so much light, and love, and power filling you that it overflows and spreads out from this dimension of light and envelops the world below. All people are touched by this light. As the light spreads, it brings them peace, comfort, and hope.

Now the light coming to you from God takes the shape of a brilliant white laser. This laser light is so strong, it pierces through the deepest darkness, touching all souls, cleansing them, healing them, and restoring their faith.

God's light is transformative. You are a lighthouse, a pure and reflective mirror of His Grace.

EPILOGUE: YOUR RIGHT TO SOUL POWER

SOUL POWER begins with an intention. It can be as simple as wanting to become a better person, or as big as choosing to be an agent of change for the world. Each person has to come to an understanding of his or her spiritual purpose.

Just by reading this book you will have begun to experience a change in consciousness. If you used the exercises and meditations you will have experienced peace and inner wisdom and your capacity for self-healing will have increased. Once you move into making meditation a regular part of your life, and commit to deepening that practice, you will continue to grow in self-knowledge and stature.

Each morning spend fifteen minutes or more focusing on who you are and what you have come here to be and do. Through attention and practice you can claim the soul power that is yours. Everyone has soul power.

Just because you are on a spiritual path does not mean that you will not be challenged. The challenges you face, the lessons you learn, are all part of a divine plan to help you to become more powerful.

The human heart is capable of forgiveness. The human being is capable of thinking in new ways. Soul power is about finding yourself. Release the past, and realize the beauty of your inner being.

It is said that we are living in a spiritual age. And yet we are also living in a world torn apart by the haves and the have-nots, by turmoil, suffering, and pain. This is not a world in which many of us would choose to live, which is why, I believe, we have chosen it again.

At the center of this spiritual revival is the mystic heart, a heart that is brimming with kindness, compassion and love. God's love is the greatest healing power. A modern mystic will draw on this love and become a light for the world.

Spiritual revival does not happen in isolation, it is a communal act. Just as a carpet of wild buttercups starts in one place and then spreads across a green field, in the same way, a wave of kindness and compassion can spread across the world. It starts with you.

This is what modern spirituality is all about. If each of us can tap into our pure energies of soul, and unite as one powerful force for good, we can change the course of the world.

Then there will be light, so much light on the face of the earth.

ABOUT THE AUTHOR

If you would like further information about Nikki de Carteret's Soul Power Seminars, or would like to organize a local study group, visit her website at www.soulpowerseminars.com

If you would like to know more about Raja Yoga meditation visit www.bkpublications.com

SOURCES

We would like to thank the following:

Brahma Kumaris World Spiritual Organization for kind permission to use extracts from their teachings at the start of each chapter.

STAGE ONE: AWAKENING

St Catherine of Genoa (Evelyn Underhill, *Mystics of the Church*, James Clarke and Co, Ltd, 1925); Way of the Pilgrim (*The Way of the Pilgrim* and *The Pilgrim Continues His Way*, translated by R.M. French, Quality Paperback Book Club by arrangement with HarperSanFrancisco, 1998).

STAGE 2: SPIRITUAL KNOWLEDGE

St Augustine (*The Confessions of St Augustine*, translated by F. J. Sheed, Sheed and Ward, London & New York, 1944); St Francis of Assisi (Evelyn Underhill, *Mystics of the Church*, James Clarke and Co, Ltd, 1925); Richard Rolle ("Fire of Love," see: *The English Mystics of the 14th Century*, Karen Armstrong, Kyle Cathie, 1991); Cloud of Unknowing ("The Cloud of Unknowing" see: *The English Mystics of 14th Century*, Karen Armstrong, Kyle Cathie, 1991); Julian of Norwich *(Revelations of Divine Love*, Julian of Norwich, edited by Grace Warrack, Methuen & Co, London,1949); Hildegard (Scivias: *Hildegard von Bingen's Mystical Visions*, translated from Scivias by Bruce Hozeski, Bear and Company Publishing, Santa Fe, 1986); St. Catherine of Genoa (Evelyn Underhill, *Mystics of the Church,* James Clarke and Co, Ltd, 1925); St John of the Cross (Stephen Clissold, *Wisdom of the Spanish Mystics,* A New Direction Book, 1997); Akdamut Millin, hymn by the eleventh-century Jewish preacher Meir ben Isaac Nehora'i (reproduced from: *A Book of Jewish Thoughts* by J. H. Hertz, London, 1944); Upanishads (Evelyn Underhill, *Mystics of the Church*, James Clarke and Co, Ltd, 1925); Rumi (*A Garden beyond Paradise: the Mystical poetry of Rumi*, translated by Jonathan Star and Shahram Shiva, Bantam, 1992); Suso (Margaret Smith, *Rabi'a: The Life and Work of Rabi'a and other Women Mystics in Islam*, One World, Oxford, 1994); Rusbroeck (John of Ruysbroeck, *Book of Supreme Truth).*

STAGE THREE: SPIRITUAL PRACTICE

Thomas Merton (Thomas Merton, *The Springs of Contemplation: A Retreat at the Abbey of Gethsemani*, Farrar, Straus, Giroux, New York, 1992, X111);Desert Fathers (translated by Thomas Merton, *The Wisdom of the Desert*, Shambhalla Pocket Classics, Boston & London, 1994); St Teresa of Avila (*The Life of Saint Teresa of Avila by Herself,* Penguin Classics, London, 1957); T. S. Eliot (T. S. Eliot, "Burnt Norton," *Four Quartets*, Faber & Faber, London, 1994).

STAGE FOUR: DARK NIGHT OF THE SOUL

Ecclesiastes 3:1; Voluspa (E. O. G Turville-Petre, trans. *Myths and Religion of the North*, London, Weidenfeld and Nicolson, 1964); Revelation 21:3-4; I have retold in my own words the alchemy tale of the king (from: Hazrat Inayat Khan, *Spiritual Dimensions of Psychology*, Omega Uniform Edition, 1988); Rumi (*Travelling the path of Love: Sayings of the Sufi masters*, edited by Llewellyn Vaughan-Lee, The Golden Sufi Center, 1995); Fritjof Capra (Fritjof Capra, *The Tao of Physics*, Shambhalla, Boston, 1991); Rumi (*The Essential Rumi*, translated by Coleman Barks, Quality Paperback Book Club, New York, 1995); Angela of Foligna (*The Book of Divine Consolation of the Blessed Angela of Foligna*, translated from the Italian by Mary G. Steegmann, Introduction by Algar Thorold, Cooper Square Publishers, New York, 1966); St John of the Cross (St John of the Cross, *Dark Night of the Soul*, translated and edited with an introduction by E. Allison Peers, Doubleday, 1959); Joseph Campbell (Joseph Campbell, *Hero with a Thousand Faces*); Carl Jung (*Aion*, 1951, CW 9); Frederick Pierce (Frederick Pierce, *Dreams and Personality* as quoted in Joseph Campbell, *Hero with a Thousand Faces*); I have retold the Handless Maiden tale in my own words (based on Robert Johnson, *The Fisher King/The Handless Maiden*, HarperCollins, 1993).

STAGE FIVE: ILLUMINATION

Music of the Mind (Darryl Reanney, *Music of the Mind, an Adventure into Consciousness*, Hill of Content, 1994); Lusseyran ("Seeing Without Eyes," Wayne Constantineau translates Jacques Lusseyran, *The Idler*, no 26 1989); Meister Eckhart (Meister Eckhart, *On Detachment*); Caroline Myss (Caroline Myss, *Why People don't Heal and how they Can*, Three Rivers Press, New York, 1997); Richard of St Victor (Evelyn Underhill, *The Essentials of Mysticism*); St Teresa of Avila (Tessa Bielecki, *Teresa of Avila: Mystical Writings*, Crossroad, New York, 1996); St Augustine (Evelyn Underhill, *Mystics of the Church*, James Clarke and Co, Ltd, 1925); Proverbs 3:5; Al-Hallaj (*Travelling the Path of Love: Sayings of the Sufi masters*, edited by Llewellyn Vaughan-Lee, The Golden Sufi Center, 1995); Indries Shah (Indries Shah, *Way of the Sufi*, E. P. Dutton & Co, Ltd, 1968); Jami (from: *Travelling the Path of Love: Sayings of the Sufi masters*, edited by Llewellyn Vaughan-Lee, The Golden Sufi Center, 1995); Lao-tzu (Lao-tzu's *Treatise on the Response of the Tao*, (*T'ai-shang Kan-ying P'ien*) by Ling Yi-Chang, translated by Dr Eva Wong, edited by Kerry Brown and Sima Sharma, The Sacred Literature Series, HarperCollins, 1994); St John of the Cross (St John of the Cross, *Dark Night of the Soul*, translated and edited with an introduction by E. Allison Peers, Doubleday, 1959).

STAGE 6: SURRENDER

Herbert Benson (Herbert Benson, MD, *Timeless Healing*, Simon and Schuster, 1996); Evagrios the Solitatary (*The Philokalia: The Complete Text, Volume 1*, compiled by St Nikodimos of the Holy Mountain & St Makarios of Corinth, trans. by G. E. H. Palmer, Philip Sherrard, Kallistos Ware, Faber and Faber, London, 1979); W. H. Murray (The Scottish Himalayan Expedition by W. H. Murray, 1951); Rabi'a (Margaret Smith, *Rabi'a: The Life and Work of Rabi'a and other Women Mystics in Islam*, One World, Oxford, 1994); Meera (from: *In the Dark of the Heart, Songs of Meera*, translated with an introduction by Shama Futehally, HarperCollins, New York, 1994); St Teresa of Avila (St Teresa of Avila, Interior Castle: from Tessa Bielecki, *Teresa of Avila: Mystical Writings*, Crossroad, New York, 1996); Evagrios (Evagrios the Solitary, *"On Prayer,"* *The Philokalia: The Complete Text, Volume 1*, compiled by St Nikodimos of the Holy Mountain & St Makarios of Corinth, trans by G. E. H. Palmer, Philip Sherrard, Kallistos Ware, Faber and Faber,

London, 1979); Music of the Mind (Darryl Reanney, *Music of the Mind, an Adventure into Consciousness,* Hill of Content, 1994); St Catherine of Genoa (*The Life and Sayings of Saint Catherine of Genoa,* trans. Paul Garvin, Staten Island, Alba House, 1964); Nizami (*Travelling the Path of Love: Sayings of the Sufi Masters,* edited by Llewellyn Vaughan-Lee, The Golden Sufi Center, 1995); Irving Stone (Irving Stone, *The Agony and Ecstasy,* Collins, 1961); Michelangelo (*Artists in Quotation* compiled by Donna Ward La Cour, quotes taken from: *The Complete Poems and selected letters of Michaelangelo,* edited by Robert N. Linscott, 1963).

STAGE SEVEN: WALKING THE TALK

Angela of Foligna (*The Book of Divine Consolation of the Blessed Angela of Foligna,* translated from the Italian by Mary G. Steegmann; Introduction by Algar Thorold, Cooper Square Publishers, New York, 1966); St Hildegard of Bingen (*Meditations with Hildegard of Bingen,* introduction and versions by Gabriele Uhlein, Bear and Company, Santa Fe, 1983); Lao-tzu (from Lao-tzu's *Treatise on the Response of the Tao,* (*T'ai-shang Kan-ying P'ien*) by Ling Yi-Chang, translated by Dr Eva Wong, edited by Kerry Brown and Sima Sharma, The Sacred Literature Series, HarperCollins, 1994); Lusseyran (Jacques Lusseyran, *And There Was Light* translated from the French by Elizabeth R. Cameron, Heinemann, London, 1963); Maya Angelou *Oprah* (US TV).

STAGE EIGHT: BLISS

Ziyab Al Arabi (Kenneth Walker, *The Mystic Mind,* Emerson books, New York, 1965); Murasaki Shikibu (from: Liza Dalby, *The Tale of Murasaki,* London, Vintage, 2001); Viktor Frankl (Viktor Frankl, *Man's Search for Meaning,* Beacon Press, Boston, 1962); Dr Edith Eva Egar ("Phoenix of Auschwitz," *Usana Magazine,* July/August, 1998); Brother Lawrence (The Second Conversation, *The Practice of the Presence of God* by Brother Lawrence of the Resurrection, newly translated with an introduction by John J. Delaney, foreword by Henri J. M. Nouwen, Images Books, a division of Doubleday, New York, 1977); Angela of Foligna (*The Book of Divine Consolation of the Blessed Angela of Foligna,* Cooper Square Publishers, New York, 1966); Catherine of Genoa (*The Life and Sayings of Saint Catherine of Genoa,* trans. Paul Garvin, Staten Island, Alba House, 1964); Theresa of Avila (*The Life of Saint Teresa of Avila by Herself,* Penguin Classics, London, 1957; translated with an Introduction by J. M. Cohen); Kabir (*The vision of Kabir: Love poems of a 15th century weaver-sage,* by Sehdev Kumar); St Teresa (from: Stephen Clissold, *Wisdom of the Spanish Mystics,* A New Direction Book, 1997).

STAGE NINE: PERFECTION OF SPIRIT

St Teresa (Stephen Clissold, *Wisdom of the Spanish Mystics,* A New Direction Book, 1997); St Teresa of Avila (Evelyn Underhill, *Mystics of the Church,* James Clarke and Co, Ltd, 1925); I have adapted the tale of the wise sage from Anthony De Mello's *The Heart of the Enlightened* (from: *Quotes and Anecdotes: the essential reference for preachers and teachers,* Anthony P. Castle, Kevin Mayhew Ltd, Bury St. Edmonds, 1979, 1994); Ruysbroeck (John of Ruysbroeck, *Sparkling Stone,* introduction by Evelyn Underhill); Ruysbroeck (John of Ruysbroeck, *The Adornement of Spiritual Marriage*); The 14th Dalai Lama ("The True Expression of Non-Violence is Compassion," The 14th Dalai Lama Speaking in India www.spiritsound.com/bhikshu.html).